A Text Book of Irish Literature,

VOL. II.

AMS PRESS
NEW YORK

A Text Book of Irish Literature

Part II.

ELEANOR HULL

AUTHOR OF "THE CUCHULLIN SAGA IN IRISH LITERATURE,"
"PAGAN IRELAND," ETC.

M. H. GILL & SON, Ltd.
London
DAVID NUTT.
1908

Library of Congress Cataloging in Publication Data

Hull, Eleanor, 1860-1935.
  A text book of Irish literature.

  Bibliography: p.

  1. Irish literature—History and criticism. I. Title.
PB1306.H75 1974   820'.9   70-153595
ISBN 0-404-09244-6

Reprinted from the edition of 1906-1908, Dublin
First AMS edition published in 1974
Manufactured in the United States of America

International Standard Book Number:
Complete Set: 0-404-09244-6
Volume II: 0-404-09246-2

AMS PRESS INC.
NEW YORK, N.Y. 10003

CONTENTS.

PREFACE.

THE general outline of the theory here advanced as to the origin and spread of the Fenian Legends was suggested to me by reading in proof, some time ago, Mr. John Mac Neill's introduction to his volume containing a portion of the collection of Ossianic poems known as " Duanaire Finn," just published by the Irish Texts Society. I had long been pondering the special features presented by these legends and endeavouring to construct some theory of their origin which would combine such facts as are at present known. The suggestions offered in Mr. Mac Neill's essay regarding the genealogies of Finn, and the general consensus of opinion among the Irish mediæval genealogists that he was sprung from the pre-Milesian or old inhabitants of the country, known by the name of the Firbolg race, seemed worthy of consideration, and I endeavoured to work out the idea in greater detail. The result will be found in the notes on the legends which occupy the first five chapters of this volume. The theory seems to explain much that was obscure as to the early origin of the tales and their very general hold on the people, in spite of the fact that they do not seem, until a late period, to have been considered by the official scribes as worthy of a place in their collections. It may be objected that a text book for students is not the place in which to advance or discuss new theories of any kind ; but whether the explanation here offered be finally accepted or not, it has at least this advantage, that it brings to light and combines a large number of details met with in the tales themselves which could not without some such theory be satisfactorily presented to the student at all. Thus cohesion is gained in what is otherwise a mere confused mass of data. To my mind, a theory which explains many difficulties, and which takes its stand on the historical conceptions of the writers who recorded the legends is likely to have some foundation of truth. It would be singularly improbable that the highly popular tradition of Finn and his followers should be connected in all the genealogies with the despised races who had been conquered by the Gaels and who were regarded by them as inferior, unless the tradition of their connection were very strong ; unless, in fact, these later settlers had themselves received the traditions from or through the older races. The genealogies are not to be regarded as the pedigrees of real personages ; but they are real in the sense that they represent the opinion of the learned of an earlier day upon the origin and source of the legends ; and they are unanimous in ascribing the origin of Finn to the Firbolg races, that is, to the pre-Milesian tribes then still scattered through the country. It is interesting to reflect that the memory of these despised and conquered people, in describing whom their successors could find no words sufficiently black, has survived in a great body of legend which is as fondly regarded by their conquerors as it ever could have been by the races among whom it first sprang up.

Mr. John Mac Neill has kindly read the chapters relating to the Fenian legends, and I have also to thank Mr. J. J. O'Kelly and Tadhg O'Donnchadha for helpful suggestions in the chapter on Geoffrey Keating and in the Chronology, and Mr. A. Nutt for assistance in the Bibliography.

CHRONOLOGY.

———

(The references are to pages in the text, which the Chronology is intended only to supplement.)

fl. 1560. FEARFLATHA O'GNIVE, bard of the O'Neills of Clannaboy, accompanied Shane O'Neill to London in 1562, when he was summoned by Elizabeth. His poems had much influence in rousing O'Neill to action in the North, and in stirring up the Irish nobles in other parts of the kingdom. His best known poem is the " Downfall (or ' stepping-down ') of the Gael," a lament over the condition of Ireland and the inaction of the chiefs. This O'Gnive, or more probably another bard of the same name, wrote a lament on the death of Teigue Dall O'Higgin, who was murdered in 1617 by the O'Haras.

1550 (?). LOGHLIN óG O'DALY. O'Reilly gives the above date, but he seems from his poem, " Whither are gone the Gael ? " to have lived on into the period of the Ulster plantations (*infra* p.159). He wrote also an address to Owny O'Loghlin of Burren in Clare, and a poem on the expulsion of the Franciscan friars from their convents.

d. 1570. ANGUS O'DALY FIONN, called *na diadhachta* or " The Divine," a voluminous religious poet. O'Reilly gives fifteen poems by him chiefly penitential or in praise of the Blessed Virgin, and others are known. A particularly sweet

poem is his *Grian na maighdean mathair Dé,*
" Sun of all Virgins the mother of God."

d. 1617. ANGUS O'DALY, called the " Red Bard " or
" Angus of the Satires," wrote a poem lam-
pooning the chief families of Ireland (pp.174-6)
for Carew, in whose service he seems to have
been retained. He lived at Ballyovrone, Co.
Cork. Stabbed in revenge by one of the
servants of O'Meagher.

fl. 1566. JOHN MAC TORNA O'MULCHONAIRE of Ardchoill
in Thomond. A fine ode on the inauguration
of Brian na Murtha " of the Bulwarks "
O'Rourke, as chief of Breifney, on the death of
his brother Hugh in 1566, was written by him.
It is in a difficult dialect, and a gloss was added
by Thaddeus O'Rody in the seventeenth century.
O'Rourke was one of the most powerful and
determined opponents of Elizabeth. In 1592
he was delivered over to the English queen
by James VI. of Scotland, to whom he had fled
for refuge, and was hanged at Tyburn.

fl. 1600. FLANN MAGRATH OR M'CRAITH. Poem on
Ireland's shepherdless condition, beginning
" Many the complaints that Ireland utters."
Poems on Thomas Butler, tenth Earl of Ormond
(d. 1614), and on Death and Judgment. Some
of the M'Craiths were poets to the O'Byrnes
of Co. Wicklow, and of Ranelagh, near Dublin,
and there are numerous poems by them to
members of the family.

fl. 1584. DERMOT O'COBHTHAIGH (O'Coffey), poet of
the barony of Rathconrate, Co. Westmeath.
Lament for the death of his kinsman Uaithne

and his wife, who were murdered in 1556, and five religious poems. Another of the family, Murtough, wrote about the same time poems addressed to the Nugents, Lords of Delvin.

The troubles that befel the great families of the O'Neills, Earls of Tyrone, and O'Donnells, Lords of Tyrconnel, made the Northern bardic family of the Mac Wards especially active at this period. Chief among them are the following:

fl 1587. MAELMUIRE MAC AN BHAIRD (Ward) who wrote (1) an address to Red Hugh O'Donnell, encouraging him to bravely support his afflictions; (2) to the same, remonstrating with him on having forsaken Mac Ward, who protests that he was always his faithful friend; (3) on the deserted castle of Donegal after it had been dismantled by Red Hugh, for fear it should fall into the hands of the English.

d. 1609. EOGHAN ROE MAC AN BHAIRD (Owen Ward the Red) flourished about the same time. He was head of his family and died at an advanced age. He wrote (1) an address to Red Hugh O'Donnell on his flight into Spain after the defeat of the Irish at Kinsale in 1602; (2) a warning to Rory O'Donnell on his placing himself in the hands of the English in Dublin; (3) the celebrated address to Nuala weeping over the grave of her brother, Rory O'Donnell, Earl of Tyrconnel (1603-1608) at Rome. Rory was brother to Red Hugh, and succeeded him after his death in Spain in 1602; (4) Address to Niall Garbh (d. 1626) when confined in the

Tower by King James in 1608, after the flight
of the Earls, and other poems to members of
the O'Donnell, O'Neill and Mac Sweeney
families (pp. 165, 166).

fl. 1600. FERGHAL OG MAC AN BHAIRD (Ferrall Ward)
appears to have been still living when the Four
Masters closed their annals in 1616.   He wrote
(1) Four poems in praise of the Maguires, Lords
of Fermanagh ;   (2) Poem in expectation of
the descent by Hugh, Earl of Tyrone, from
Italy upon Ireland ;   (3) another on the death
of O'Donnell in Spain ;   another (4) urging
Turlough Luineach O'Neill to claim the leadership of Ireland.   Mac Ward seems to have
either exiled himself voluntarily to Scotland
for safety, or to have been exiled thither by
others, for among his compositions are a poem
beginning (5) " Sorrowful my journey to Alba "
(Scotland) ;   (6) a Benediction to Ireland and
his friends there, written from that country,
and (7) a lament on the people of Scotland
renouncing the religion of their forefathers.

Another family of Northern bards were the O'Husseys,
chief poets and genealogists to the Maguires of Fermanagh.   Prominent among these are :—

d. 1614. MAELBRIGHDE O'HEOGHUSA OR O'HUSSEY.
He entered the Franciscan Order and took the
name of Bonaventura.   He was born in Donegal,
and after being for some time at Douay, he asked
to be transferred to Louvain, which he entered
as one of the original members on Nov. 1st,
1607.   He became lecturer in philosophy and

theology at Louvain, and was Guardian of the College until his death by smallpox in 1614. Among his poems are one on entering the Order of St. Frances ; a translation into Irish of St. Bernard's Latin hymn " On the vanity of the world," and some personal poems to friends. He wrote also a catechism in prose and another in verse containing an abridgment of Christian Doctrine.

fl. 1630. EOCHADH O'HUSSEY was educated in Munster. He began to write at an early age, his earliest poem having been written in 1593 on the escape of Red Hugh O'Donnell from Dublin Castle the year before. He was chief bard to the Maguires, and wrote four poems on Cuchonnacht Maguire and seven on his son Hugh. He travelled much and wrote laudations on his hosts, besides addresses to Hugh O'Neill and Rory O'Donnell, Earl of Tyrconnel, and some poems on general subjects. He was a voluminous writer. O'Reilly mentions twenty-eight poems by him, many of them of great merit and beauty, and there are others extant unknown to him (pp. 172–174).

d. before 1617. TADHG DALL O'HIGGIN, born on the Southern borders of Ulster. His earliest poem was written before 1554. The most important of his poems urging the laying aside of old feuds and re-union of the Irish clans for the expulsion of the English were : (1) Address to Owen Oge Mac Sweeney ; (2) a plea for the fusion of the " Seed of Colla," i.e., the Maguires, O'Kellys and Mac Mahons under one head ; (3) Address to

Turlough Luineach O'Neill; (4) to Sir Shane Mac William Burke, and (5) Richard mac Oliver Burke; (6) Warlike Ode to Sir Brian O'Rourke; (7) to Aedh mac Manus O'Donnell. Poems for convivial occasions are : (8) In praise of the residence of Shane O'Neill; (9) on a Christmas party (1577) at Turlough O'Neill's house, on the Bann ; (10) on a night at the house of Maelmora Mac Sweeney; (11) on a visit to Cuchonnacht Oge Maguire. Other poems are : (12) laments for Cathal O'Conor Sligo, d. 1587 ; (13) an earlier poem to More, Cathal's wife, to beg her to intercede for his restoration to his office as bard ; (14) poem lamenting a battle about to be fought in June, 1583, between Sir Hugh O'Donnell and Turlough O'Neill, encamped on the R. Finn. He advises O'Donnell to dismiss his clansmen and return home. (15) poem in praise of Lifford, Co. Donegal ; (16) satire on the six O'Haras. Tadhg with his wife and child were brutally murdered by the O'Haras some time before 1617 (pp. 176-180).

Of the Fitzgerald family several attained a good position as poets. Chief among them were :—

circa 1612. MAURICE MAC DAVID DUFF FITZGERALD. Two poems by him (1) on the degeneracy of his own times, and (2) an address to his ship on setting out for Spain, are very fine. There are a number of poems also on minor subjects, such as his verses on a French cat, two sets of verses giving advice, and verses giving thanks for gifts received by him. A spirited address to one of the Mac Carthys seems also to be from his hand.

1709 (?) d. after 1791. PIERCE FITZGERALD. A Cork poet and gentleman of good position. He was the fourth son in his family, but for some cause which is not quite clear, his father's inheritance was, in 1722, made over to him. Pierce married twice, and he seems to have eventually settled in Co. Waterford in the neighbourhood of his wife's relations. Most of his poems were composed between the years 1742-1775. His verses, which are visions, Jacobite songs, or poems on personal events, run pleasantly and without effort.

d. 1653 (?) PIERCE FERRITER. A chieftain of Co. Kerry who took part in the rebellion of 1641, and besieged and took the Castle of Tralee in 1642. He was the last Irish chieftain to hold out against the Cromwellian army. After the fall of Ross Castle, he was induced to come to Killarney to arrange terms of peace, but on his way back he was seized and brought a prisoner into Killarney, where he was hanged about the year 1653. He was an accomplished scholar, poet and musician, a humane man and a brave soldier. He wrote in the older classical and elegiac metres. His poems are love songs, elegies and verses on current events.

Of the family of O'Brody or O'Brodin two are worthy of special notice :—

d. 1602. MAOILIN MAC BRUAIDEDH or O'BRODIN. The O'Brodins were ollaves and bards of the

O'Briens and allied families, such as the O'Gradys and O'Gormans, in Thomond. Maoilin was born at Ballybrodin, Co. Clare. When the Northern chiefs raided Munster in 1599, O'Donnell carried off the cattle of the bard along with the stock of the neighbouring farmers, but he returned them on receiving a poetical epistle from the poet, claiming the exemption of literature from the laws of war. His poems are chiefly addressed to the heads of the families with which he was connected, and are historical compositions relating the history of their ancestors.

d. 1652. TADHG MAC DAIRE MAC BRODIN (b. 1570), who succeeded him in 1603 as poet of the O'Briens of Thomond. His poems were :—(1) Nine poems on the history and pretensions of Munster contributed to the " Contention of the Bards ; " (2) poems on the inauguration and death of the Fourth Earl of Thomond, and other verses addressed to the O'Briens ; (3) Religious verses. He lived on his own estate at the Castle of Dunogan, Co. Clare, and was killed by a Crom-wellian soldier, to whom the property was granted about the year 1652 (pp. 169–171).

d. before 1632. LUGAIDH O'CLERY, chief bard of Tyr-connel. He took part in the " Contention of the Bards," defending the claims of the North of Ireland against Tadhg mac Daire mac Brodin. To this he contributed four poems. His chief work is his " Life of Red Hugh O'Donnell," written from his dictation by his sons (pp. 93-4.)

d. 1664. CUCOGRY OR PEREGRINE O'CLERY, son of Lugaidh, an industrious collector and transcriber

of manuscripts. His autograph copy of his
father's life of Red Hugh O'Donnell and of
Michael's " Leabhar Gabhála " are in the R. I.
Academy. He wrote poems addressed to two
of the O'Donnell family. He assisted in the
compilation of the Annals of the Four Masters
(pp. 94-97).

1575-1643. MICHAEL O'CLERY, fourth s. of Donnchad
O'Clery, and third cousin to Lugaidh (above).
Educated in the Franciscan Convent of Louvain.
An industrious and learned collector of manu-
scripts and compiler of Irish chronicles. His
chief works are :—(1) Reim Rioghraidhe, or
Royal List of the Succession of Kings of Ireland,
1603 ; (2) Leabhar Gabhála, or " Book of
Invasions," dedicated to Brian Maguire (1631) ;
(3) Annales Dungallensis, called also Annala
Rioghachta Eirenn, and Annals of the Four
Masters in 1636 (pp. 104-114) ; (4) Martyrologium
Sanctorum Hiberniæ, or Calendar of the Saints
of Ireland (1636) ; a glossary of difficult Irish
words (1643). O'Clery died at Louvain in 1643
(pp. 97-103).

1580-5 (?) 1660. DUGALD MAC FIRBIS, last of the ollaves
of the O'Dowds of Co. Sligo, chronicler and
genealogist. In 1645 he settled in Galway
as tutor to John Lynch and R. O'Flaherty.
He transcribed many chronicles for Sir James
Ware. His chief works and compilations are :—
(1) Genealogies of the families of Ireland, 1650 ;
(2) A Treatise on Irish authors, 1656 (incom-
plete) ; (3) Catalogue of extinct Irish Bishoprics ;
(4) A collection of Irish glossaries, original

B

and transcribed ; (5) A Martyrology in verse ;
(6) Transcripts of the Chronicum Scotorum ; (7)
Transcript of portions of Annals belonging to the
Mac Egans of Ormonde, with copies and translations of many other Annals.   In the latter
part of his life he was engaged in compiling a
glossary of old Irish law-terms, but this is lost
(see pp. 88-91).

1629-30—1718. RODERIC O'FLAHERTY of Galway.
Studied under the father of John Lynch and
under D. Mac Firbis.   His chief work is the
" Ogygia," a history of Ireland, written in
Latin in 1685.   He wrote also an " Ogygia
Christiana," which is lost, and a description
of West Connacht (see pp. 91-93).

fl. 1607. TEIGUE O'KEENAN, companion of O'Neill and
O'Donnell in their flight to Rome in 1607.   He
wrote a detailed account of their journey
known as the " Flight of the Earls."   O'Keenan
was a member of the family who were hereditary
bards of Maguire (pp. 129-130).

b. about 1590-1660 (?). PHILIP O'SULLIVAN BEARE, s. of
Dermot O'Sullivan, and nephew of Donell
O'Sullivan Beare, Lord of Dunboy (1560-1618).
He was sent for refuge into Spain while still
a lad, in 1602, where after the fall of Dunboy
he was joined by his father and family.   He
became a soldier in the Spanish forces, but his
predilection was for literature.   His chief
works are :—(1) Historiæ Catholicæ Iberniæ
Compendium, Lisbon (1621) ;   (2) Patriciana
Decas, a life of St. Patrick (1629).   He also
wrote many Saints' lives, some of which he sent

to the Bollandists in 1634. He entered into a heated controversy with Ussher, whose works he attacked. He has been identified by Webb with the Earl of Bearhaven who died at Madrid in 1659 or 1660, leaving one daughter, but this is uncertain (pp. 130-131).

1575-1647 (?). STEPHEN WHITE, native of Clonmel, and Jesuit. In 1606 he was appointed Professor of Scholastic Theology at Ingoldstadt, but returned to Spain in 1609. He became Rector of Cassel College, but was in Ireland from 1638-1640. He travelled much, and everywhere spent much labour in searching for and transcribing Irish MSS. in foreign libraries. To his researches is owing the re-discovery of a valuable copy of Adamnan's Life of St. Columcille in a chest in the town library at Schaffhausen in Switzerland. Most of his transcripts he sent to Colgan and Ussher for their works on the ancient Church of Ireland. A letter to Colgan, dated Jan. 31st, 1640, gives an account of his studies. He wrote an "Apologia pro Hibernia adversus Cambri Calumnicis" in 1615. His other works are religious.

1588-1657. LUKE WADDING, Franciscan and priest. He went from Waterford, his native town, to Lisbon in 1604, and became President of the Irish College at Salamanca in 1617. In 1618 he went to Rome and founded the College and Monastery of St. Isidore for the reception of Irish students, with four lecturers from Ireland. He died and is buried at the College, to which he presented 5,000 printed books and

800 MSS.   He was so much regarded at home
for his devotion to the Irish cause and care of
Irish exiles that the Confederate Catholics drew
up a petition to Pope Urban VIII., desiring him
to bestow upon the President of St. Isidore's
a Cardinal's hat.   Wadding, however, managed
to intercept the petition, which never reached
Rome.   His voluminous works, published in
thirty-six volumes, at Rome, Lyons, and
Antwerp, are religious and ecclesiastical.

d. 1657 (?). JOHN COLGAN was a native of Donegal, priest
and Franciscan.   He was one of the most
famous of the learned band of men whose
industry and talents were enlisted by the
enthusiasm of Rev. Hugh Ward, or Aedh mac
an Bhaird, Guardian of the Irish Minorite
Convent at Louvain, in the service of their
native land.   Among the other labourers
under the same auspices were Michael O'Clery,
Fr. Luke Wadding, Fr. Stephen White, and
Br. Patrick Fleming, who assisted each other
in various ways by collecting and transcribing
manuscripts and compiling their voluminous
works.   Colgan, though delicate in health,
projected a vast collection of the lives of Irish
Saints in six volumes, only two of which, the
second and third, actually appeared.   The
first to be published was Volume III., containing the lives of Irish Saints from Jan. to
March in the Calendar.   It was published at
Louvain in 1645.   The second volume, which
succeeded it, contains the lives of SS. Patrick,
Columcille, and Brigit.   It is known under

the title " Trias Thaumaturga," and was
published at Louvain in 1647. The first volume,
which was to contain a general introduction,
and the fourth and following volumes, which
were to continue the Calendar of Saints for the
rest of the year under the general title of "Acta
Sanctorum veteris et majoris Scotiæ en
Hiberniæ," were not completed, though Wadding mentions in his bibliography of the Minorite
writers, published in 1650, that the fourth
volume was in the press. Fr. Colgan succeeded
Fr. Hugh Ward as Professor of Theology in
Louvain, but he retired from the office in 1645.
He desired to publish the work under the
name of his master and predecessor, to whom
the original conception of the undertaking was
due, but he was dissuaded from this. He
published a small volume on Duns Scotus,
maintaining his Irish origin, and some theological lectures. He died at Louvain about
the year 1657.

1599 (?) 1673 (?). JOHN LYNCH was born in Galway, and
he was probably son of Alexander Lynch of that
town, whose fame as a schoolmaster attracted
pupils even from the Pale. John was educated
partly by D. mac Firbis and partly by the
Jesuits. He became a secular priest about
1622, and celebrated mass in private houses
and secret places until the re-opening of the
Catholic churches in 1642. He was Archdeacon
of Tuam, but not, as generally stated, Bishop
of Killala. He did not mix in politics, but lived
secluded in the old castle of Ruadhri O'Conor,

and for some time kept a school. On the surrender of Galway (1652) he fled to France, probably to Brittany, which allotted public support to Irish exiles. Most of his works were published at St. Malo. He died abroad before 1674. His chief works are :—(1) A translation into Latin of Keating's History ; (2) " Cambrensis Eversus," published under the name of " Gratianus Lucius," and dedicated to Charles II. This great work, though primarily intended to refute the statements of Giraldus Cambrensis, or Gerald of Wales, about Ireland, is designed on a large scale and embraces a great variety of well-digested information on every period of Irish history. Lynch was a strong Loyalist, and he wrote two treatises against Richard Farral, a Capuchin who had endeavoured to renew divisions between the native Irish and old Anglo-Irish settlers.

1570-1646 (?). GEOFFREY KEATING, b. at Burgess, Co. Tipperary, and educated abroad. Returning to Ireland about 1610, he was appointed Curate of Tubrid. He was driven from his work and wandered about Ireland. He is buried at Tubrid. His chief works (all in Irish), are :—(1) Forus feasa ar Eirinn, or " History of Ireland" (1634) ; (2) Trí Bior-ghaethe an Bháis, or " Three Shafts of Death ; " (3) Eochair-sciath an Aifrinn, or " Defence of the Mass ; " (4) Short tract on the Rosary. He wrote a number of poems, some of which are addressed to friends or are laments on their deaths ; others are songs or are verses on the state of the country (pp. 133-142).

1581-1656. JAMES USSHER, Archbishop of Armagh. Educated at Trin. Coll., Dub., of which foundation he was one of the earliest students. He afterwards became Fellow and Vice-Chancellor of the University (1614). He was successively Chancellor of St. Patrick's, Bishop of Meath (1621), and Primate. He was a fiery controversialist, but a man of profound learning. Seldon says he was "learned to a miracle." He took special interest in chronology and is responsible for the chronology attached to the English Bible of James I. (Authorized Version). His large library, purchased for £2,200, was deposited in T.C.D. His works, published in Dublin, 1847-64, in seventeen volumes, are mostly ecclesiastical and controversial. His chief contributions to Irish studies are: A Discourse of the Religion anciently professed by the Irish (1623); Veterum Epistolarum Hibernicarum Sylloge (1632), being a collection of ancient Irish Epistles and documents; Britannicarum Ecclesiarum Antiquitates (1639); and a treatise on the ancient Irish Ecclesiastical terms "Corbes," "Erenachs," and "Termon Lands" (1609).

1594-1666. SIR JAMES WARE, eldest son of the Sir James Ware who went to Ireland as Secretary to Sir Wm. Fitzwilliam, Lord Deputy (1526-1599). He was educated in T.C.D. and succeeded his father as auditor-general. He had a troubled career, having been imprisoned in the Tower by the Parliamentarians, and after his return to Dublin given up as a hostage to the same party on the surrender of Dublin to their forces in 1647.   He was again expelled by General M. Jones, Parliamentary Governor, and lived for some time in London and France, spending much of his leisure in public and private libraries collecting materials for his works relating to Ireland.   At the Restoration he finally returned to his own house in Dublin and took up his old post as auditor-general.   His interest in Irish history and antiquities had been fostered by Ussher, and he made a large collection of Irish charters and manuscripts, employing Mac Firbis to make transcripts of chronicles and documents in the Irish language, which he could not read. His chief works on Ireland are : (1) Archie-piscoporum Casseliensium et Tuamensium Vitæ, published (1626) ; (2) De Hibernia et Anti-quitatibus ejus Disquisitiones (1654) ; (3) De Scriptoribus Hiberniæ, dedicated to Strafford, (1639) ; (4) S. Patricio adscripta Opuscula (1646) ; Rerum Hibernicarum Annales, 1485-1558 (1664) ; De Præsulibus Hiberniæ Commentarus (1665). He also collected and published together the histories and chronicles of Campion, Hanmer, and Marlborough, and Spenser's " View of the State of Ireland."   To his influence is largely due the recognition of Irish history as a subject of general interest.

fl. 1620. PATRICK HACKETT, native of S. Tipperary. He spent a good deal of his early life on the Continent, and was a protégé of Edmund Butler, lord of Hy Currin. Poems, many in praise of his patrons : (1) A beautiful panegyric of Ireland, written on the

Continent ; (2) Calling on the people of Ireland to take up arms, 1645 ; (3) On d. of Richard Butler, of Dunboyne ; (4) On the dispersion of the Irish nobility by Cromwell. Like Keating and O'Bruadair, he was master of both old and modern metres.

fl. 1600. JOHN MAC WALTER WALSH, s. of the chief of the sept of " Walsh of the Mountains," in Co. Kilkenny. Wrote an affecting elegy on the d. of Oliver Grace, the youthful heir of the baronial house of Courtstown, Kilkenny, in 1604, and many other poems which have not been collected.

fl. 1670. FATHER DONALL O'COLMAN, wrote a well-known religious piece called " The Parliament of Women," on the abandoning of vices and practising of virtues.

1650-1694 (?). O'BRUADAIR, DAVID, b. in Limerick or Co. Cork. The chronological order of the more important of his poems is : (1) Epithalamium in prose and verse on the marriage of Oliver Stephen, of Co. Cork, to Eleanora Bourke, of Co. Limerick, 1674 ; (2) Political poem on the ills of Ireland from 1641-84 ; (3) Advice to a trooper, 1686 ; (4) Triumphs of the second King James, 1686 ; (5) In praise of James II., and dispraise of William III., 1688 ; (6) On Sarsfield's destruction of the siege-train at Ballineety, 1690 ; (7) " Ireland's Hurly-burly," 1691 ; (8) On the exile of the native gentry, and (9) on those who became Protestants after the Siege of Limerick ; (10) Lament for the loss of his old patrons, 1692 ; (11) Epithalamium on the m. of Dominic

Roche and Una Bourke, of Cahirmoyle. (See pp. 195-197).

d. after 1718. JOHN O'NEACHTAN, a learned man and good poet. Born in Meath. Among his poems are an elegy on the death of Mary D'Este, widow of James II. ; " Maggie Laidir," a convivial piece ; " Battle of St. Bridget's Gap," a humorous piece. He wrote numerous other songs and elegies, besides translations of Latin verses into Irish. Among his prose pieces are an extravaganza called " The Strong-armed Wrestler," and " The History of Edmond O'Clery." Many of his poems are addressed to priests imprisoned for their religion (pp. 218, 219).

d. after 1750. TEIGE O'NEACHTAN.   He compiled an Irish-English Dictionary between the years 1734-39, and some fragmentary prose pieces. Twenty-five poems are mentioned by O'Reilly.

fl. 1700. EGAN O'RAHILLY. Dates of birth and death unknown, but most of his poems were produced between the years 1694-1734. Lived in the neighbourhood of Killarney. A voluminous writer. Among his more important poems are : (a) Visions and poems on the woes of Ireland (1) The Wounds of the Land of Fodla ; (2) The Ruin that befell the great families of Erin ; (3) The Merchant's Son ; (4) Brightness of Brightness ; (5) An Illusive Vision ; (6) The Assembly of Munstermen ; (b) Personal Poems (7) On his removal to Duibhneacha ; (8) On a pair of shoes presented to him ; (9) Poem written on his deathbed ; (c) Elegies and poems to friends (10) Valentine Brown ; (11) On the death of Tadhg O'Cronin's three children ; (12) On John Brown ; (13) On Diarmuid O'Leary ; (14) Epithalamium for Lord Kenmare ; (d) Satires and political pieces (15) Adventures of Clan Thomas ; (16) Parliament of Clan Thomas ; (17) Adventures of Tadhg Dubh, etc. (pp. 197-200).

fl. 1700. GEOFFREY O'DONOGHUE, of Glenflask, Co. Kerry, belonged to the same or a slightly earlier period. Wrote chiefly in the old *dán díreach* and in the elegiac metres. An accomplished and dignified poet, but wanting in movement and feeling. His poems are elegies, laments, and verses in praise of Glenflask. A lighter poem is a lament addressed to his spaniel, killed in hunting a mouse.

1670-1738. TURLOUGH CAROLAN, b. at Newtown, Co. Meath. Song-writer and composer. His songs are principally odes to women and to his friends and patrons (pp. 214-218). Among his friends and contemporaries were : *Cahir mac Cabe*, harper and song-writer, who wrote an elegy on Carolan's death in 1738 ; *James Dall mac Cuarta*, of Louth, a prolific song-writer : his pieces are love-songs, religious poems and dialogues ; *Patrick mac Alindon*, writer of love-songs and satirical pieces ; *Peter O'Durnan*, of Meath, who also wrote satirical and amatory pieces.

d. 1740 (?). ANDREW M'CURTIN, a poet of Clare, composed a poetic address to a fairy, Donn of the Sandpits, asking him to take him into his service, as he has been neglected by the gentry of the country. Among his poems are a Jacobite song, an elegy on the d. of Sir Donagh O'Brien (1717), and an address to Sorley mac Donnell, complaining of the difficulty of composing in the new metres (pp. 211, 212).

d. after 1750. HUGH M'CURTIN, author of an English-Irish Dictionary, published in Paris, 1732, and of an Irish Grammar published at Louvain, 1728; a native of Co. Clare. He composed several elegies. He seems to have been imprisoned for some cause unknown during part of his life (pp. 212, 213).

1688 (?) d. 1760. MICHAEL COMYN, b. at Kilcorcoran in Co. Clare. In 1750 he produced his Ossianic poem *Laoi Oisín ar Thir na n-Og*, or "The Lay of Oisín in the Land of Youth." Besides some minor poems, he wrote two prose tales, the "Adventures of Turlough, s. of Starn," and "The Adventures of Turlough's Three Sons."

Among the poets and bards who took part in the bardic sessions at Blarney are:

1668-1724. WILLIAM MAC CURTAIN, called William of Doon, though of an Ulster family. He served through the Williamite war in one of King James' cavalry regiments. After the war he settled down at Carrignavar, where he taught a school, transcribed books, and wrote poetry. He became chief of the bardic school on the death of Dermot, s. of John Boy mac Carthy, in 1705. The bardic school was moved after William Doon's death, in 1724, from Blarney to White-church. He was a close friend of Bishop mac Sleyne, of Cork, who was banished over seas, and wrote many poems to him in terms of affectionate lament. Others of his poems are on the depressed condition of the native gentry. A vigorous poem praises the courage of Sir James Cotter, an Irishman who had shot Lyle, one of the regicides of Charles I., who had taken refuge abroad.

fl. 1760. EDMOND WALL, of Dungourney, Co. Cork, was also a member of the bardic sessions at White-church and Carrignavar. He wrote a lament on the death of William Cotter, who was chief of the school between 1724 and 1738, and other pieces.

1656-1726. FATHER OWEN O'KEEFE, b. at Glenville, Co. Cork; he married early and had a son, Art, who died in a seminary at Rochelle in 1709, and on whom he wrote a beautiful elegy. His wife died in 1707, and he then took holy orders and died parish priest of Doneraile. Among his other pieces are a poem written after the Battle of Aughrim, 1692; and one of the many poems composed in sympathy with John mac Sleyne, Bishop of Cork, who was driven across to the Continent in a small boat in 1703, and took refuge in Lisbon, where he died.

1700-1762. JOHN MURPHY (Séan O'Murchadha na Raithineach), was born in Carrignavar, five miles N.E. of Cork, and lived in the same neighbourhood. He exercised the professions of schoolmaster and scribe, but acted for a short time as bailiff to Donnall Spáineach mac

Carthy. He succeeded William Cotter, of Castlelyons, as President of the bardic sessions of
Blarney in 1738, and remained leader till the
year of his death. He was a cheerful, kindly
man, fluent of speech, and wrote simply and
naturally in the modern metres. Most of his
verses are written to friends, or are laments on
the death of the priests and fellow-bards whom
he met at the bardic sessions or who were
personally known to him.

fl. 1700. DONNCHADH CAOCH O'MAHONY, the Reachtaire
or Registrar of the Bardic Court at Blarney.
Poems, many satirical: (1) On the Earl of
Mar's Insurrection, 1709 ; (2) In praise of the
Irish Language ; (3) In praise of the harper,
Donn O'Falvey ; (4) In praise of Father Donogh
M'Carthy, Bishop of Cork. He spent the
greater portion of his life in the City of Cork.

fl. 1769. FR. JOHN O'BRIEN, Bishop of Cork, Cloyne
and Ross. Published at Paris, 1769 (?) an
Irish-English Dictionary. Author of a number
of poems ; some unpublished sketches on Irish
History, Literature and Prosody.

fl. 1738. WILLIAM COTTER, a tailor-poet of Castle
Lehane, Co. Cork. Another of the same name,
Thomas Cotter, wrote the famous Jacobite song,
"Leather away with the wattle, O ! "

1682-1768. PETER O'DORNIN, of Cashel, wrote a long
poem on the ancient divisions of Ireland, and
other pieces. He spent most of his life as a
schoolmaster in Forkhill, Co. Armagh.

(fl. ?). HENRY MAC AULIFFE wrote Jacobite songs,
addressed to Prince Charlie.

(fl. ?). JOHN O'CONNELL. Popular poem on the history of Ireland called " Ireland's Elegy."

1691-1754. JOHN CLARAGH MAC DONNELL, b. near Rath Lurc, Co. Cork. Jacobite poet, writer of songs and elegies, and visions. He was chief of the bardic sessions at Charleville. Among his best elegies are one on Sir James Cotter, who was hanged in 1720 for his adherence to the Jacobite cause, and one on James O'Donnell, murdered near Ardpatrick, Co. Limerick. Among his pieces on foreign topics are a poem on the European war of 1740-48. His two most virulent satires are those on the death of Philip Duke of Orleans, in 1723, and on the death of Colonel Dawson of Aherlow. He was chief poet of Munster in his day, and was a man of greater learning than most of his fellows (pp. 200-203).

1706-1775. JOHN TUOMY succeeded Mac Donnell as chief bard of the district of the Maigue in Co. Limerick. He kept an inn at Croom where the bards of N. Munster assembled for poetical contests. Later in life he moved to Limerick. His compositions resemble those of John Claragh in their ease and gaiety, and their authorship has frequently been mistaken. His subjects are similar ; poems to Ireland, to the Stuarts, and to friends, drinking and convivial songs, and poetical disputes or conversations carried on with different bards (pp. 206, 207).

fl. 1750. WILLIAM HEFFERNAN, called Dall " the Blind," a native of Shronehill, Co. Tipperary. Contemporary with Tuomy and Mac Donnell, with whom he often contended in the bardic sessions.

Among his poems are, Clioона na Cappaige, Caiclín ní Uallacáin, 'be n-eirinn í, Uaill-gut an aoibnir, all beautiful and popular songs. He was of old and respectable family, and lived till near the beginning of the eighteenth century.

d. after 1790. ANDREW MAGRATH, called " An Mangaire Súgach " or the Jolly Pedlar. A contemporary Munster bard with Tuomy. Born in Limerick. His poems are satirical, amatory, bacchanalian and political. His love-songs are full of pathos, and usually free from loose expressions, but he lived a wild and irregular life. His wit was keen and his satire dreaded. Among his sweetest poems is his " Farewell to the Maigue," and his spirited " Song of Freedom." His " Lament " was written when, after being expelled from the Catholic Church, he was also refused admittance into the Protestant Communion (pp. 207-209).

1748 (?) 1784. OWEN ROE O'SULLIVAN, b. at Meentogues, near Killarney. Of a wild and restless disposition. His songs are *aislingi*, satires, elegies and religious verses (pp. 203-205).

d. 1795. TADHG GAEDHEALACH O'SULLIVAN, a popular and sweet writer of religious verse. He lived chiefly near Youghal and in Co. Waterford. His youth was spent in gaiety, but in middle life he devoted himself to religious exercises, attaching himself to a confraternity at Dungarvan, and leading a life of penance and piety. Six editions of his religious poems were published before 1822, under the title of " The Pious Miscellany." His early verse consisted chiefly of love-songs. He was probably called ᵹaeᵭeaᴛaċ from his rustic manners or purely Irish speech (pp. 209-211).

d. 1778. FATHER WILLIAM ENGLISH, b. in Limerick, and took the habit of an Augustinian friar as one of the community in Cork in 1749. He had to renounce song-writing on taking holy orders. Among his songs are " ᴀn ᵱeᴀn-ᵭuine Seoᵱᵱᵳe," " Caiᵱioᴛ ᵯúᵯan," and " Coiᵳ na bᵱiᵹᵭe." A political song headed " Father W. English's loud lamentation after his shoes, stolen by some nimble-handed thief," brought forth two replies from Edward Nagle, a tailor poet of Cork, who composed some pieces with Tadhg Gaedhealach in 1756. One piece, " The Friar's Butter," was written by Fr. English later in life. He was a wit and humorist as well as a poet.

Among the wandering bards who frequently composed airs as well as songs, and who lived on the alms of those whose tables they enlivened by their singing and recitation of old tales, we may mention CORMAC COMMON, called Cormac Dall, b. in 1703 at Woodstock, Co. Mayo. In infancy small-pox deprived him of his sight, and Walker tells us that in his old age he had frequently found him going about the country led by a grandchild. He was an uneducated man, but he played the harp and sang the native airs. He also chanted Ossianic Poems, and was known as a professional story-teller. His best long poem is an elegy on the death of John Bourke, of Carntryle (d. 1746).

d. 1808. BRIAN MERRIMAN. A Clare poet and school-

B1

master.   His chief poem is the long satire
" The Midnight Court," Cúi⟨ρ⟩c ⟨an⟩ ⟨mead⟩om oⁱⱷⱺe,
composed in 1780, which runs to 1070 lines
in some copies. He died in Limerick in 1808
(pp. 150-152).

d. 1814. DONOGH MAC CON MARA or MACNAMARA,
native of Cratloe, Co. Clare, but spent most
of his life in the Counties of Waterford and Cork.
It is said that he was destined for the priesthood,
but he was dismissed from his college. He led a
wild life, occasionally supporting himself by
school-teaching.   In 1745 he embarked for Newfoundland, but the vessel was driven on the coast
of France, where it fell in with a French frigate
and was forced to return to Ireland.   He, however, went there at a later date. He made three
voyages across the Atlantic, and kept a school
at Hamburg.   His chief poem is eⱥⱷⱺⱥ Ꝫⁱoⱡⱡⱥ
⟨an⟩ ⟨Amⱥⱬⱥⁱn⟩ or the " Adventures of a Luckless
Fellow," called the Mock Æneid, founded on
his adventures ; he wrote also " Ⴆⱥn-ⱷnoⁱc
Ⴆⁱⱬeⱥnn óⁱꝪ ! " humorous pieces, partly in Irish
and partly in English, and political songs and
verses on his own life. He composed a Latin
elegy on the d. of Tadhg Gaedhealach O'Sullivan.
He became blind in his old age (pp. 147-150).

b. 1754 (?) d. 1816. JOHN COLLINS, a schoolmaster in
Skibbereen, Co. Cork.   His best poem is the
beautiful " Soliloquy on the Ruins of Timo-
league Abbey," in S. Munster, but there are
minor pieces by his hand, including an Irish
translation of Campbell's " Exile of Erin."
He belonged to the Irish sept of the O'Cullanes,

formerly Lords of Castlelyons. He had a good education, and his poems show that he was a man of refined and cultivated mind.

1784 (?) 1835. ANTHONY RAFTERY (Antoine O Reachtúire), b. at Killeadan, Co. Mayo, and spent most of his life near Gort, Co. Galway. He lost his sight in childhood through an attack of small-pox. Poems: (1) On the drowning of Annach Doon; (2) Laments on Thomas O'Daly, and two to William O'Kelly; (3) Political: The Catholic Rent, and two on The Whiteboys; O'Connell's Victory; (4) Historical: The Bush; (5) Religious: The Cholera Morbus; (6) To Women: The Wife of the Red-haired Man, Nancy Walsh, Breedyeen Vesey, Peggy Mitchell, Mary Staunton, Mary Hynes, etc.; (7) Drinking-songs: In praise of Whiskey, Dispute with Whiskey, etc. (pp. 231-233).

1776-1857. PATRICK CONDON, a Cork poet who emigrated to N. America, where he died. He wrote a great number of pieces in Irish, the only language which he spoke or understood.

A Text Book of Irish Literature

———◆———

CHAPTER I.

The Fenian Tales.

TRADITION tells that in the ancient fortress called the Grianan of Aileach, in Donegal, there sit for ever a thousand armed men resting in a magic sleep, their right hands laid upon their swords. There they will sit until the time shall come when they shall be called forth to take their part in the struggle for Erin's freedom. From time to time they stir themselves in their sleep, and the hollow chambers of the Grianan echo with the words, " Is the time yet come ? " and the resounding answer is borne back again, " The time is not as yet." And so the heroes sink again to sleep.

In like manner the Scot of Inverness holds fast to the belief that close at hand, in a boat-shaped mound called Tom na Hurich, Finn mac Cool and his followers are couched, each one reposing on his left elbow and enjoying unbroken sleep until the time of their awakening. A stranger entering their abode once chanced to strike an iron chain suspended from the roof, whereupon these ancient Fians rose upon their elbows and their great dogs began to bark.

So the Briton dreamed of Arthur, who " passed but

could not die ; " so the Teuton thought of Barbarossa and the Spaniard of the Cid Rodrigo ; so even yet it is told in Ireland that the O'Donoghue sleeps to wake again beneath the waters of Killarney.

No nation in whom the gift of imagination is yet alive ever wholly loses its heroes of the past.   They never really die.   From hill and slope and valley they call back the modern world to the dreams of the nation's childhood, when life seemed large and simple, and men were valorous and hospitable and kind ; when

> " We, the Fianna, never told a lie,
>   Falsehood to us was never known ;
>   But by truth and the might of our arms
>   We came unhurt from the conflict."

It was a happy inspiration which made Oisín, son of Fionn, warrior and poet, live into the times of St. Patrick, and bridge over in his own person the gap between the old world and the new ; no change from Paganism to Christianity, no passage of events from the ancient to the modern world, has sufficed to stamp out the memories of Fionn and his compeers.   In isolated places spots are shown called The Cooking-places or Kitchens of the Fianna (*Fulachta-na-Fiann*) and cromlechs, still called the " Beds of Diarmuid and Grainne " (*Leapthacha Dhiamada agus Ghrainne*), recall the ancient love-tale of the wandering and hunted lovers ; Ben Gulbans in Sligo, and other mountains of the same name in Scotland, vie with each other in claiming to be the classic ground where the hunt of the wild magic boar brought Diarmuid to his death ; and among a peasantry whose historic memories of actual events are vague and dim, the deeds of Fionn and Oscar are clearly known and " Oisín after the Fianna " is yet alive to-day.

Historic Tradition.—It will be convenient at the outset of our inquiry into the origin and growth of the Ossianic or Fenian Literature to give the commonly received semi-historic account of Fionn and his followers. Fionn is supposed to have lived in the third century, and to have been leader of a band of professional soldiers called " Fianna,"* who seem to have been independent of the monarchy of Tara and to have lived exclusively for war and hunting. Fionn was leader of the Fianna of Leinster or Clann Baeiscne. He was son of Cumhall, who had been leader of the Leinster warriors before him, and his chief opponent was Aedh or Iollann, later called Goll mac Morna, head of the Connacht Fianna. In the two chief battles waged by the Leinster troops, the Battle of Cnucha or Castleknock (now Rathcoole, near Dublin), and the Battle of Gabhra, or Gaura, we find the Clann Baeiscne arrayed against the central monarchy of Tara, which was supported by the Clann Morna of Connacht. The feud with the High Monarchy is said to have been caused by the creation of Crimthann of the Yellow Hair as King of Leinster, to the exclusion of the race of

---

* The separate warriors were called *féinnid* or fiann, and the whole band *fianna*. The word *féinnid* is very old, and is used even in tales of the Cuchulain Saga to denote a professional warrior moving about the country with an armed band. Cf. *Togail Bruidne Da Derga*, Ed. Stokes, secs. 141, 144, etc., and *Compert Concobair*, Ed. Hennessy, Rev. Celt, vi., pp. 90-2. The word is not used in the annals to describe any contemporary institution. It was revived in modern times by John O'Mahony to designate the political body which he called the " Fenians." The word Fian, fianna, or féinne has nothing to do with the name of Fionn.

Cathair Mór, whom Conn of the Hundred Battles had slain in the year 122 A.D. and whose cause was espoused by Cumhall and the Clann Baeiscne. Cumhall fell in the Battle of Cnucha by the hand of Goll mac Morna, and the feud with Tara continued during the reign of Cormac mac Airt, who came to the throne in 227 A.D., and that of his son, Cairbre, who was killed in the Battle of Gaura, in which Oscar, Fionn's grandson, also fell.

Fionn's death is usually placed in the years 252 or 283 (Annals of the Four Masters, 286 A.D.). He is said to have fallen at Ath Brea on the Boinn (Boyne), by the darts or fishing gaffs of Aichlech, son of Duibhrenn, one of the sons of that Uirgrenn of the Luaighni of Tara, who had in former days disputed the high-stewardship of Erin with Cumhall and brought about the Battle of Cnucha.*

His most famous son was Oisín, called in Scotland Ossian, father of Oscar, to whom in later days many ballads of the Fianna were attributed. Fionn's chief abode was at Almhain (now the Hill of Allen, in Co. Kildare), or at Magh-Elle (now Moyelly, in King's County). His wooing of Grainne, daughter of his enemy, Cormac, High King of Tara, and her flight with Diarmuid, is the theme of one of the longest tales of the cycle. He eventually brought about the death of his rival and married Grainne in his old age.

The poems and prose pieces give brilliant accounts of the glories of Almhain and of the strength of the Fenian forces and the hospitality and courage of their leaders. Lists of his chief warriors and of the hounds belonging to Fionn are also given.

* See " The Boyish Exploits of Fionn," which gives the original account of this battle.

Foundation of the Fianna.—More important still is the account given by Caeilte, one of the chief leaders, of the origin and early history of the Fianna, and of the captains who held command over them.

According to this tradition, they were apparently already organised in the reign of a king of Ireland named Feradach fechtnach (reigned A.D. 15-36), one of whose two sons preferred to cast in his lot with the Fianna, who seem to have been regarded as outlaws, and " to inherit the rivers, wastes and wilds and woods and precipices and estuaries " of Erin, while the other son assumed the monarchy and entered into possession of the forts, the houses and temporal wealth pertaining to the kingdom. On the death of his elder brother, Fiacha, the second son, who had hitherto followed the life of a Fian chief, became King of Tara, and he committed the charge of the Fianna troops to Morna of Connacht. Four of this tribe succeeded, and then, after thirty-two years of Connacht leadership, the High Chieftaincy passed to Ulster for a short period. Two Munster chiefs, " sons of plebeian men of Ara," succeeded, " in reward of guileful arts," and then came Trénmhór ua Baeiscne, the grandfather of Fionn, who won so great affection among the troops that the whole of the Fianna of Ireland united themselves under his command. For seventeen years he held together the hosts of North and South. Cumhall succeeded him, and fought thirty battles before he fell at Cnucha. After him, for ten years, Goll Mòr mac Morna held the command, until it was wrested from him by " The Golden Salmon, Fionn, son of Cumhall, son of Trénmhór," who, according to this account, lived " two hundred years in flourishing condition and thirty more

free of debility," before he took " the leap of his old
age." *

Conditions of Enrolment.—In Fionn's time the
strength of the Fianna was said to be a hundred and
fifty officers, each man of whom commanded twenty-
seven warriors, who were bound to the special conditions
of service laid upon all troops in the Fianna.   These
were (1) That they should be satisfied with no ordinary
' eric ' or recompense if their guarantee was violated ;
(2) that they should not deny to any wealth or food ;
and (3) that no one of them should turn his back or
fly even if attacked by nine warriors at once.   They
were also bound never to receive a portion with a wife,
but to choose her for good manners and virtue alone,
and never to hurt or distress any woman.   A Fenian
was not permitted to be avenged by his relations in
the event of his death by murder or treachery, as any
ordinary clansman would have been ; he seems indeed
to have been cut off from all connection with his family
and clan from the moment he entered the forces of
the Fians and to have been bound by no tribal laws
or obligations.   This did not prevent bitter and almost
interminable blood feuds between the different divisions
of the Fenian forces themselves, such as that between
the Clann Morna and Clann Baeiscne after the Battle of
Cnucha, but these were entirely apart from tribal disputes.

* The Colloquy, *Silva Gadelica* ii., pp. 165-166.   According
to some accounts Fionn, when quite old, and in order to test
his strength, attempted to leap across the Boyne at a spot which
bore the name of *Léim Finn* or " Fionn's Leap."   He fell, and
was dashed between two rocks.   It was there that the fishermen
dragged up his body with gaffs and cut off his head.

As the tribe was not called upon to revenge an injury
or murder committed on a warrior of the Fians, neither
could it exact any punishment or ' Eric ' from the
Fians no matter what injury they might inflict on the
tribe.   The clansmen were at the mercy of these troops,
whose exactions, waxing greater as their power and
irresponsibility increased, finally brought about their
downfall.   Among their demands (which were enforced
by the whole strength of their arms), was one that
permitted no woman to be given in marriage to any
man in Ireland until she had been offered to and refused
by the Fenians.   Cairbre, King of Ireland, had a fair
daughter named Sgeimh-sholais, " Light of Beauty."
She was wooed by the King of the Decies, with the
consent of her father.   The Fenians interfered,
demanding the princess for one of themselves, or, in
the event of refusal, a ransom of twenty *ungas* of gold
for her.   Cairbre was so enraged that he determined
once and for all to lower their pride and, if possible,
to extirpate the entire force.   The armies met at
Gabhra, or Gaura (Gowran, in Kilkenny ?) about the
year 283 A.D.,* and a furious battle, the theme of many
ballads and prose pieces, was fought.   In it Cairbre
was slain, but the Fenian losses were so severe that the
troops never recovered their former position.   Oscar,
son of Oisín, a grandson of Fionn, one of the bravest
leaders of the Fians, fell in this battle.

The conditions under which a young aspirant might
gain admission to the Fianship were exacting.   Tests
of all kinds were applied to him to prove his mental
and physical fitness.   He must have passed through

* O'Flaherty gives 296 A.D.

CHAPTER II.

Characteristics of the Fenian Legends.

The Ulster period of literary activity, with which a
large part of our first volume was concerned, closed
about the twelfth or the thirteenth century.   Though
the tales of the Ulster cycle continued to be copied
and repeated long after this period, few new tales were
added, and they became in a far less degree than the
cycle of tales relating to the early gods or to that
relating to Fionn and his companions the foundation
of the country's folklore.   The tales of the Champions
of the Red Branch continued to form the chief portion
of the repertoire of an accomplished professional story-
teller, and the chief delight of princes and chiefs at
feasts, but upon the people at large they took no very
strong hold.   The single combats, the chariot-riding,
the great barbarian feasts, belonged to a system of
things too far apart from the life of the people, too
archaic, and too aristocratic to appeal to them as a
native expression of sentiment.

The fierce barbarisms and the splendid chivalries of
the Ulster heroes alike unfitted them to take their place
as the companions of the people's thought ;   they
represented the ideas and manners of a free aristocracy
set in the framework of an archaic age, and they in no
way represented the interests of the folk at large.

Comparison with the Ulster Cycle.—To fill this
want another cycle, the Fenian or Ossianic cycle,
sprang up among the people themselves.   It bears
the marks of the folk-element strong upon it, and it

remains to this day the best expression of the folk-belief of the Gaelic-speaking peoples both of Ireland and the Western Highlands of Scotland, and their favourite imaginative food.

Although the Fenian tales appear to have had their origin quite as early as those of the Ulster cycle, for we find allusions to them and fragments of stories in the oldest manuscripts we possess, the Leabhar na h-Uidhre and the Book of Leinster, they represent a totally different order of ideas and of society, as well as a totally different method of expression and literary form. Indeed the conditions of life to which they bear witness are so unlike those which we meet in the stories of the Northern cycle that it is difficult to conceive of them as having arisen at a similar epoch or among the same people.

Of cattle-lifting raids or Táins, which formed the subject of a large part of the Ulster romance, we hear nothing at all ; though cattle-lifting went on in Ireland for centuries, it was the occupation of chiefs and large owners, not of the poorer classes, and it did not occupy the minds of the tale-tellers of the Ossianic legends. The splendid march of the Milesian freemen, swinging into battle clan by clan, the nobly-attired heroes flinging up the sod with the on-rush of their double-horsed chariots, the challenges to single combat at the ford, the primitive ferocity which obliged an instant attack upon any warrior belonging to another province, or which showed itself in the carrying of the skulls of slaughtered enemies at the belt, all this is gone by.

Warfare.—The popular tale has another complexion. The Fenian leader is not the chief of a provincial tribe

or sept ; he is the officer of men who own no stake in
the country save that which a soldier quartered on a
district he is engaged to defend might be supposed to
feel towards the inhabitants among whom his lot is
thrown, but from whose interests he is otherwise
detached.   Fighting is no longer the challenge of
champion with champion, or a test of personal courage,
nor is it the pursuit of war waged in defence of provincial
territories ; it is either the struggle for mastery between
two opposing bands of trained and disciplined warriors,
as in the Battles of Cnucha or Gaura, or, in the later
tales, it is the defence of the shores of Ireland against
a foreign over-sea invader, as in the Battle of Ventry.

The Chase.—Bloodshedding, either for defence or
for personal glory, is no longer the dominant note
of the legends, it sinks into a secondary place ; and
the chief position of importance is assigned to the
more peaceful pursuits of venery and the chase.   There
are a far larger number of Fenian tales of the hunt of
stags and deer than there are accounts of battles.   The
horn of the chase has succeeded to the war-cry, and
the hound has taken the place of the chariot-horse.
In the Ulster tales the hound seems to have been only
used for warfare or for defence.   We hear of the dead
bodies of battle-hounds lying heaped together with
those of men and horses after a scene of carnage, and
we hear of hounds being used to guard a dwelling.
Such was the ferocious mastiff " brought out of Spain,"*
which guarded the fort of Culann the smith, and from

* *Cóir Anmann*, sec. 266 ; a gloss in L. U. version of the
Táin bó Cualnge, says that the hound came from over-seas,
facs. 60b.

the destruction of which Cuchulain, "The Hound of Culann," got his name.   Among the Ulster heroes the chase was looked down upon as a trivial and ignominious pursuit.   Cú himself indignantly refuses to be thought of as a peaceful hound of the chase, and contends that he is in truth one of the " dogs of war " let loose upon his enemies.   He says of himself :

> " I was not a hound for the coursing of a deer,
> I was a hound strong for combat ;
> I was not a cur licking up broken bits,
> I was a hound who dwelt among the troops ;
> I was not a watch-dog left to herd the calves ;
> I was a hound guarding Emain Macha."

But in the Fenian tales the chase attains a new dignity.   The greatest leaders awaken morning after morning to the cheerful bugle-call, rejoicing in the vigorous and peaceful pursuit to which the day has called them.

The baying of the hounds is to Fionn the most attractive of all the sounds of nature, and his large pack of dogs, all bearing individual names, and, we might almost say, individual characters, are his beloved friends and constant companions.   The interest shown in dogs in this group of tales is very remarkable.   The horse is used for racing, but as a means of warfare it has completely dropped out, for the Fenian warriors fight on foot ; they are totally unaware of the use of chariots, and they do not ride into battle.   But the dog is to them, as he became actually in later times in Ireland, the companion of the hearth, the sharer in the pursuits and the affections of man.   Bran, Fionn's chief hound, is credited with an intelligence which is superhuman, and which is only explained by her superhuman origin and birth. The touching story of Bran's affection for and efforts to save Diarmuid when he is fleeing with Grainne before Fionn, will be remembered.

Fairy Element.—There is a strong fairy element in the Fenian tales which differs altogether from the feeling of aloofness and awe with which the ancient gods are regarded in the Northern cycle. The view of the gods in the Ossianic ballads and tales is much more modern and familiar. They are usually regarded as troops of fairy beings who abide underground in the *Sídh* dwellings, but who are in constant communication with the bands of the Fenian warriors. They have meetings with them for games or war ; we find the Fenian heroes and the troops of the Tuatha Dé Danann playing hurley on the same immortal playing-fields, or they feast and converse together, or they destroy each other on the battle-field ; they even intermarry with each other. Fionn had for seven years a shee-wife who was alive by day and dead at night, and several of his followers had wives of fairy birth.

This fairy element is one of the most distinctive notes of the whole Fenian Saga. When the heroes go out hunting, the hind of which they are in pursuit turns out frequently to be a witch woman disguised, who plunges into a lake or conducts them to some fairy habitation underground where they are feasted and entertained, or, more frequently, imprisoned and held in bondage.

On the rare occasions in which one of the older gods appears in his original aspect as a being apart from and elevated above mortal life, we find that Angus, the god of Youth and Beauty, usually replaces Lugh as the guardian and protector of the heroes. In the tale of the " Pursuit of Diarmuid and Grainne," it is Angus who protects Grainne and carries her off under his invisible cloak when Fionn is seeking her and she can no longer escape from him by other means; Diarmuid is indeed in some sense Angus himself under a new form. In one of the poems in the collection called *Duanaire Finn* we are told that Angus, the " young son of the Dagda of the clean roads," himself led a party of Fenian warriors to Tara and " drove the spoil before them." Like the gods in the Homeric wars, he " plied a hidden shooting " and carried off the spoils of the slain.

As a rule, however, the Tuatha Dé Danann do not interfere as single deities in the affairs of the Fenian warriors, though they are constantly present in large bodies as hosts of fairy warriors. The conception of them in these tales is almost precisely the popular fairy idea of the present day.

Belief in Phantoms.—Along with this belief in the Fairy-people we find the popular superstitions about witches, monsters, giants and dwarfs, huge serpents and phantoms of all kinds. Though a large number of these folk-tales are known only in a modern form we cannot suppose that the ideas they contain are modern; they are those which have held their place from immemorial time in a certain stratum of society. Many incidents that have survived only as folk-tales preserve a very ancient tradition, which may or may not have been written down at an earlier stage. The tale of Fionn and the Phantoms, a grotesque account of the trapping of Fionn and his companions by the Nine Phantoms of the Valley of Yew-trees, is one of the very earliest Fenian stories that has come down to us, for it is found in the Book of Leinster ; yet it is a purely popular folk-tale with a modern tone. In it Fionn, with Caeilte and Oisín, become separated from their companions towards night-fall and seek shelter in a house that they perceive before them in the valley, but which they have never noticed before. They find themselves in a hut filled with the most horrid sounds of screeching and wailing. In the midst stands a grey churl, and along with him are a grim old hag with three heads and a man who has no head, but a single eye in the middle of his breast. The churl calls on some unseen beings to sing a song for the king-warriors of the Fianna, upon which nine bodies without heads rise up on one side of the dark cottage, and nine heads without bodies rise on the other side, and together they raise nine horrid screeches which fill the heroes with terror.

" Though each rough strain of theirs was bad, the headless
    bodies' strain was worse ;
No strain of all so ill to hear, as the whistle of the one-eyed man,
The song they sang for us that night would wake the dead from
    out the clay,
It well-nigh split our heads in twain, that chorus was not melody."

These verses are taken from the *Duanaire Finn*, which preserves the poem.* The phantoms attack the Fian chiefs and fight them all night long, but with the first

* Many of these poems are written in the ancient syllabic non-accented metres. In this poem there are seven syllables to the line, and four lines to the quatrain.

break of day the whole dismal crew, the house and all its inhabitants vanish into thin air, leaving Fionn and the other heroes in a swoon upon the ground, from which, however, they revive in course of time and return home none the worse.

Its Popularity.—The Fenian Saga, with its love of the chase, of song and war, with its pure delight in nature, its strong fairy element, its love of the humorous, the grotesque, and the bombastic, and its markedly democratic tone, is the creation of the people, and it holds its place among them in ballad and song and story wherever the Gael is found.   In Scotland, as in Ireland, tales of the Fenian heroes are familiar at every gathering and are told around every turf fire.   It became a saying that if the Fians were twenty-four hours without anyone mentioning them, they would rise again.   " Old men, hearing these tales, lift their bonnets for reverence," said Roderick MacFadyen, of Tiree, in 1868 ; a reverence not so much perhaps for the matter of the tale, which is often long and tedious, as for the fact that it links them with their own long-distant past—

> " The old days that seem to be
> Much older than any history
> That is written in any book."

Something of the same feeling haunts the Gaelic auditor when he hears the recitation of the deeds of the Fenian heroes as that which is expressed in such touching language, in words ascribed to Oisín in one of his dialogues with St. Patrick.   The Pagan hero and the Christian saint listen together to the song of a bird above them, and the old hero exclaims—

> " If thou, as I, but knew the tale
> It tells of all this ancient isle,
> Thy tears would cease, and thou would'st fail
> To mind thy God, awhile.

> (Sigerson's Translation).

And yet the surprising problem presents itself that while these tales seem best to express the Gaelic spirit, the Fenian Saga, as a whole, does not seem to have had its origin among the Gaelic population proper, but among some tribes dispersed in early times among the general population and looked down upon by them as the remnants of an earlier and inferior race ; the people whom the genealogists of the tenth century called the Firbolg.

This will become apparent if we consider the legend in the oldest form in which it has come down to us, and enquire of what elements it was originally composed.

CHAPTER III.

Origin of the Fenian Tales.

The tales of the Fianna fall naturally into three divisions, embodying a Leinster, a Connacht, and a Munster tradition.

The Leinster tradition became by far the most popular, and the adventures of the Leinster Fianna and of their leaders, Fionn himself, his son, Oisín, and his grandson, Oscar, and of their relative, Caeilte, form the subject of the main bulk of the legends. But the story of Diarmuid and Grainne seems to preserve traces of a Munster tradition, and the frequent localising of the scene of Fionn's exploits around the borders of Loch Lein, or Killarney, and the Kerry neighbourhood, appears to show that many of the legends originated in Kerry or West Munster. The fact that Fionn has a Munster as well as a Leinster genealogy also shows the desire to identify his legend with the Southern Province.

The Connacht Tradition and Goll mac Morna. —The Connacht legend, of which Aedh or Goll mac Morna was the hero, would seem to have originally occupied a large place in the cycle, but to have gradually given way before the more popular Leinster legend. The poems in praise of Goll form a good share of the collection known as *Duanaire Finn*, or the " Poem-book of Fionn," and are found also in Scotland ; while Goll still retains his early position of importance in the folk-tradition of the north-west and west of Ireland.

In a rhapsody in praise of this Connacht leader, found in the Scottish Book of the Dean of Lismore, Goll is extolled quite as highly as is Fionn himself in the companion eulogy on the Leinster chief :

> " Highminded Goll,
> Sworn foe of Finn,
> Hero in might,
> Bold in assault ;
> Free in his gifts,
> Fierce in his hate,
> By all beloved,
> Goll, gentle, brave ;
> Morna's great son,   .   .   .
> First in the school,
> Of gentle blood,
> Of noble race,
> Liberal, kind,
> Untired in fight,
> No prince so wise   .   .   .
> Of fairest face,
> No king like Goll."

He is frequently spoken of as the " great-souled son of Morna," and in the tale called " The Little Brawl at Almhain (Allen) " he is placed next to Fionn himself in the list of Fenian warriors and takes equal rank with him as leader of his own Connacht troops. Sometimes he is represented as the friend and ally of Fionn ; he rids Fionn of a terrible deformed hag of whom all the host declare themselves afraid, in order to prove to the chief that " when the need is greatest, 'tis then the friend is proven ; "* and his trustworthiness is commented on frequently in the Ossianic poems :

* Tale of the Cave of Keshcorran, *Silva Gadelica*, Ed. S. H. O'Grady, ii., p. 347.

" We were staunch, relying on Goll ; now that Goll
of the feasts lives not, every man is bold against us."
There is a touching story of Goll's protection of his
adversary, Fionn, when the latter had ventured alone
one evening across the ford and found Goll sleeping
in the midst of his hosts.   Fionn awakens and challenges
Goll, but the chief of the Connacht warriors points to
the array of his hosts who have placed themselves
between Fionn and his retreat.   Fionn appeals to his
protection, and Goll nobly responds by conducting
Fionn safely back into the midst of his own army
(*Duanaire Finn iii.*).   The incident may be compared
to Cuchulain's protection of Meave's army during its
retreat across the Shannon.   Fionn even bestows on
Goll his own daughter to wife.*

But there were causes of jealousy between the two
chieftains.   In the tale called " The Little Brawl
at Allen " Fionn is represented as jealous of Goll's
wealth, and of the rents which he had exacted
independently of the Leinster chief from the King of
Lochlann,† and there were other causes of quarrel
between them.   Nor was it possible that Fionn should
forget that Goll it was who had killed his father in the
Battle of Cnucha.   This deed was always coming up
between them, and it ended in a violent feud in which
Fionn pursued Goll with persistent enmity and finally
drove him to death.   Goll is found pent up at last on
a narrow crag in the wide ocean, his faithful wife by
his side still refusing to abandon him, fierce with the
pangs of hunger and with only brine to drink, yet still
untamed, and slaying one by one the warriors sent
against him.   One of the most pathetic poems in the

* *Ibid.*, ii., p. 347.   † *Ibid.*, ii., p. 380.

Duanaire Finn (No. X) describes his appeal to his wife
on the evening before he is slain to leave his side and
seek safety in the tents of the enemy, and her refusal to
do so ; while another short poem of great force launches
as the refrain of each stanza his curse upon the house
of Baeiscne.

The character of Goll mac Morna is everywhere
represented as powerful, noble, and magnanimous.

Fionn.—But though Goll is lauded for magnanimity,
Oisín for wisdom and poetical gifts, and Oscar for
bravery, it is around the head of Fionn that the praises
of the poets cluster. He is the " golden salmon,"
" the gift-bestowing noble leader of the hosts," " the
diversely accomplished sage," the Fian chief whose
accomplishments exceeded those of all the fifteen Fian
leaders before him.* He is equally renowned as poet
and warrior ; most of the early Fenian poems are
ascribed to Fionn himself or to Caeilte, or to his poetic
son, Fergus True-lips ; it is only later that we find
Oisín replacing Fionn as the supposed author of the
Ossianic ballads and verses. Caeilte is regarded as
the author of nearly all the poems in the " Colloquy,"
save a few ascribed to Fionn, and he frequently composes
them in response to questions proposed by Oisín ;
while in the collection called *Duanaire Finn*, the authors
are various. The Leinster chief's generosity is such
that—

> " Were but the brown leaf that the wood sheds from it gold—
> Were but the white billow silver—
> Fionn would have given it all away ; "†

while the splendour of his equipment, his fort and

* *Silva Gad.*, ii., pp. 166-167.   † *Ibid.*, ii., p. 104.

servants, his retinue of poets, physicians, wise men and warriors is the theme of innumerable poems and eulogies. Yet the actual character of the hero as we find it set before us in the tales is strangely in contrast to these fair eulogiums. He is often represented as vindictive, tortuous in his dealings, little given to pity or to straightforward action. He would seem to have two aspects; his official character as a chieftain, and his less pleasing character as a private individual. As we may regard the personality of Fionn to be compounded out of many different ideals, this need not disturb us.

Leinster Tradition.—The great number of poems and tales dealing with the adventures of Fionn, or ascribed to the hero himself, amply prove that the Ossianic cycle is in the main a Leinster product. Fionn himself is a Leinster man, his palace is at Almhain (Allen), in the present County of Kildare, and the tales deal for the greater part with the wars and deeds of the Leinster Fianna. It will be necessary to look a little more closely into the matter in order to discover among what section of this Leinster population the tales arose and under what circumstances the cycle was formed. The genealogies of Finn will aid us in determining this. They are not very easy to understand, because he has at least three distinct genealogies, and there are also considerable differences between the various accounts even of these three. The oldest account is probably that which makes him one of the Ui Tairrsigh of Failge (Offaley, a great district comprising the present counties of Kildare and parts of King's and Queen's Counties), sometimes identified with the

Luaigne of Tara, or more properly with the Gaileoin, a distinct race of people settled in parts of Leinster. This is his Leinster pedigree, and by much the oldest and most important.

Munster Tradition.—The two others connect him with Munster. The first gives him a descent from the Corca-Oiche Ui Fidhgeinte,* from whom the tribe of the Ui Tairrsigh branched. The second makes him a descendant of the Orbhraighe, of Druim Imnocht, probably the people of the barony of Orrery in Co. Cork. These are only three of the most important out of the six different descents assigned to Fionn mac Cumhall in Mac Firbis' great collection of genealogies. Evidently there was much uncertainty about his real origin, and he was claimed as champion by both the Southern Provinces and assigned a place among their tribes. We may discard here the theories of his Munster origin, which seem to have been invented at some late date, probably when the kingdom of Cashel rose into prominence, or when the family of the Dal Cais came to the front with the rapid rise of Brian Boru to power.† It may well have seemed a necessity to be able to claim one of the national heroes as the head

---

* Intended in the later genealogies to designate the sept of that name in Co. Limerick.

† The only sept that claimed descent from Fionn is the Dal Cais, *i.e.*, the O'Briens of Munster. It is said that Fearcorb, their progenitor, was son of one of Finn's daughters by Grainne, d. of Cormac mac Airt. As the Dal Cais, or Dalcassians, were unknown to fame until shortly before the time of Brian Boromhe (Boru) and his brothers, it is clear that this Munster genealogy was invented after that time to dignify the ancestry of their race.

of the Southern clans; but the general tradition has
always made Fionn a Leinsterman, and there is good
manuscript authority for adhering to this tradition.
It is not only supported by Mac Firbis, but also more
explicitly in the Book of Leinster.*

We give here this pedigree from the Book of Leinster,
with some additions from other sources to make it more
complete.

Leinster Pedigree.

Bresal *brec*

Connla, ancestor   Lughaid, ancestor
of Ossory   of Leinster

Setna *Sithbhrac*, k. of Leinster; his 4th son was

Nuada necht, who killed Eterscel mòr, and became k. of Tara; m.
                                    Almu

Baeiscne   Dond-duma

Eltan   Tadhg   m. Rairiu

Sualt

Trenmhór (m. Bàine, d. of Scúl *balbh*)

Cumhall, m. —   —   —   Muirn *munchaemh*

Fionn

We must remark on this pedigree that the names
Eltan and Sualt are usually omitted.   In one of Mac
Firbis' genealogies they are given as one word, " Sab-
halt," but the real explanation of them is found in
a tract on Fionn in MS. Egerton, 1782, in which Fionn's
pedigree is given thus: " Fionn, s. of Cumhall, s. of
Sualtach, s. of Baeiscne, s. of Nuada Necht."   It is
clear that this is no other than the father of Cuchulain

* cf. *Silva Gadelica*, ii., Extracts X. (iv.), *a. b.*, p. 519; and the
" Colloquy with the Ancient Men," *ibid*. ii., p. 245.

transferred into the genealogy of Fionn.* To show the wide differences which exist in Fionn's pedigrees we give one of the Munster genealogies from the Book of Lecan (col. 768).

Sen
|
Dedad (mythical ancestor of the Ivernians of Munster,
| who were called Clann Dedad).
Daire
|
Irgoll (or " Forgoll," Mac Firbis).
|
Goll
|
Fir-da-Roth
|
Baeiscne
|
Cumhall
|
Fionn

A note to this adds, " This is not the Leinster pedigree."

Difficulties in the Pedigrees.

—The variety in his pedigrees was evidently long ago a matter of difficulty to the scribes, for in MS. Egerton, 1782, after relating that Fionn fell in battle with the three sons of Uirgrenn and Aichlech mòr, son of Duibhrenn, the third son of Uirgrenn, at Ath Brea on the Boyne, the scribe adds : " His origin the experts declare variously ; some of them say that he was of the Corca-oiche in Ua Fidh-geinte ; others again assert (and this is the truth of the matter) that he was of the úi Tairrsigh of Offaley, which were of the Aithech Tuatha, as Maelmura has

* This reading of the name was conjectured by Dr. Kuno Meyer in an article on Fionn's genealogy which appeared in the *Academy*, February 21st, 1885 ; but he does not seem to have been aware of the references which confirm his supposition.

said in the chronicle : Six stocks there are that shall have territorial settlement, but are not of Breogan's people, viz. : the Gabhraidhe of the Suca ; the Ui Tairrsigh, the Gaileoin of Leinster [and others]." (Sil. Gad, ii., p. 99.)

In the piece called " The Boyish Exploits of Fionn " (*Mac-ghniomhartha Fhinn*) Cumhall is said to be " of the Corca-oiche, a tribe of Cuil Contuinn, and it was from these that the Ui Tairrsigh, the tribe of Cumhall, branched."* This tale is a very old one, being found in the Psalter of Cashel. The Leinster origin of the tribe we may consider to have been the oldest tradition, and it corresponds to all we otherwise know of the Ui Tairrsigh, *i.e.*, the people of Cumhall, who were a Leinster sept of the Ui Failghe, the traditional descendants of Ros Failghe, eldest son of Cathair mòr. Their country was very extensive before the English invasion, and from them the O'Conor Falys and O'Dempseys claim descent. It comprised the present baronies of East and West Offaley in Kildare and other districts in King's and Queen's Counties.† There is, however, considerable difference in the account of the exact home of the úi Tairrsigh. In the " Colloquy " Drum Cree (Druim Criaich) in Westmeath is said to be in their territory. It is evident that Fionn has been localized in various districts of Leinster. Accepting

---

* O'Donovan locates this tribe " on the borders of Meath and Cavan," which would have been within the ancient borders of Ulster, but his opinion is unauthenticated.

† In the " Colloquy " this pedigree is given thus : " Fionn, s. of Cumhall, s. of Tredhorn, s. of Cairbre *garbshrón* " rough nose," s. of Fiacha *fóbhreac*, " slightly freckled," of the úi Fhailge. *Sil. Gad*, ii., p. 245.

this general tradition of the race of Fionn and Cumhall
as the one usually accounted most correct, we must
ask, who were these peoples, the Ui Tairrsigh, the
Gaileoin, the Gabhraidhe, and the Luaigne of Tara
from whom this great hero was popularly believed to
be descended ?

It will be remembered that in the quotation made
above from the account of Fionn's death, found in
MS. Egerton, 1782, these three stocks are said to be not
of Breogan's people, that is, not of the Milesian race,*
though they were settled among them, but to be of the
Aithech Tuatha or unfree tribes, who were a subject race.
This is said to be quoted from Maelmura of Fathan,
a writer of genealogical and historical poems, who
died in 884.   It is possible that in Maelmura's time
these remnants of a subject race may still have remained
in Leinster and have been known to him.   In any
case their tradition was still alive.   Keating repeats
the same account of them in his chapter on the Firbolg.
He says : " Some antiquaries say that it is from the
Firbolg come these three tribes which are in Ireland,
but are not of the Gael, namely, the Gabhraidhe of
Suca (R. Suck) in Connacht, the Ui Tairrsigh in the
country of the O'Failge and the Gaileoin of Leinster."†

The Firbolg.—The people from whom Fionn was
believed to be descended were then a subjected race,
not of the true Gaels or Milesians, but belonging to those
vassal tribes scattered through the country who were
known under the general name of Firbolg, and who

---

* Breogan was father of Bili, whose son was Galamh or
Milesius, the ancestor of the Milesians.

† History of Ireland, Ed. Comyn, for Ir. T. Society, p. 201.

were popularly believed to have inhabited the whole
of Ireland at an earlier period of its history.

They are more commonly divided into the Fir Galian,
the Fir Domhnann, and the Fir Bolg,* but were gathered
under the general name of Fir Bolg.   These people
were looked down upon by the true Gaels, and were
regarded by them with the utmost contempt and hatred.
Mac Firbis, in his introduction to his great Book of
Genealogies, says of them : " Everyone who is black-
haired, who is a tattler, guileful, tale-telling, noisy,
contemptible ;   every wretched, mean, strolling, un-
steady, harsh and inhospitable person ;   every slave,
every mean thief, every churl, everyone who loves not
to listen to music and entertainment, the disturbers of
every council and assembly and the promoters of
discord among men, these are the descendants of the
Firbolg, of the Gaileoin, of Liogairne and of the
Fir Domhnann, in Erin.   But, however, the descendants
of the Firbolg are the most numerous of all these."

But though this was the official verdict of the
conquerors upon the races they had conquered, but
who remained scattered among them up and down
the country, the occasional glimpses that we get of
these people in the stories give us quite a different idea
of them.   As a matter of fact, the Gaels seem to have
been jealous of their activity, courage and energy.
In the opening account of the forces collected by Queen
Meave for the war of the *Táin bó Cuailnge*, we find
the Gaileoin or Gailiana exceeding all the other troops
of Ireland in these qualities.   When King Ailell, her

* *Ibid*, p. 195.   Cf. The Irish Nennius, Ed. Todd, 1848, pp. 44,
49 ; and for a list of the unfree or rent-paying tribes, cf. O'Curry
Mans. Cust., Intro., p. xxvii. *n.*

husband, questions her as to the spirit and disposition
of the various contingents, she is forced angrily to
acknowledge that in comparison with the Gailiana or
Gaileoin all the others were but a poor set ; when the
other troops had but just halted to encamp, the Gailiana
had finished pitching their tents and bothies ; when
others had set up their shelters the Gailiana had made
an end of cooking ; when others were beginning to eat,
the Gailiana had finished their meal ; while others were
still eating, the Gailiana were already in bed and asleep.
Ailell congratulates himself that they have such excellent
troops on their side, but Meave protests that she would
like to exterminate the whole of them, as she considers
them to be a danger in the host.   She is only dissuaded
from this vengeful and unjust act by the persuasions
of Fergus and her husband, and on condition that they
are dispersed through the army and are not allowed
to remain more than five men together in any one
place.   It was the policy of the free tribes or Milesians
in every way to depress and hold down their powerful
predecessors.   Like Meave, they feared that a com-
bination of these active warriors might at some time
threaten their authority, and they took the same course
as Meave pursued with the Gaileoin to weaken them,
by dispersing them throughout all Erin and taking
their lands from them.*

It seems to have been among this brave but unfree
race that the legends of the Fianna had their origin.
It is impossible to suppose that the Gael would
deliberately have made Fionn, who became a national
hero for the whole country, a member of the race they

* See Mac Firbis' Introduction to the Book of Genealogies ;
O'Curry, *Mans. Cust.*, Intro., xxvii. *n.*

despised, unless some early tradition had existed identifying the legends with these people. But if they had learned the stories from these warlike remnants of older races living beside and among themselves and among whom probably their children were fostered, a people who were their servants, nurses and hired troops, the theories of Fionn's origin would become comprehensible. They traced his descent from the septs among whom his legends were first repeated.

Slow Acceptance of the Tales.—If we accept this theory of the rise of the Fenian legends among a subject race it would help us also to explain the otherwise curious fact of their slow acceptance by the learned men and the deliberate preference shown by them for the literature of the Cuchulain cycle, which arose among the free and dominant Gaelic peoples and is marked by a haughty independence. That a number of the stories were known in the time of the gathering of the great collections of romance in the eleventh and twelfth centuries, and even long before this, is certain ; the tales, poems and allusions found in our earliest remaining books, the Psaltair of Cashel, the Book of the Dun, and the Book of Leinster prove this abundantly. But though they were known, they are only sparsely represented among the great mass of Cuchulain tales or of tales of independent origin. They seem to have been unwillingly admitted as part of the national literary heritage and to have been dependent almost entirely upon oral transmission through several centuries. Though a single allusion in an old poem makes us aware that the love tale of Diarmuid and Grainne is as old at least as the ninth century, the oldest copy that we have of the whole story is of the fifteenth century. The great bulk of the stories of the Cuchulain cycle which has come down to us dates, in its written form, from the twelfth and thirteenth centuries, but the great bulk of the written Ossianic Literature comes to us from the late fifteenth century onward, the largest portion being comparatively recent and dating only from the seventeenth and eighteenth centuries. Yet it is quite possible that of the two the Fenian legend is in its origin older than the Cuchulain cycle. There are proofs that the general outline, already half-historic, half-romantic, was formed at least by the eighth or ninth century. The tales of Mongan-Fionn are thought to belong to the eighth century; there are allusions to Fionn in the Eulogy on St. Colum-cille (*Amra Choluimb Chille*), and in Cormac's Glossary, which cannot be more than a century later, and Cinaedh hui Artacain (d. 975), and Tighernach the Annalist (d. 1088), both mention the death of Fionn at Ath-Brea on the Boyne.

No doubt, the legends themselves are far older than any written record we have of them. The fact that they were generally known, but not considered to be worthy of insertion in the great collections, is easily understood on the supposition that they were looked upon as the popular folk-beliefs and stories of the people who were regarded by the ruling and dominant class as their vassals, an inferior race whom they at once feared and despised; it is not easily explained on any other ground. Its rise and location in different parts of Ireland is also natural when we consider how these people were dispersed through the country. Starting with a common tradition the cycle would develop along independent lines in Leinster, in Connacht, and in Munster, and in each province localities would be identified with the deeds of Fionn and his heroes, and special stories would be invented to illustrate them. With the dying out of the more splendid Cuchulain cycle, and with the gradual absorption of the subject races in the general population and the loss of those distinctive marks of vassalage which had divided them off as a separate race from the aristocratic families, the tales of Fionn would work their way upward and begin to receive wider notice. The Ulster cycle was too local to retain a permanent place, and it had never touched the people at all ; it remained as the ideal and pastime of the well-to-do and ruling classes. When Ulster ceased to give its kings to Tara and Munster princes replaced the long succession of Ui Néill, a fresh heroic legend, representing southern Ireland, was needed ; perhaps we may take the adoption of Fionn as head of the house of Dal Cais, whose chief, Brian, rose to be first Southern King of Ireland, as a mark of the change of feeling. At any rate it was about this time that the cycle underwent its greatest expansion.

The Norse invasions brought into it a new and wider element. Fionn and Goll were no longer mere local leaders of mercenary bands, engaged in carrying on interminable blood-feuds between themselves, and occupied during the months in which they could not fight in the more peaceful arts of venery ; they became national warriors, engaged in defending the coasts against foreign invasion, or extending a world-power outside Ireland. The Lochlannach is no longer a fairy-being, dwelling beneath the waters of the inland lakes; he is the Norse invader against whom Brian and the whole country must wage never-ceasing war.

Second Period.—To this second period of Ossianic revival belong a large number of tales and ballads which have as their subject fights with over-sea warriors, excursions into distant lands, and the rescue of fair women from foreign tyrants.

These tales and ballads, having the Norse invasions as their subject, continued to be invented at least up to the twelfth century, for several mention the name of Manus or King Magnus of Norway, who fell in battle in Ireland in 1103 A.D. After the middle of the twelfth century, though Norse raids continued, they were rather isolated attacks than national efforts to conquer the country. The coming of the Normans directed attention in another direction, and we may consider that the second epoch of the Ossianic legend closed about this time. There is no mention in any of the poems or prose tales of the Norman invaders; we may therefore presume that they ceased for a time to be invented.

The third period of Ossianic production extends from before the fifteenth century down almost to our own day. The great body of Scottish and Irish Ossianic ballads belongs to this period, with numerous prose tales, usually of an extravagant and bombastic nature, intended chiefly for entertainment and retaining little trace of the historic tone of the ancient tales.

CHAPTER IV.

Historical Probability of the Fenian Legend.

Before examining the separate tales more closely, let us return for a moment to the traditions of Fionn's ancestry and personality. We have said that the Fenian legends appear to have arisen among the Firbolg peoples, but the question still remains : was Fionn an actual chief of Leinster warriors, and did such a body of troops ever actually exist as we hear of in the traditions of the Fianna, over whom Fionn is represented as presiding either as captain of a local militia or as an over-sea conqueror and guardian of Ireland in the Norse period ? To answer the latter part of the question we can appeal to the history of the period. The method of attack by the Norse and the defence offered by the Irish are well known, and we may say at once that there is no notice in the history of a force organised under its own leaders for the defence of the country, independent of the tribal and provincial chiefs or of the Kings of Tara. The tribal system, in which each chief called out and sustained his own tribesmen in the field, himself leading them to battle, was in full sway during the Norse period and was the ordinary method of defence. There was, indeed, just such quartering of soldiers upon the people as was complained of under the Fenian *régime*, but it was Norse or Norse-Irish fighting-men from whose exactions the native inhabitants suffered. There is no sign during the Norse period of the existence of an organised militia for purposes of national defence such as is pictured in the Fenian tales. But for purposes of foreign warfare it is probable that in Ireland, as elsewhere, bodies of mercenary troops under powerful leaders would constantly be raised, who would be independent of the claims of the sept and would be ready for service whenever required. Whether they were also used within the country is uncertain.

Such semi-historical stories as the Battle of Magh Rath, or the Battles of Rosnaree or Clontarf, or the account of the Battle of Chester in 912, show that mixed mercenary forces were always available when any special military expedition was in progress. Going further back, the constant wars of the Irish " Scots," in union with the Picts and Britons, against the Romans during the fourth and early fifth centuries, make the existence at that time of large levies of trained troops in Ireland fit and ready for foreign service and fighting under recognised leaders extremely probable. The ordinary system of military service would probably have been unsuited to troops employed in continuous foreign warfare ; and forced levies entirely at the disposal of their leaders and whose services were repaid in money or its equivalent would become a necessity. Nothing is more likely than that the unfree populace would be largely drawn upon for such military service. They could be ordered abroad or wherever required with a facility which would not have been possible in dealing with free and independent tribesmen. The fact that these septs had been in large part deprived of their lands and that they were a naturally active and military race would dispose them to turn to fighting as a natural outlet to their energies. Their condition of dependence is expressed in such comments as that in the Dindsenchus of Druim n-Dairbrech, where we read of some of these unfree tribes : " The Fidgai, the Fochmaind, the Gaileoin, were not their own masters early or late."[*]

It therefore seems natural to suppose that the Fenian tradition may have arisen out of an actual condition of things, probably existing in Ireland through a considerable period of time, and the idea of which was a familiar one to the people at large.

Actual Existence of the Fenian Leaders.— But when we pass from the general question of the existence of a militia quartered upon the clans but owning obedience only to their own leaders and not to the chiefs of the clans, to consider that of special personages mentioned in the legends, we must approach the subject with greater caution. Let us return to the genealogy of Fionn himself. It will strike us at once, even if we confine ourselves entirely to the best authenticated Leinster pedigree, that it is a pedigree concocted from mixed sources and that it contains a very large element of the supernatural. The introduction of the name of Sualtach or Sualtam, Cuchulain's father, broken into two and filling two links, is curious, and it becomes more interesting in connection with the whole question of Fionn's genealogy when we remember that though Sualtach is usually regarded as the mortal father of Cuchulain, he is called more than once in old Irish literature, " Sualtach sídhe," or Sualtach sídhech, *i.e.*, " Sualtach of the fairy mounds," and is spoken of

[*] Metrical Dind., Part II., p. 47, Ed. E. Gwynn, R.I.A. Todd Lecture Series.

as possessing, through the power of his mother, who was an elf woman, " the magical might of an elf."*

Discarding the name of Sualtach, which is clearly an innovation, and does not occur in most of the genealogies, we come to the name of Cumhall's father, Trenmhór, or " great strength," which sounds suspiciously like a concocted name ; and when, further on, mounting to the head of the pedigree, we find that Fionn was removed by but few intermediate steps (in many of the genealogies by three only, viz., Baeiscne, Trenmhór, and Cumhall) from the god Nuada, from whom most of the Leinster tribes traced their descent, we feel that we are on ground that is not far separated from pure mythology. It will be noticed that Nuada Necht is also Fionn's great grandfather on the female side, through Muirn " of the smooth-neck," whom Cumhall married, and who was daughter of Tadhg, son of Nuada and his wife, Almu.

Now all these persons are purely mythological figures and are always regarded in Irish literature as gods and goddesses. In the " Colloquy " we read, in answer to the query, " Who was Fionn's mother ? " " She was Muirne smooth-neck, daughter of Tadhg, son of Nuada, of the Tuatha dé Danann ;"† and elsewhere, in reckoning up the chief princes of the Tuatha dé Danann, Tadhg's name is mentioned with such well-known deities as Bodhb Derg, Angus Og, Lir of sídh Fionnachaidh, etc., as " Tadhg, son of Nuada, out of the beautiful sídh of Almhain."‡

A similar mythical origin is given for Scál balbh, whose daughter, Baine, was wife to Trenmhór and

---

* LL. 58a, 24 ; Cóir Anmann, *Irische Texte,* Sec. 282.

† Silva Gad. II., p. 245.   ‡ *Ibid.,* p. 225.

mother of Cumhall.   He is said in one place to have
been " King of the Fomori," or gods of the sea ; and
yet again he is father of the god Lugh *Lámh-fhada*, the
god of light.*

Nuada Necht himself appears in legend under a
double personality ; he is sometimes a god and sometimes the powerful Druid and magician of Cathair
mòr.†   Under both forms his wife was Almu or Almha,
who dwelt in the sídh in Leinster, to which she gave her
name.   This hill of Allen, in Kildare, became traditionally
the central fort and residence of Fionn.   It is called
in the older form, Almu, and in the later Ossianic
ballads, Almhain, but though certain spots in the
neighbourhood are still traditionally associated with
incidents in the Fenian stories, there is no sign of any
ancient rath or mound on the hill itself.   Like other
places associated with the Fenian legends, it vanishes
into a fairy haunt when we approach it more closely.
When, in the " Colloquy," Caeilte is questioned as to
the origin of the name, he replies : " It was a warrior
of the Tuatha dé Danann that lived in the teeming,
glittering brugh : Bracon (or Becan) was his name,
and he had a daughter that was still a virgin ; her
name was Almha."   What comes next is erroneous.
" Cumhall, son of Trenmhór, took her to wife ; in

* Book of Ballymote, fac. 403*a*, 33 ; we find him said to be " of
the Saxons " in B. Lec., p. 385*b*, 41.   *Silva Gad*. II., Extracts
XXIV. (ii.) ; *ibid* VI. (v.)

† The pedigree of Nuada, the Druid of Cathair mòr, is : Son
of Achi, s. of Dathi, s. of Brocan, s. of Fintan of Tuath-Dathi
in Brega.   His wife was Almu, who, according to this story,
died of grief for the destruction of her castle and death of her
husband.   *Fotha Catha Cnucha*, or Causes of the Battle of
Cnucha, *Rev. Celt*. II., p. 86.

bearing him a son she died, and this green-surfaced
tulach was closed in over her. From her, therefore,
it is now named, whereas until then it had been called
' the Look-out Hill.' "*

The same atmosphere of fairy-lore comes into the
description of every personage and of every act of the
Saga. Diarmuid O'Duibhne, called in *Duanaire-
Finn* " Diarmuid O'Duibhne from the Brugh," had been
brought up among the gods, " with the powerful Manannán mac Lir in the land of promise ; " " with Angus
Og, the Dagda's son, he had learned knowledge."
Cnú Dheireoil, Fionn's dwarf harper, is " son of Lugh
of comely form ; " Oisín's mother, Blai, daughter of
Derc " of the forcible language," is a sídh-woman.
(Colloquy, *Silva Gad.* II., p. 102). Even Bran, Fionn's
hound, is superhuman. In *Duanaire-Finn* xvii., we
read :

> " Bran though a hound was yet no hound ;
> Good was her valour, fair her fame ;
> She was no hound's offspring, from no hound sprang ;
> No hunting-dog's offspring was her mother."

But the most important among the traditions
regarding Fionn himself is that which connects him
with a mysterious being called Mongan, who was,

* *Silva Gad.* II., p. 131.

Almu was wife to Nuada, not to Cumhall, and the true story
is told in the Dindsenchus of Almu :

> " Almu, beautiful the woman !
> Wife of Nuada mòr, son of Achi ;
> She entreated—just the award—
> That her name should be on the entire hill." †

† Todd Lecture Series, Vol. IX., p. 73, and *cf.* Dind : of
Rennes, *Rev. Celt.* XV., p. 309.

according to the historical accounts, son of Fiachna Finn, a King of Ulster in the early part of the seventh century, but, according to the old traditions, a son of Manannán mac Lir, and a man gifted, like his supernatural father, with surpassing knowledge and subtle intelligence and the power of shape-shifting.   It is hinted in one story that this Mongan was, in reality, Fionn mac Cumhall, re-born four centuries after his death.   He is addressed as Fionn by a distinguished warrior, who says he is Caeilte, Fionn's foster-son.   It does not seem clear that this Mongan is always regarded as Fionn, but the suggestion is a curious one, and is one more link connecting his personality with the mythological world.   It is the only tradition connecting the Leinster leader with Ulster, and was, perhaps, invented for this special purpose.*

Now, the fact that Fionn's genealogy is traced up to Nuada Necht and Tadhg, his son, who are both gods, need not necessarily mean that he himself is superhuman, any more than the fact that many of the rulers of Europe trace their descent from Woden and other deities makes them gods themselves ; but in the case of Fionn and his compeers the genealogies are so near to the fountain-head and are, like all his history, so closely interwoven with the supernatural, that it becomes difficult to regard him and his followers otherwise than as products of the poetic imagination.   In this instance it is the imagination of a subjected race, regarded as outcast by their conquerors, but whose traditions, as the race distinction slowly died out, became the heritage of the entire nation.   It was a tradition looked down upon by the official story-tellers

*For this legend, see " Voyage of Bran," by A. Nutt, pp. 45-51.

as unworthy of their notice ; they did not recite the tales or copy them into their books ; but the legend nevertheless gradually made its way, was added to and expanded, until from the fifteenth century onward it formed the most voluminous portion of the country's literature. To deal separately with each piece in this vast collection of ballads and stories would be impossible, but a few of them must be mentioned separately.

CHAPTER V.

Longer Fenian Romances.

The Causes of the Battle of Cnucha (*Fotha Catha Cnucha*).—This piece describes the causes of the heredi-tary feud that existed between the sons of Morna, or Connacht Fianna, led by Aedh or Goll mac Morna, and the Leinster Fianna. After giving the genealogy of Nuada and Tadhg, his son, it describes the beauty of Tadhg's daughter, Muirn Munchaemh, and Cum-hall's desire to marry her. Being refused, he carried her off by force. He was ordered by Conn, King of Tara, to give up Muirn, but instead of doing so he eloped with her to Scotland. Then Conn gathered his forces and united with the Luaigne of Tara under Urgrend, or Uirgrenn, s. of Lugaidh Corr, together with Aedh mac Morna and the Connacht warriors to attack Cumhall. They met in the Battle of Cnucha and Cum-hall was slain. Aedh's eye was put out in the fight by Luchet, who, in revenge, was slain by Aedh. This was the beginning of a feud between the Leinster and Con-nacht Fianna which afterwards completely separated them and made of the hitherto united band two hostile troops. Aedh was henceforth called Goll " the blind " on account of the loss of his eye. After the battle Muirn returned to her father, Tadhg, but he gave orders that she should be burned alive in punishment for her flight with Cumhall. She fled to Conn for protection, and he sent her into the care of a sister of Cumhall, Bodhmall the Druidess, Fiacail's wife. Here Fionn was born, and was first named Deimne ; as soon as he was old enough he proclaimed war with Tadhg and demanded full eric for his father's death.   Tadhg gave up to him Almu for ever and a portion of his own hereditary land. A peace was patched up between Fionn and Goll, which lasted until " the slaying of the Sucking-Pig of Slanga," on the plain of Teamhair Luachra (parish of Dysart, Co. Kerry).*

The Boyish Exploits of Fionn (*Mac-ghníomhartha Fhinn*).—This tale opens with an account of the Battle of Cnucha similar to the above, save that Conn is not mentioned.   The simplicity and directness of both pieces are a sign of their age ; there is none of the redundancy of the later tales.   They give a brief narration of events, couched in short sentences, and show no effort after literary style.   The story goes on to relate the rearing of Fionn in the forest and his early adventures, his boyish feats of courage, and the adoption of his name Fionn " fair " in place of Deimne on account of the fairness of his appearance.   He visits the plain of the Liffey (Magh Life) and takes part in hurling on the lawn, hunts deer in the Slieve Bloom Mountains (Sléibhe Bládhma), and hires himself into military service to the King of Bantry in S. Munster ; he also remains some time with a king in Co. Kerry, and passes thence

* These were magical swine which re-appeared as often as they were killed and eaten.   The last Slanga pig is said to have satisfied twenty-five battalions.   Tadhg is here erroneously called " Tadhg of the Towers," which suggests that the version must be later than the reign of the celebrated King of Connacht of that name who died 954 A.D., and with whom he seems to have been confused.

into Connacht. Afterwards he seeks the R. Boyne, to study with Finn-eigeas and to watch for the " Salmon of Knowledge " from the pool of Feic, the eating of which was to endue him with wisdom and with the gifts of magic and prophecy. When the salmon was caught, Fionn was put to cook it, but happening to touch it with his thumb, he burned himself and put the thumb into his mouth, by which means all magical knowledge became revealed to him. Henceforth, whenever he was in difficulty he had recourse to his " Thumb of Knowledge ; " when he put it under his tooth he obtained the direction he was in need of. The allegory of the Salmon of Knowledge, which must be caught in youth and which is watched over by the aged sage of learning, is repeated in Irish Literature under many forms. The piece closes with Fionn's well-known poem in praise of Spring.*

Battle of Gaura (*Cath Gabhra*).—There are both prose and poetical versions of this tale in existence. It must be an ancient tale, for there is a short poem referring to it in the Book of Leinster. The causes of this battle, which closed the period of Fenian power, have been already stated. One of the finest passages in Ossianic Literature is the account in the poetical version of the death of Oscar, and of the grief of Oisín, his father, and the Fians for their chief.

Some portions of the Scottish version of the poem are identical with the form preserved in Ireland.

* There are manifest imitations of the boyish feats of Cuchulain in this piece ; this is even more evident in a poem on the subject in the *Duanaire Finn* XV., where the prophecy of Cuchulain's future greatness is repeated for Fionn ; but there is no mention of the combats or slaughter. The feats are all peaceful.

The Colloquy with the Ancient Men (*Agallamh na Senorach*).—This is by far the longest and most important of all the prose pieces belonging to the Fenian cycle. It is a collection or corpus of stories relating to the Fianna and their chiefs thrown together in the form of a Dindsenchus or geographical guide. The stories are supposed to be related by Caeilte mac Ronan to St. Patrick as they travel together with their companies of followers through the Provinces of Ireland, each place at which they stop suggesting to Caeilte some reminiscence of the ancient days when Fionn and his people were yet alive and when the Fianna were in their glory. By one of those fortunate chances to which the Irish loved to attribute the preservation of their old legends, Caeilte and Oisín, with twice nine companions, are supposed to have survived by a hundred and fifty years the destruction of their comrades at the Battle of Gaura (Gabhra), and after wandering through Meath they meet St. Patrick at Drumderg, an old fort belonging to Fionn. As Patrick is finishing his chanting of the canon, he perceives drawing near him a band of enormous men attended by huge wolf-dogs, both men and dogs being evidently of another age and time. None of the clergy reached to the shoulders of the newcomers, and as they came up and sat down the priests gazed on them in terror. By degrees they take courage to ask their names and origin. In a few words Caeilte replies to these questions, and he adds that they, with the Fianna, were sustained through life by " the truth that was in their hearts, the strength in their arms and the fulfilment in their tongues." Patrick grows curious to hear tales of the bygone days in which they lived, but he fears that such worldly converse will distract the mind from religion. "Were it not for us an impairing of the devout life, an occasion of neglecting prayer and of deserting converse with God, we should feel the time pass quickly as we talked with thee, O warriors." And again : "Success and benediction attend thee, Caeilte, thy tale is to me a lightening of spirit and of mind, tell us now another tale." This friendly eagerness of the saint to hear the old Pagan legends is the key to the whole of this long tale. There are none of the contentious and wrangling passages which occur in the Ossianic poems proper, that is, in those in which Oisín converses with St. Patrick. Caeilte and the Saint have the most perfect appreciation of and respect for each other and a beautiful courtesy is shown in all their dealings together. Patrick's hesitation is allayed by the appearance of his two guardian angels, who assure him emphatically that so far from it being displeasing to God that he should listen to all that the old warriors can tell of their former life, he is divinely commanded to write down their tales " on tabular poet's staffs and in the words of ollaves," because it will be " a pastime to the nobles and companies of the latter time to give ear to these stories." Thus reassured, the Saint throws himself with zest into the occasion and, having first baptized the visitors, he and his band accompany them round Ireland, each glen and wood and hillock bringing up reminiscences and tales of long ago.

The tales are of different ages, and gathered evidently from many sources ; there is no connection between them beyond their subject and the manner of their telling : some are brief and fragmentary, others are told at great length. At frequent intervals Caeilte

breaks out into some song which arises naturally out
of the subject of his tale. These songs are often of
great beauty and prove a deep and sympathetic love
of natural scenery. The fairy element enters largely
into the stories. We have innumerable tales in which
the Tuatha dé Danann mingle with the concerns of
the Fenian heroes ; they are no longer inaccessible
deities set far apart from human life ; they come as
troops of beautiful half-divine, half-human, beings to
take their part in it. They are placed on the same
level with the sons of Milesius as " two tribes that are
equal ; " they enter into combat with the Fenian
warriors and can be slain by them, or they can suffer
death by drowning and in other ways. They fall in
love with human beings and are wedded to them. We
learn in the Battle of Ventry that there " was not a
leader or chief of the Fians of Erin whose wife or mother
or fostermother was not of the Tuatha dé Danann ;
hostages of the Tuatha dé Danann are taken by the
Fenian warriors, and it is even possible to use towards
them the old Irish custom of " fasting upon them "
in order to obtain some demand. Like Caeilte himself,
these fairy people submit themselves to Patrick and
give the Saint a general command over their hosts ;
all sense of impossible distance between the race of
mortals and the fairy people is done away, and " the
Fianna of Ireland had not more frequent and free
intercourse with the men of settled habitation than
with the Tuatha dé Danann." Very close to earth,
too, is " the flock-abounding Land of Promise," and
the birds of that land are constantly heard making
melody. The Fenian heroes pass in and out of the
sídh-dwellings, which are no longer confined to one or

two special spots, as in the older times, but are thought
of, as they are thought of by the peasantry to-day,
as found everywhere beneath the grassy hills and slopes
or Erin.*

Towards the close of the " Colloquy " Caeilte and Oisín
meet again at Tara, and here the remnant of the Fianna
who had accompanied them " lay their lips to earth
and die " amid the silent grief of the whole of Ireland.
It is characteristic of the piece that Dermot mac Cearbhal
is reigning at Tara, and we thus have three separate
epochs, that of the Fians, that of Patrick, and that of
Dermot and Columcille, united together.

The Battle of Ventry (*Cath Finntrága*).—This
long tale is still familiarly known in the part of Kerry
in which the scene is placed.   It is a comparatively
modern tale, probably not much older than the oldest
manuscript in which it is contained, which is of the
fifteenth century, but it is found in numerous late paper
manuscripts.   It describes an invasion of Ireland by
Daire Donn, King of the World, accompanied by the
Kings of France, Greece, India, Spain, Norway, and
numerous other potentates, in order to avenge the
dishonour done to the King of France, Bolcan or Vulcan,
whose wife and daughter had been carried off by Fionn.
Among the host is a daughter of the King of Greece,
who is described as " the best woman-warrior who ever
came into the world," and who has a terrible hand-to-
hand struggle with Fionn himself.

The hosts are guided by Glas, a warrior of the Fenian
band, who had been expelled by Fionn from Ireland

---

* Here, as elsewhere, the gods or fairy-folk are regarded by
the Christian teachers as " demons."

in consequence of an endeavour he had made to betray the Fenian leader to King Cormac mac Airt. He leads them round the southern shores of Ireland into Ventry Harbour (Finntraigh or " White Strand ") in Co. Kerry, which is said to be the property of the King of Spain, and there they ride on smooth water, " filling the borders of the whole harbour, so that the sea was not visible between the boats," the great bark of the King of the World sailing first into the harbour. All the landing-places in Ireland are said to have had Fenian watchmen guarding them, but the watchman of Ventry is a son of Bran, son of Febal,* of the Tuatha dé Danann, and before warning Fionn and his troops—who are in the north of Ireland—of the arrival of the foreigners, he arouses the fairy hosts, who come in great armies, led by their chiefs, the gods Lir, Bodhb Derg, etc., to attack the hosts of the invaders.

The foreigners are described as inquiring whether these are the armies of the Fianna, and Glas replies : " Not so, but they are another troop of the men of Erin who dare not be above ground, but live in the sídh-brughs (fairy palaces) underground." When the troops of Fionn arrive on the scene a lengthened and terrific conflict (it lasts for a year and a day) ensues, in which the foreigners, who are armed with the most strange and venomous weapons, usually get the best of it, in spite of a succession of brilliant deeds done by Fionn himself and all his chief warriors. The most picturesque passage in this long story is that at the close, which describes the death of Cael and the lament of Gelges (called also Crede), his wife, over his body. The passage is, however, only found entire in one copy (Rawl. B. 487).

---

* See *The Voyage of Bran*, Vol I., p. 127.

F

" Fergus went where Cael was, and asked him how he was." " Sad is that, O Fergus," said Cael. " I pledge my word, that if my breastplate and my helmet were taken off me and all my armour, there would not be a particle of me that would not fall asunder ; but I swear that I am more grieved that yon warrior that I see should get away alive to the foreigners, than I myself to be as I am. I leave my blessing with thee, O Fergus," said Cael, " and take me on thy back towards the sea, that I may swim after the foreigner, and he will not know that I am not one of his own people ; for it would be well with me if that foreigner fell by me before my soul were parted from my body."

Fergus lifted him up and took him to the sea and set him swimming after the foreigner (" Allmurach "). The Allmurach waited for him till he reached the vessel, because he thought he was one of his own people. Cael raised himself up, however, and he swimming alongside the ship.   The foreigner stretched out his hand to him.   Cael grasped it by the slender wrist and closed around it his firm-clenching inseparable fingers, and gave a manly truly-valiant tug at him, so that he pulled him out overboard.   Then they clasped their graceful heroes' hands across one another's bodies, and went together to the sand and gravel of the clear sea, and neither of them were seen from that time forth.

Then came the women of rank and the gentlewomen, and the minstrels and gleemen and skilled men of the Fianna of Erin to search for and to bury the kings and princes of the Fiann, and everyone of them that could be cured was carried where he might be healed. And Gelges, daughter of Mac Lugach, the wife of Cael,

son of Crimthan of the Harbours, came, and over all
the borders of the land were heard the feeble cries and
the truly sorrowful sobs that she uttered aloud in
seeking her gentle mate amongst the slaughter. And
as she was there, she saw a crane of the meadow and her
two young, and the wily creature that is called the
fox, watching her young, and while she covered one
of the birds to shelter him, he made a dart at the other
bird, so that she had to stretch herself between the
birds, and she would rather have got and suffered
death by the wild beast than that her birds should
have been killed by him. And Gelges mused greatly
on this, and she said: " I wonder not that my fair
lover is so loved by me, since the little bird is in such
distress about her birds."

Then she heard a stag on Druim Ruiglenn above the
harbour, and it was bewailing its hind vehemently
from one pass to the other. For they had been nine
years together and had dwelt in the wood that was
at the foot of the harbour, to wit, Fidh Leis, and the
hind had been killed by Fionn, and the stag was nineteen
days without tasting grass or water, lamenting its hind.
" It were no shame for me," said Gelges, " that I should
die of grief for Cael, when the stag is shortening his life
for grief of the hind. . . . Small need is there,"
she said, " for me to bewail Cael and the Clanna
Baeiscne, for mightily the birds and the waves bewail
them."

We have to remark in the Battle of Ventry Harbour
the introduction of matter taken directly from the older
Cuchulain stories. The descent from Ulster of the
Boy-corps to aid Fionn in the fight, and their brave
effort and sad destruction, is an incident precisely

parallel to their defence of Cuchulain during his period of exhaustion in the *Táin bó Cuailnge*. There are other examples in the Literature of the transference of episodes from the one cycle into the other. The Scottish Book of the Dean of Lismore contains a fine poetical rendering of this piece. It represents the hosts of the Fianna as having accomplished a greater slaughter of the foreigners than they are represented as having made in the prose account. The leader of the foreigners, Daire Donn, is here called sometimes, as in the prose version, King of the World; sometimes King of Lochlann. It was usually Greek or Scandinavian princes who were thought of as Kings of the World in the Irish tales, but we find the British King Arthur sometimes so named.

The Pursuit of Diarmuid and Grainne (*Tóruigheacht Dhiarmuda agus Ghráinne*).—One of the longest and most imaginative tales of the Fenian literature. Though we possess no copy of it earlier than the fifteenth century, the incidents on which it is founded must have been known as early, at least, as the tenth century, for in the eulogy supposed to be written for St. Columcille by Dallan Forgall, a bard of the sixth and seventh centuries, and which in its existing form is believed to be of the ninth century, there occurs a gloss which quotes this verse : " As Grainne, daughter of Cormac, said to Fionn—

> There lives one
> From whom I would love a long look.
> For whom I would give the whole world
> O, Son of Mary ! though it be a privation ! "

This quatrain evidently alludes to the love of Grainne for Diarmuid, which is the subject of this story, and shows that the story itself was a familiar one when the tenth-century scribe wrote his glosses and explanations on the old poem whose words had already become obscure to readers in his own day. Such a chance survival as this of a single verse proving the existence of a legend centuries before any written version that we have of it, should warn us that care must be exercised in dating the origin of tales or pieces merely by the manuscripts of them that have come down to us. It is especially necessary to remember this in regard to the Fenian tales, which seem to have been familiar to the people long before they were recognised by the professional scribes or admitted into the written litera- ture. The tale is told with much simplicity and with none of the long adjectival passages which deface a portion of Irish prose romance. It describes Fionn's intention in his old age to marry again after the loss of his wife, Maighneis, daughter of Garadh mac Moirne,* and the advice of his friends that he should wed Grainne, the young daughter of Cormac mac Airt, King of Tara. Fionn agrees, and although since the Battle of Cnucha there had been constant enmity between Cormac and Fionn, the King consents to the old man's wooing of his daughter, and for this purpose he comes with a troop of his foremost warriors to Tara and they sit down to the banquet prepared for them by the King in the Miodhchuarta or Banqueting Hall of Tara. Now Grainne had never seen Fionn, and when her father

---

* The matrimonial arrangements of Fionn are exceedingly involved ; one MS. mentions five wives, but Maighneis is not one of them. We could add others from other accounts.

had announced to his daughter the Fenian chief's intention of marrying her, she had merely replied : " If he be a fitting son-in-law for thee, why should he not be a fitting husband and mate for me ? " But when she finds that her future husband is " a man older than her father," she lays her plan to escape from the bargain she has made. " Then Daire ' of the Poems,' son of Morna, arose and stood before Grainne, and sang her the songs and the verses and sweet poems of her fathers and of her ancestors ; and then Grainne spoke and asked the Druid, ' What is the thing or matter wherefore Fionn is come to this place to-night ? ' " " If thou knowest not that," said the Druid, " it would be no wonder if I knew it not." " I would like to learn it of thee," said Grainne. " Well, then," said the Druid, " it is to ask thee as wife and as mate that Fionn is come to this place to-night." " It is a great marvel to me," said Grainne, " that it is not for Oisín that Fionn asks me, for it would be fitter to give me to such as he than to a man that is older than my father." " Say not that," said the Druid, " for were Fionn to hear thee, he himself would not have thee, neither would Oisín dare to take thee."

Grainne then inquires the names and status of each of the guests, and she sends to her Grianan or women's house for a chased goblet which she fills with medicated wine and sends round the table, putting the larger number of the guests into a deep sleep. While the others are unconscious she approaches Oisín and Diarmuid O'Duibhne, offering herself alternately to each as wife, provided that either will take her away from Fionn. They both stoutly refuse ; and Grainne then puts Diarmuid under those " heavy Druidical bonds," or *geasa* from obeying which there was believed to be no escape for a true hero, to take her away that night; the unwillingness of Diarmuid being shown in every way when at last he is obliged to obey. The rest of the tale describes their wanderings and their pursuit by Fionn, with the efforts made by their friends among the Fianna to arrange for their escape.

The character of Grainne is an uncommon one in Irish Literature. She is selfish, frivolous, and light-minded; the contrast between her vain and coquettish disposition and Diarmuid's noble conduct towards her is very well brought out. Although she obliges Diarmuid to sacrifice his honour and renown, and his place in the Fenian forces for her, the lightness of her affection is shown by her consent to marry Fionn, from whom she had fled, and who had compassed the death of Diarmuid, immediately she was free to do so. It is curious that a very unfavourable opinion of women should be ascribed to Grainne's father, Cormac. Among the dicta with which he is credited is the following on women. " I know them, but I cannot describe them. Their counsel is foolish, they are forgetful of love, headstrong in their desires, fond of folly, prone to enter rashly into engagements—of much garrulity. Until evil be good, until the sun hide his light, until the stars of heaven fall, women shall remain as we have said. Woe to him, my son, who desires or serves a bad woman, woe to everyone who has got a bad wife ! " The opinion held of Grainne by the Fenian troops is shown by the reception they accorded her when, not long after Diarmuid's death by the treachery of Fionn, he goes to seek her out, and " left not plying her with sweet words and loving gentle discourse, until he brought her to his will.   When the Fians of Erin saw their old chief and Grainne coming towards them in that guise they gave one shout of derision and mocking at her, so that Grainne bowed her head with shame. ' We trow, O Fionn,' quoth Oisín, ' that thou wilt keep Grainne well from henceforth.' "

We should like to draw attention to the close similarities that exist between portions of this tale and that of Tristrem and Iseult (Isolda).   They are too remarkable to be explained except by the supposition that both derived, in part at least, their inspiration from Ireland.   It will be remembered that Iseult lived in Dublin, and that it was there that Tristrem or Tristan (Pictish, Drostan ?) sought her as bride for the aged king Mark, who was his uncle.   In both cases it is the woman who tempts the man to unfaithfulness, and the man for a long time resists ; in both they fly into the forests and wander from hiding to hiding, and in both they are helped by a faithful hound.   As the love-philtre binds the lovers together in a bond they are powerless to break, so the " love-spot " of Diarmuid, if seen by a woman, cannot fail to awaken a passion of affection.   He is on this account called *Diarmuid na m-ban*, or " Dermot of the Women."   In both stories, also, the lover's passion is expressed with a force and sentiment found elsewhere in no part of the literature of contemporary Europe.   The atmosphere of the story of Tristrem and Iseult is, like that of the Fenian tales, one of sylvan pleasures and the chase rather than of war and turmoil.   We can hardly refrain from imagining that this tale of Iseult's love, whose passion and intensity so caught the imagination of the mediæval world that it may justly be styled the first love-story of modern Europe, arose out of similar conditions and about the same period as that of the famous but less widely known story of Grainne.   There is, at least, no doubt that at a time when as yet the attention of heroic literature elsewhere was centred upon themes of war or bravery, or concerned itself with religious subjects, Ireland had evoked from her own imagination a series of the most touching and tender tales of love.

The episode of the death of Diarmuid has become classic.   Diarmuid being a foster son of Angus of the Brugh and brought up in the company of the gods, was not subject to the natural ills of life.   Like Achilles, he was vulnerable only in the heel, and in the popular traditions of his death, after having killed the boar of Ben Gulban, he is bidden by Fionn to measure the length of the hide.   This he did by pacing the skin from the head to the tail, but Fionn, who was determined on his death, required him to measure it a second time in the contrary direction, and in walking against the bristles his foot was pierced by one of them, and of this he died.   In the longer story he dies of wounds inflicted by the boar in the chase, to which he had been incited by Fionn, who was his own house-guest at the time, and who knew that *geasa* or prohibitions had been laid upon Diarmuid by the god Angus, his foster-father, that he never should hunt a boar.

As he lies in the agonies of death, Fionn and his followers come up and gaze upon Diarmuid.   " It likes me well to see thee in this plight, O Diarmuid," said Fionn ; " and I grieve that the women of Erin are not now gazing upon thee ; for thy excellent beauty is turned to ugliness, and thy choice form to deformity."

" Nevertheless it is in thy power to heal me, O Fionn,"
said Diarmuid, " for when the noble gift of divination
was bestowed upon thee at the Boyne, it was given
thee that to whomsoever thou should'st give a drink
out of the palms of thy hands, should be restored to
youthfulness and health from any sickness that might
happen to him at the time." For a long time Fionn
refuses to fetch the drink that Diarmuid craves,
but he is at last forced through shame, and because
of the urgency of his followers, to go and look for
water.

" I know no well whatever upon this mountain,"
quoth Fionn.

" That is not true," said Diarmuid ; " for but nine
paces from thee is the best well of pure water in the
world."

Then Fionn went to the well, and raised the full of
his two hands of the water ; but he had not returned
more than half-way when he let the water run down
through his hands, and he said that he could not carry
the water.

" I swear," said Diarmuid, " that it was by thine own
will thou didst let it run away."

A second time Fionn went for water, but when he
had come about the same distance, a thought of Grainne
came to him, and he let the water trickle through his
hands.   Then Diarmuid let fall a piteous sigh of anguish
when he saw that.

" I swear before my arms," said Oscar, grandson
of Fionn, " that if thou bring not the water speedily,
O Fionn, only one of us twain shall leave this hill alive."
Because of that speech which Oscar made, Fionn returned
to the well a third time, and brought the water to

Diarmuid ; but as he came up the life parted from the body of Diarmuid. Then the company of the Fians of Erin that were on the spot raised three great exceeding mighty shouts, wailing for Diarmuid O'Duibhne, and Oscar looked fiercely and wrathfully upon Fionn, and he said that it was a greater pity that Diarmuid should be dead than were it he himself who had perished, and that the Fianna had lost their mainstay of battle through his death."

Ben Gulbain (Anglicised Ben Bulban) is a long low mountain between Roscommon and Sligo, but Scotland also claims to possess the spot on which Diarmuid died. There is a Tor Gulbin in the braes of Lochaber, but his grave is pointed out in Glenshee in the eastern part of Perthshire. He was, in fact, a semi-divine personage, a re-incarnation of Angus Og, the god of Youth and Beauty, and he is the Adonis of the Gael. From the accident of the name of his grandfather he became identified with the district of Corca Ui Dhuibhne in Kerry, but he seems to have been of the tribe of the Decies. The traditions of him have, however, become associated with the south-west of Ireland, where he is still most vividly remembered, and some of his genealogies connect him with Munster.* A poetical rendering of this tale found in Scotland gives the more popular account of the death of Diarmuid from a prick of the bristle in the foot when measuring the boar's skin backward. The account of Fionn's refusal to bring water to the dying man is, however, omitted.

* The Campbells of Argyllshire are called, fancifully, " Clann Diarmuid."

Among the more popular Fenian tales and ballads are the following :—

The Little Brawl at Allen.
The Battle of Cnoc an Air.
The Chase of Sliabh Guilleann.
The Pursuit of the Giolla Decair.
The Festivities at the House of Conan of Ceann Sleibhe.
The Enchanted Fort of the Quicken Tree.
The Adventures of the Lomnochtan of Slieve Riffé.
The Enchanted Cave of Keshcorran.
The Kern of the Narrow Stripes.
The Carle of the Coat.

CHAPTER VI.

Ossianic Poetry.

The poetry belonging to the Ossianic literature may be roughly divided into two parts : the long ballads, which frequently contain the same incidents as those found in the prose pieces, and the shorter lyrics found interspersed in the prose narrations, and particularly in the " Colloquy," or else detached as separate poems. It is only the long descriptive ballads that can properly be called Ossianic. The larger number of them are supposed to be composed by Oisín, Fionn's son, and take the form of dialogues carried on between him and St. Patrick, but others are simple lays uttered in connection with the events out of which they take their rise. Fionn was regarded quite as much in the light of a poet as of a warrior, and one of the earliest and most charming poems found in Gaelic Literature is his lyric " In praise of May," which is said to have been written in his youth to test his learning. It is found both separately and at the close of " The Boyish Exploits of Fionn."*

Duanaire Finn.—Two collections, one made by Irish scribes early in the seventeenth century, the other by a Scottish ecclesiastic early in the sixteenth century, have, fortunately, preserved for us a number of the ballads ; others are found separately and are contained

* *Textbook*, Part I., pp. 225-6.

in a multitude of manuscripts, mostly of modern date (*i.e.*, from the fifteenth century onward), scattered throughout the country.   These two collections, which we may consider together, are known as the *Duanaire-Finn*, or Poem Book of Fionn, and the Book of the Dean of Lismore.   The former was written, according to notes on the margin, by three different scribes at Louvain during the years 1626-27 for a certain Captain Somhairle or Sorley MacDonnell, who was probably serving in the Netherlands at that time.   It is now preserved in the Franciscan Library, Dublin.   The poems must have been collected in Ireland and transcribed for him into a book which also contains, among other matter, a copy of the prose " Colloquy with the Ancient Men " and another Fenian ballad.   Several of the poems in this collection do not seem to exist elsewhere, so that we have special cause to commend the love of his native literature shown by this Irish soldier on foreign service.

Few of them are ascribed to Oisín ; they are usually supposed to be spoken by Fionn himself or by Caeilte or Goll mac Morna.   It is possible that they are older than the Ossianic ballads proper, as many of the poems refer to Goll, and they represent him in an altogether more favourable light than that under which he appears in the poems ascribed to Oisín.   They show little sign of that grotesque element which marks the later ballads ; Conan, the comic figure of the more modern poems, being here represented as a brave warrior and faithful friend.   Nor is there any sign at all in them of the contentious wrangling between Oisín and St. Patrick, which is the most marked feature of the ballads ascribed to the latter poet.

There is a greater seriousness about these earlier poems than in those of a later age ; the bombastic element does not take so large a place. The heroes are still regarded as men of renown, whose history is dignified and grave ; later they often degenerate into merely comic figures, whose exploits are designed chiefly as a pastime or to raise a sociable laugh around the turf fire on a winter's night.

The Irish collection contains, in addition to the true Fenian lays, a large number of poems loosely connected with the history of the Fians, but strictly dealing with the mythological cycle. These are of peculiar interest, as they contain allusions and traditions otherwise unknown to us. Such is the curious poem of the Crane-Bag which carried the treasures of Manannán, or the poem of the Hunt of Balor's Pig, or the still more interesting " Song of Fionn's Shield," which carries the history of this weapon back to the pre-historic Battle of Moytura.

The battles in which the shield played a conspicuous part are related, and the great personages are named to whom it successively belonged. Among them were the Dagda, Tadhg, s. of Nuada, Cumhall, and finally Fionn himself, by whom a long series of battles were fought with it. Among them are said to have been thirty-five battles outside Ireland, and eighteen gained over the Tuatha dé Danann.

The Book of the Dean of Lismore.—The second collection of which we have to speak is that made by Sir James M'Gregor, Dean of Lismore, Argyleshire, about the year 1512, and called from this circumstance the " Book of the Dean of Lismore." The poems were

collected in the Western Highlands and are of the same
type as those preserved in *Duanaire-Finn ;* together
they form a great corpus of Fenian poetry.   The Irish
collection is written in middle Irish with the spelling
somewhat modernised, but retaining the older spelling
in some places ; the twenty-eight Ossianic poems found
in Argyleshire were written down by the Dean in the
Roman character of the fifteenth century, but the
spelling is phonetic.   This, while it is valuable as
preserving the pronunciation of the words, made the
manuscript a difficult one to decipher, especially as
it contained many obsolete words.   Some of the poems
are in pure Irish, some in pure Scotch Gaelic, and
others are in a mixed dialect and preserve the Irish
or Scottish idiom according to the closeness with which
the writers kept to the written form of the ballad.
Of the purely Irish origin of many of the poems there
can be no doubt.   There are productions by such
well-known Irish bards as Tadhg óg O'Higgin (d. 1448),
Muireadach O'Daly, called Muireadach Albanach, or
" Murray the Scotchman " (d. about 1224), and several
others of the O'Daly family ; and there are copies of
poems found in the Irish annals, some of them attributed
to very early writers, such as the Lay of Queen Gormliath, lamenting the death of her husband, Niall
Glunduth, or " Black-knee," who died early in the tenth
century.   There are several poems in this Scottish
collection which are either entirely or in part identical
with copies known in Ireland.   Such are the poems
on the Battle of Gaura and on the Hill of the Fair
Women (*Sliabh na m-ban fionn*).   The use of the word
" sliabh " is a sign, if any were needed, of the direct
Irish origin of this piece, for it is never used in Scotland

to signify a mountain, " Beinn," anglicised " Ben,"
being the invariable Scottish word.   A very amusing
poem also found in *Duanaire Finn* is that which describes
the efforts of Caeilte to obtain from King Cormac the
release of Fionn mac Cumhall from the confinement
in which he held him, by capturing two of every sort
of beast and fowl known at that time in Ireland.   This
duty had been imposed on him by the monarch of
Ireland as the only condition on which his chief's release
could be procured.   The King believed that he had
demanded an impossible task, and it was indeed only
by extraordinary efforts that Caeilte succeeded in driving
before him to Tara his modern Noah's Ark of birds
and beasts, for as soon as he had got together one set
of animals he found that the others had dispersed themselves over the plain or taken to flight through the air.
A short prose version of this legend, which preserves
what is possibly a complete record of the birds and
animals known in Ireland at the time it was composed,
gives a different motive to Caeilte's efforts.   Here it
was Grainne who insisted on the apparently impossible
task being accomplished before she would consent to
marry Fionn, whom she disliked.

Among Scottish poetical versions of stories best
known in Ireland in their prose forms are the Death
of Diarmuid, the Battle of Ventry, and fragments of
the Sickbed of Cuchulain.   There is more of the mingling
of the two cycles in these Scottish poems than is usual
in Ireland.   For instance, Emer is, in one poem, made
to fall in love with one of the Ulster Fians ; and there
are certain whole poems mixed with the Ossianic
ballads that belong properly to the Cuchulain period.
Such are, for instance, the poem on the Death of

G

Conlaech, and Conall Cernach's "Lay of the Heads," both known also in Irish copies.*

MacPherson's "Fingal" and "Temora."—When MacPherson, in 1762 and 1763, composed his "Fingal," and "Temora," which purported to be, and doubtless were, founded on fragments of these old ballads learned by him in the Highlands, he was much blamed for having confused the two cycles of tales and thrown together ideas and incidents belonging to distinct periods of composition and different historical traditions. But although he probably carried this confusion to a degree hitherto unknown, he did not do so of set purpose; he merely used all the fragments of legends and poems that had come in his way, combining them into long poems without any pretence of historical accuracy. The chief error for which he is to be blamed was that he altogether changed the style and character of the poems he pretended merely to reproduce, and yet persisted in presenting them to the public as old Gaelic ballads collected by himself in the Highlands; while, in fact, they were original poems composed by him upon subjects suggested by the old floating traditions still alive in his day among the Gaelic-speaking people, and with some fragments of which he had become familiar in travelling through the West of Scotland and the Isles. His work had the merit of attracting attention to a great body of tradition existing both in Ireland and Scotland which had hitherto only been locally known, and of inspiring Gaelic societies and

---

* In Ireland it is usually the Tuatha dé Danann cycle that is mixed up with that of the Fians; but confusion between the Cuchulain and Fian cycle is not uncommon.

North of Ireland and the South-Western Districts and Isles of Scotland had been of the closest possible kind. The establishment of the Dalriadic princes in Argyle-shire, and of St. Columba and his followers at Iona, had been only the first steps in a union which grew closer age by age.   It was strengthened not only by constant intercourse, but by frequent inter-marriages between the princes of the powerful and almost independent Celtic dynasty of the Lords of the Isles, who ruled in the Western Highlands from the twelfth to the sixteenth century, with daughters of the great Irish houses of the North of Ireland.   At the marriage of one of the most powerful Lords with a lady of the Irish family of O'Cathan towards the close of the thirteenth century, tradition says that twenty-four families from Ulster settled in the Scottish Highlands, and at a later date, a scion of the House of the Isles acquired land in Ireland and founded the Antrim branch of the family.   It seems reasonable to suppose that it was during the time of this later intercourse, that is, from the thirteenth century onward, rather than in the sixth and seventh centuries, that the tradition of the Fianna became rooted in Scotland.   Only a few stories belonging to the Cuchulain cycle, such as the Death of Conlaech and the Tragical Death of the Sons of Usnach, were invented in Scotland, or rooted themselves there and became localised in various spots ; but the whole Fenian cycle in its historical outline appears to have been known, though the folk-stories underwent special late develop-ments in the two different countries.   For a very long period, from the twelfth to the seventeenth centuries, just when the expansion of the Fenian legend was most rapidly going on and manuscripts containing the poems and legends were multiplying, the literary connection between Ireland and Western Scotland was of the closest kind. Many well-known bards and minstrels and several heads of bardic schools are mentioned in the Annals as having been chief preceptors or poets of Erin and Alba, *i.e.*, of Ireland and Scotland, and the careers of men like Muireadach Albanach or Giolla Brighde mac Conmidhe, show how constantly these teachers and poets travelled to and fro between the two countries. Among the men holding this distinguished position were Maclose O'Daly (d. 1185), O'Carroll the blind minstrel (d. 1328), Tadhg óg O'Higgin (d. 1448), and Tadhg O'Coffey (d. 1554).

The hereditary bards and ollavs of the Macleans were O'Neills of the North of Ireland, and the M'Vurichs, who occupied a similar position in the family of the Clanranalds, were of Irish descent, and had received their education in Irish Colleges of poetry and scribal learning. A large number of manuscripts and poems bear the names of Irish scribes and poets, and the oldest of the Gaelic manuscripts preserved in Edinburgh are written in Irish Gaelic and in the Irish character. Through a part of this period, those students who desired to perfect themselves in writing and in the knowledge of their day, appear to have resorted to the Irish schools.

The Ossianic Ballads.—It is probable that most of the long ballads which form the Ossianic Poems proper are later than and are formed upon the prose tales on the same subjects, and that these again come later in time than the simple narrative lays. The dialogue form, into which most of them are thrown, is much less dignified than the earlier style of plain narration, and the actual story is constantly interrupted by disquisitions on the part of Oisín, who compares in a petulant tone the excellence of the household and hospitality of Fionn with the privations endured and enforced by the monks, while St. Patrick replies by extolling the happiness of heaven into which, he says, the Fenian warriors, on account of their Pagan beliefs, cannot enter. These comparisons lead to a constant wrangling between the Christian Saint and the Pagan warrior which is quite unlike the deference shown to St. Patrick by Caeilte in the prose " Colloquy with the Ancient Men." Passages of this kind occupy so large a place in these poems that it is necessary to give a specimen.

In the poem known as " The Colloquy of Oisín and Patrick " (*Agallamh Oisín agus Phadraig*) the old hero begins by recounting the feats of his companions in the old time, and bewails his own loneliness and the mournful and quiet life he is now living among the clergy, where fasting and the ringing of church bells have replaced the great feasts and the outdoor life of the Fenian epoch. Some of the stanzas in this poem are very smooth and charming.

> " I have heard music sweeter far
> Than hymns and psalms of clerics are ;
> The blackbird's pipe on Letterlea,
> The Dord Finn's wailing melody.*
>
> The thrush's song of Glenna-Scàl,
> The hound's deep bay at twilight's fall,
> The barque's sharp grating on the shore,
> Than clerics' chants delight me more."

> * " Do chualas ceól ba bhinne ná bhur g-ceól
> Gidh mór mholas tu an chliar ;
> Sgaltarnach loin Leitreach Laoi,
> 'S an faoidh do ghnídh an Dord Fhiann."

He then recounts the battles of Fionn and bewails the death of the heroes, their hounds, and their followers, and he says, if Fionn were alive he, Oisín, would speedily abandon the clerics and their prayers and follow once more the wild deer with the dogs through the glen. He asks Patrick to pray that Fionn and the Fenians may enter heaven, but Patrick stoutly refuses to offer any petition for Fionn, and says that he is bound fast in hell with all his companions. This leads to a violent altercation, Oisín asserting that no bonds could hold one so mighty as Fionn, nor would his followers permit him to lie in pain for a single instant. When this dies down Oisín begins again by enquiring whether the hounds of the heroes will be let into heaven.

> Tell me in confidence, O Priest,
> If Fionn is left without, at least,
> Will they let Bran and Sgeolan in
> Those gates of heaven fast shut on Fionn ?

Patrick replies :—

> Old man, who lackest grace and sense
> From whom I get no recompense,
> The courts of heaven and heaven's King
> Will never let these creatures in.

And so the interminable discourse goes on. Patrick, as a rule, is represented as a hard and stern old man lacking in kindliness and sympathy, but fine words are occasionally put into his mouth, as when he declares with dignity :

> " It is my King who made the heavens,
> It is He who gives might to the hero,
> It is He that created the universe,
> It is He that showers the blossoms on the trees."

This poem may be taken as a general model upon which many of the longer Ossianic ballads are formed,

CHAPTER VII.

Lyric Poems.

There are found interspersed in the prose narratives of all this period, as well as separately, a great number of charming lyrics, lullabies, hunting-songs, and poems in praise of natural scenery. A good number of these pieces occur in " The Colloquy," or are connected with the names of the Fenian heroes or with their deeds, and may fitly be classed with the Ossianic literature. It will be convenient here to throw into the same chapter some other poems by unknown authors which belong to the period with which we are dealing. There seems to have been a large amount of genuine poetry produced, some portions of which have grown out of, or been introduced into, prose narratives, such as lives of saints, fairy legends or folk-lore and Fenian tales, while others seem unconnected with any prose recital. Caeilte's Hymn to the Island of Arran in Scotland which occurs in the " Colloquy " is full of descriptive power. It would seem that from Lammas-tide (called in Ireland Lughnasadh, or the feast of the god Lugh) until " the call of the cuckoo from the tree-tops in Ireland " the battalions were accustomed to repair to the Isle of Arran for hunting. Caeilte in describing this island to St. Patrick becomes eloquent of its delights. " More melodious than all music ever heard were the voices of the birds as they rose from the billows, and from the coast-line of the island, thrice fifty flocks of winged fowl encircled her, clad in gay brilliance of every colour," he begins, and then he breaks forth into this lay :—

> " Arran of many stags, the sea her very shoulders washes,
>   Island that feeds whole companies, among whose ridges blue spears redden,
>   Skittish deer are on her mountain peaks, soft blae-berries among her moving undergrowth,
>   Cool water flowing in her streams, and mast upon her russet oaks."

He goes on to describe the search of the greyhounds and hunting dogs amongst the thickets, the crimson crop of berries on the rocks, the smooth grass of the glades and the leaping of the fawns over the crags. The poem ends as follows :

> " Right pleasant their condition (*i.e.*, the wild fruits and animals and the vessels sailing past the Isle) when fair weather sets in ; under her river brinks lie the trout, round her grand cliffs to one another wheeling sea-gulls call ; at such a time as this, right pleasant is the Isle."*

Elsewhere the cold of the weather and the deep snow, often commented upon in Irish writings, calls forth a song from Caeilte :

> " Cold is the winter, the wind is risen, the high-couraged unquelled stag is on foot ; 'tis bitter cold to-night the mountain o'er, yet still bells out the ungovernable stag. Well sleeps the ruddy deer stretched out upon the rock, hidden from sight as though beneath the soil, all in the latter end of chilly night."†

He compares his own old age to the chill cold of winter, and he ends by bewailing the Fianna, once so bold and vigorous, now lying dead and cold beneath the ground.

---

* Silva Gadelica, i., p. 102 ; ii., p. 109.
† *Ibid* i., p. 172 ; ii., p. 192.

Very charming also are the poems in praise of Benn Edair, or Howth Hill, a headland stretching along the outer side of Dublin Bay, and a favourite haunt of the heroes. One of these begins as follows :

> " The loveliest hill on Erin's ground,
>   Bright as its sea-gulls circling round,
>   Sore grief to me my thoughts to tear
>   From old Benn Edair, grave and fair."

These poems show, like those of an earlier age, a pure delight in natural things, a love which lingers round its object, giving to every aspect of it a meaning and poetic significance. The feeling for symbolism is strong in Ireland. The winds, for instance, are symbolised by colours, and a mediæval poem describes the character and destiny of a child as being fixed by the point from which the wind blew at its birth. Even states of the mind are characterised in the same way ; there are red, white and green martyrdoms in ecclesiastical literature, and by these different kinds and degrees of self-sacrifice are designated. In a long poem full of charming fancy the trees of the forest are rehearsed in turn, and to each a poetical significance is attached. The woodbine is, curiously enough, called the " Monarch of the forests of Inisfail," and this because none may hold it captive, while in its embrace it hugs the toughest trees ; " no effort of a feeble ruler this." The noble willow is sacred to poems, and may not be burned, " within his bloom bees are a-sucking, to each his little prison-house is dear " ; " the graceful tree with berries called the rowan is the wizards' tree ; " " the precious and low-sweeping apple-bough is a tree ever decked in bloom of white, against whose fair head all men put forth the hand," and so on through all the trees of the wood.

One of the finest of these long poems is the splendid " Hymn to Morning " which occurs in a mediæval Life of St. Cellach, of Killala. It purports to have been written at the rising of the sun on the morning on which he was to be put to death. The Saint had been seized by his murderers the day before his death and carried by them into the deepest recesses of the forest, where he was shut up in the hollow trunk of a tree, there to await his end. His murderers, who had been his former friends and fellow-pupils, but who had been induced by bribes to desert and slay him, sit in watch outside his temporary prison. His fears and his dread of death are vividly described, his sleepless night and early awakening, his dreams of flight, and his final submission to his predestined fate. With the first dawn of day he looks out only to see, sitting on the branches above him, the raven, the kite, and the scall-crow, sure harbingers of his approaching death ; on seeing him, a wolf on the track of his blood slinks back amongst the brackens. " My dream of Wednesday night was true," said Cellach, " four wild dogs (*i.e.*, his four companions) rent me and dragged me through the brackens ; adown a precipice I fell, and never more came up." Then, as the rising sun burst forth and flooded the earth with splendour, he forgot his misery for the moment and broke into a noble farewell hymn to greet the dawn of his final day of life.

" Hail to the morning fair, that falls as a flame on the green-
sward.
Hail, too, to Him who sends her, the Morn ever fruitful in
blessings.

> Morning resplendent and proud, the brilliant sun's little sister,
> Hail to thee, Dawn, thrice-hail, that lightest my book of the
> Hours."

He addresses the wild birds and beasts that are
waiting for their victim, and he ruefully suggests that
it was perhaps " the tiny wren, scant of tail, who is
piping a prophetic lay " from the branches above his
head, who had betrayed him to his enemies. The
quatrains describing his capture by his old fellow-
students, and their hurried and secret journey into the
depths of the forest might have suggested to Keats
the famous lines in his poem of Isabella, or the Pot
of Basil.* They are as follows :—

> " Wednesday night past I saw visions, the wild dogs troubled
>   my slumbers,
>   Hither and thither they dragged me, through russet ferns of
>   the coppice.
>
>   'Twas in a dream I saw it, to the lonely green glen men bore me,
>   Four men carried me thither, I saw only three returning."

Lullabies and laments are also common and appear
to have been set to old airs suited to their plaintive
melody. The lament of Fionn, the old man, over
the bier of his grandchild, Oscar, is one of these ; it
sometimes forms part of the ballad of the Battle of
Gaura, in which Oscar was killed, and is sometimes
separate.

> " Beloved of my beloved, beloved of my beloved,
>   Child of my own child, white-skinned and slender."

A weird and lovely melody which has the sound of a

---

* " So the two brothers and their murdered man, rode past
fair Florence," etc.—Stanza xxvii.

swing among the trees or of the night-wind sighing round the house is the old fairy lullaby, which begins :—

> " My cause of merriment, soft and sweet art thou
> Of the race of Coll and Conn art thou ;
> My cause of merriment, soft and sweet art thou
> Of the race of Conn art thou.
>
> My soft cause of merriment, my soft rushes,
> My lovely rock plant,
> Were it not for the charm that is on your foot
> We would lift you with us."

These are only examples of a copious literature of lyric verse.

CHAPTER VIII.

Classical and Mediæval Adaptations.

We must briefly refer to the Classical and Mediæval literature, of which versions exist in Irish. These are seldom mere translations into Gaelic; they are, as a rule, adaptations freely condensed or re-arranged, and they often become virtually new tales founded upon the foreign or classical model, and embodying the more dramatic passages, but throwing the story into a novel form and telling it in a way more congenial to the tastes of an Irish audience than the original form would have been. In fact, while the pith of the ancient story is retained, so far as incident and matter is concerned, the tale has been changed in style into an Irish romance, exhibiting many of the features of a native Gaelic story. This curious transmutation would lead us to the conclusion that it was customary to recite these classical stories just in the same manner as the native romances were recited, and that it is in this re-modelled form that they were afterwards written down. The Tale of Troy, The Alexander Saga, The Wanderings of Ulysses, The Theban War were well-known in Ireland in the fourteenth and fifteenth centuries, and possibly much earlier. Notable Irish heroes, such as Cuchulain, Conall Cernach, and King Brian Boromhe were frequently compared to Hector, Achilles, or Alexander the Great, and it seems very probable that certain incidents in the Northern romances, such as the making of Cuchulain's shield, the Hero's Light that in moments of intense excitement played about his head, or the description by the Look-out

Men* or Heralds of the appearance of the battalions
assembling before a battle in the Táin and elsewhere,
are modelled directly upon Greek parallels. If this
is so, it leads to the conclusion that the classical tales
were known at a considerably earlier date than the
fourteenth century. It is probable that the Greek
stories were known chiefly through Latin versions ;
the writer of the Irish version of the Saga of Alexander
the Great and Philip of Macedon frequently quotes
Orosius as his chief authority and the Irish Tale of Troy
is adapted from the Latin of Dares Phrygius. Possibly
old French versions of some of the Classical Tales may
also have been known. The Latin tradition has always
been strong in Ireland ; up to the sixteenth or seventeenth century Latin and Irish were equally the language
of men of any pretensions to culture and were used for
the ordinary purposes of verbal or written communication between them.

Both the omissions and additions to the original tale
are instructive. One of the most curious is the tendency
to minimise or altogether to eliminate from the stories
the supernatural element. The poetic and impressive
background of the Greek epic in which, from a vast
and exalted world of their own, the gods and goddesses
held their councils separate from but interested in the
doings and wars of men, is altogether omitted. In
consequence, the contest shrinks into an ordinary warfare
between heroic hosts. This is especially noticeable
in the Irish version of the Æneid, in the whole course
of which the Immortals hardly appear at all, while in

* Comp. Iliad xviii. with T. B. C., Windisch's Ed. l. 2611-2625.
The description of Cuchulain's Distortion is transferred back
bodily into the Irish Tale of Troy, Ir. Texte, ii., pt. I., p. 115.
Or Iliad, ii., with T. B. C., Windisch's Ed. xxv., l. 5010-5725,
or Mesca Ulad, pp. 21-41, etc.

the Troy Tale they take no active part in the contest.
Like the native gods of the Tuatha dé Danann in the
later period, they have dwindled, in the conception of
the Irish story-teller, into the " idols of the Greeks."
On the other hand we have, as in Irish romance, " Badb
and the demons of the air " screaming over the slain
and rejoicing in the slaughter of the battlefield.   The
whole atmosphere of these tales has become infused
with the Irish spirit.   But for the names and incidents
we might, in reading the Tale of Troy, be reading a
romance of the Ulster Cycle.   We have, for instance,
many passages filled with that sense of natural beauty
which pervades Irish writing.   In the Irish version
of the Æneid from the Book of Ballymote we read,
when Latinus was entering the Tiber : " Beautiful,
joyous was the morn, serene was the air, and calm the
sea.   Æneas saw afar off a lovely, sacred grove, close to
the margin of the shore where issues forth the River
Tiber.   On the clear bosom of the estuary were bird-
flocks of every sort floating on the surface of the water ;
it was enough of joy to listen to the varied strains uttered
by those birds.   He saw, too, about the estuary, the
lovely strand, sandy, beautiful, magnificent."*   This
might have been taken bodily out of an Irish romance.
Wholly Irish, too, is the display of a hero's person in
all the bravery of his best attire before the women, and
their undisguised admiration of his appearance.   As
Cuchulain appears in his splendour before Queen Meave,
so Alexander (Paris) arrays himself to come into the
presence of Helen.   " Then Alexander came before
the lady to show forth his form and habit, his garments

* Comp. for instance, The Voyage of Teigue, s. of Cian. *Sil.
Gad.* ii., p. 389.

and vesture. An embroidered vesture was that he had about him, with adornment of ridged red gold, with array of precious stones on the outer side, and within against his skin a tunic of silken cloth, with its fringes of refined gold. Stately and proud was his tread as he advanced to behold the women." (Ir. Texte, ii., p. 81).

As Etain loved Eochaid before she saw him, so Helen and the Athenian women loved Alexander for " his fame and eminence spread abroad throughout Europe, for his shape and form and joyance beyond all the men of the earth, for his splendour and eminence in battle and manslaying." In the same manner " the troops and assemblies of ladies and the joyous girls of the world loved Hector for the noble tales they had heard of him, so that they would have left their own countries to see and contemplate Hector's form, had not the great wars taken him from them." The Irish transcriber recognises no difference in race or character or dress between the Trojan heroes and heroines and his own Celtic champions. In appearance they are identical and in habits they are made to conform. Again, matters that would have been passed over as superfluous or trivial in the Greek tale are insisted upon in the Irish version. For instance, Homeric literature gives us few examples of the pure love-story ; of lovers and love-making we hear nothing in the Iliad, though we hear of the abduction of Helen and the wifely affection of Andromache. But in Ireland, where the pure love-story takes a conspicuous place, it is introduced into the Classical tale wherever occasion makes an opening.

A mark of the Irish influence exercised on the tales is the introduction of a note of tenderness and chivalry quite foreign to the Classic story, but which is of the

H

essence of Irish romance.   A remarkable instance of
this is found in the account given of the death of Hector.
Hector is the prime favourite among Classical heroes
with Irish writers.   The highest praise they can bestow
upon a brave prince or chieftain is that he was the
" Hector of his day."   This affection is shown in a
singular manner in the revised version of Hector's death
in the Troy Tale.   The author is not content that his hero
should fall in open fight with Achilles, still less can he
reconcile it with his ideas of the chivalry due to a fallen
foe that he should be ignominiously dragged round the
walls of Troy.   He therefore deliberately alters the
whole incident, making Hector fall by guile from a
thrust in the back maliciously dealt by Achilles, who
is represented as skulking behind a heap of clothes
when his enemy was unsuspiciously passing by.   After
his death, Hector is said to have been interred with
honour before the gates of the city " and funeral games
were held for him."   Thus in familiar wise the Irish
story-teller ends his tale, and he ingenuously adds,
with a tardy recognition of the advantage of
" authorities," that his novel and improved version
will be found in Virgil.*   The passage which succeeds

* The mediæval Latin versions of the Tale of Troy, and those
derived from them, are always favourable to Hector and the
Trojans.   Many of the changes mentioned above are suggested
in the authorities from which the Irish versions were taken, but
they are amplified and emphasised by the Gaelic story-teller ;
cf. Dares Phrygius, caps. xxiv., xxv. ; Dictys Cretensis, caps.
vi., viii. ; and Chaucer, *Troilus and Cressida*, v., l. 1558 ; or
Shakespeare, *Troilus and Cressida*, Act V., sc. viii.   It would
seem also, from the similarities in the tone and details, that
either the twelfth century *Roman de Troie* of Benôit de Sainte-
More, or the still more famous *Historia Troiana* of Guido delle
Colonne must have been known in Ireland.

the account of the death of Hector is a characteristically Irish one. "Sad, in sooth, was the wailing and lamentation that night in Troy . . . because their hearts' nut, and the bush of safe-guarding, their battle-axe of combat, their shield of protection and their boundary line against their enemies was gone from them. . . . For he surpassed the heroes of the world in splendour and dignity, in wisdom and valour, in dexterity and affluence, etc." This piling up of similes is a peculiarly Gaelic feature. The Classic writer evolves a simile and plays with it, presenting it under various aspects and pressing out of it all that it can be made to yield, but the Irish writer crushes together simile after simile, heaping them rapidly upon one another to secure a cumulative effect. The similes are usually of a stereotyped nature, and in the later literature they tend to become fixed "runs," reappearing whenever an appropriate opportunity offers. In the early literature they are rare and have not yet become fixed, nor are they thrown together in the same rapid way.*

In addition to the Classical tales there are Irish mediæval translations of various works well-known in the middle ages, among the most important of which is a Gaelic version of *Sir John Maundeville's Travels*, made in 1475, by Fingin O'Mahony (d. 1496), and an abridgment of the *Book of Ser Marco Polo* which is found in the Book of Lismore. These are, however, of much less interest from a literary point of view than the

---

* Some of these mediæval Irish "runs" are very quaint. For instance, to express anxiety or anger, it is frequently said that the persons under their influence will "exchange a good form for an evil form, and beauty for ugliness, and go into swoons and fainting-fits of death."

versions of the Greek and Latin stories, as they show few markedly Irish features, and are simply condensed reproductions of the original without any wide variations of style or matter. Fingin seems to have translated from an English text and the author of the Irish version of Marco Polo from the Latin, but the latter condenses freely.

There are also Irish versions of Turpin's Chronicle, Guy of Warwick, Bevis of Southampton, and of a number of French and Spanish romances, such as the Triumphs of Charlemagne from the French, and Richard and Lisarda, a Spanish tale.* The chief general interest of these versions of foreign texts is the testimony they bear to the fact that from the fourteenth to the six-teenth centuries Ireland kept in touch with the literary life of the Continent ; the large number of Irishmen who went for their education to the Universities of Spain and France or who repaired to the Irish monas-teries in Italy must have fostered an interest in the romances and literature of foreign countries.

Romances founded upon the Arthurian legends or dealing in a quite independent way with heroes and themes derived from Arthurian tradition are also common. Among the best of these are the Queste du Saint Gral, The Adventures of the Crop-eared Dog, and The Adventures of Eagle Boy. Many of these tales show great fertility of invention and contain picturesque and touching passages. It is common to find Irish names introduced, as in the Crop-eared Dog (*Eachtra an mhadhra mhaol*) where King Arthur is represented as reigning from the " Fort of the Red Hall," an evident reminiscence of the Red

* See Nattlau's lists in *Rev. Celt* x., pp. 184, 460-61.

Branch Hall at Emain Macha ; Sir Galahad is the hero of this story, and the " crop-eared " dog, who is endowed with superhuman intelligence, is his companion in a series of marvellous adventures, out of which he contrives by his sagacity and powers to conduct Sir Galahad in safety.

CHAPTER IX.

The Last of the Annalists.

The Irish may justly be described as a nation of annalists. The preservation of the tribal records, the recording of genealogies, and the committing to writing the local or provincial wars and raids, constituted from the earliest times the chief care of the literary class, who were trained by a long course of special studies for this particular work. The Philosophy of History was a thing of the future, and the study of history from the point of view of a general survey of the trend and course of national events can hardly be said to have begun; in the modern sense the historian had not come into existence. Nor would he have had any place in Ireland up to the seventeenth century, or even later, for the consciousness of a united nation was not sufficiently strong to make possible the construction of a record in which the bearing of each particular part upon the destinies of the whole country should be taken into account. The provincial spirit remained strongly marked up to the time of the Stuarts at least (it will probably always exist as a dividing line in Ireland), and it was only the troubles of the seventeenth and eighteenth centuries that dissolved to a certain extent these local separations and brought about fresh combinations, political, religious and social, which gave for the first time a conception of Ireland as a national whole. Possibly the records, as they have

actually come down to us, better represent the real
conditions in ancient and mediæval Ireland than any
modern history could do. For there remains to us a
large series of compilations formed out of the tribal
records, and in the number and fulness of her tribal
records Ireland can boast a superiority over any nation
of Europe. From the earliest times each sept and
province possessed its own genealogist and chronicler,
whose business it was, before the knowledge of writing,
to keep in memory, and when writing became common,
to record in special books, the deeds of the clan and
its princes and the deaths of its chief lay and ecclesiastical personages. These annalists were held by the tribe
in the highest honour. They ranked next to the chief
or head of the clan ; they fed at his table and were
supported by his bounty ; and they became his coun-
sellors and representatives in political affairs. The office
of scribe and genealogist was usually continued in
certain families, the son succeeding, as a matter of course,
to the position held by his father, and sometimes several
members of the same family being associated in the office.
These men were trained in the bardic schools or under
some well-known teacher, and they handed on from
age to age the traditions of their sept. Each annalist
added to the existing entries the events of his own lifetime, and until the break up of the tribal customs, the
records were subjected to a systematic examination
at annual or triennial gatherings of the tribe or province,
and were corrected wherever inaccuracies could be
proved. These official genealogists continued to hold
their positions in some parts of Ireland up to the middle
of the seventeenth century, but the disorganisation
of the clan life and, from the sixteenth century onward,

the poverty of their patrons, gradually made the official scribe more and more rare. Most of the annals which remain to us come to an end in the fifteenth century or earlier, though a few are continued into the following era. We may conclude that after this period the clan system was no longer sufficiently organised for the yearly entries to be considered of importance. The devastation of the country, the uncertainty of land tenure, the transference of clan property into the hands of strangers, and the general misery and poverty consequent on these things brought the clan records to an end, and with the loss of their position and duties the office of tribal historian became extinct. But in the seventeenth century there still remained a few men who retained the old knowledge of the antiquities and history of their country, and who carried on the scribal tradition into a more modern age. They were men whose learning was profound in their own department, and who had in some instances added to the antiquarian and genealogical lore of which they were the special custodians, a considerable acquaintance with the learning of other countries.

The names and work of the annalists and scribes Dugald mac Firbis and Lugaidh and Michael O'Clery are so important that they must be dealt with separately.

Dugald mac Firbis (about 1580-1660) was the last of a long family line of historiographers and scribes whose names we frequently meet with in the annals, accompanied by the memorandum that they were " chief historians of the Tir Fiachrach (Tireragh)," " learned annalists," and so on. The most important of these ancestors was Gilla-Iosa-mór mac Firbis, the compiler of the Book of Lecan, who wrote some time before 1416, and who seems also to have partly written the Yellow Book of Lecan (*Leabhar Buidhe Lecain*), so named from the district (now Lacken, in the Barony of Tireragh, Co. Sligo), in which the family were bred, and where, as he himself says, they "wrote books of history, annals, and poetry, and kept a school of history." In olden times the Mac Firbises had, along with the O'Keenes, held an honourable position next to that of their Lords, the O'Dowds, chiefs of Tir Fiachrach, in N. Sligo. At the inauguration of a chief of the family it was the duty of the Mac Firbis who happened to be poet of his day to nominate the newcomer and to touch him with his wand of office ; at the subsequent banquet, he and O'Keene drank together to the honour of the chief, and none might drink before them, and to them were given the arms and armour and steed of the elected Lord. But these days of power and dignity had passed ; the lands of the O'Dowds had been reduced by family quarrels and by confiscation, and the members of the family who remained at Lacken in Dugald's time were simple country gentlemen whose plain lives hardly needed the services of an hereditary chronicler to recount them. Still we find that Dugald was brought up to his ancestral profession, and that he was sent to study in the schools of the Mac Egans of Ormond, and of the O'Davorens at Burren, in Co. Clare. It was probably during the time that he was in the former school that he copied and thus preserved for posterity those annals of Ossory and Leinster of which Dr. O'Donovan has published the few surviving fragments.*

* Fragments of Annals, edited by J. O'Donovan for the Irish Archæological Society, 1860,

In 1645, two years after the death of his father, we find Mac Firbis settled in Galway, where he acted as tutor to John Lynch, the future author of " Cambrensis Eversus," and to Roderick O'Flaherty, then seventeen years old, both of whom he evidently imbued with his own love of the national antiquarian records. Here, in the College of St. Nicholas, he compiled his great work on the Genealogies of the Milesian race, a work still constantly referred to by the Herald's Office in our own day to trace the pedigrees of families of Irish descent. There is in this extraordinary book hardly a branch of the old Irish stock that is not traced up to its sources and followed in all its ramifications and branches.* A glance at such a work as this shows us with what care the Irish genealogical records were transmitted and preserved from the earliest times down to the seventeenth century. The chief Danish families settled in Ireland are also given, showing their inter-marriages and the names of their descendants. The work was completed in 1650. On the Surrender of Galway to the Parliamentary forces in 1652, Dr. Lynch fled to France, but Mac Firbis went quietly on with his work of collecting MSS. and compiling records both for his own purposes and for the use of Sir James Ware, in whose house at Dublin he resided for some time, and for whom he did a great deal of work that Ware had not the justice even to acknowledge ; he does not once mention his name.

* The title of this work is " The Branches of Relationship and the Genealogical Ramifications of every Colony that took possession of Ireland, . . . together with a Sanctilogium and a catalogue of the Monarchs of Ireland, etc., compiled by Dubhaltach mac Firbisigh of Lecan, 1650." The autograph is in the possession of the Earl of Roden.

On his return to Sligo, after the death of Sir J. Ware, he found himself and his companions fallen into an evil case.   O'Flaherty was in a state of absolute destitution, and he himself was not much better off. In a note to his genealogies, he says pathetically, speaking of the expedition of King Dathi to the Alps : " It is no doubt a worldly lesson to consider how the Gaels were at that time conquering far and near, and that now not one in a hundred of the Irish nobles possesses so much of his land as he could be buried in." He received no recompense for his great genealogical compilation.   He says, himself, that he wrote it only " to increase the glory of God, and for the information of the people in general."   It is mournful, indeed, to find that the last of the Irish chroniclers fell a victim to the hand of a wanton assassin.   The old man— he was past his eightieth year—was travelling on foot, as it would seem, from his native village in the West of Ireland to Dublin.   He was resting for the night at a small shop in the village of Dunflin, Co. Sligo, where he was attacked and brutally murdered, apparently without any provocation whatever, by a young gentle- man of the neighbourhood, upon whose licentious freedom of behaviour the old chronicler's presence served as an unwelcome check.   The assassination of Dugald mac Firbis closed the annals of a race of masters whose genealogical and historical labours have preserved to our time the materials upon which all future histories of Ireland must be built.

It will be well to say here a few words about his friend and pupil, O'Flaherty.

Roderic O'Flaherty was born in 1629 or 1630,

in Moycullen Castle, Co. Galway.   On the death of his
father, when he was only two years old, he became a
ward of the Crown. He was educated under the father of
John Lynch in Galway, and studied Irish History under
Dugald mac Firbis, who was living in Galway at this
time. His famous book, the **Ogygia**,* written in Latin
in 1685, appears to have arisen out of a correspondence
between himself and John Lynch, then Archdeacon of
Tuam, on the difficulties of Irish chronology.   In it
he endeavours by elaborate calculations to reconcile
the differences in the dates of the Irish records, founding
his own system upon three ancient poems, which deal
with the synchronisms of the Kings of Ireland.   This
work, diffuse and uncritical as it is, was the first History
of Ireland to find its way into the hands of the English
public.   It is dedicated to James, Duke of York, and
the English Royal family of the Stuarts is therein
traced up to the early monarchs of Ireland.   He introduces events from religious and foreign history, and his
chronology follows the usual tedious Irish system of
beginning with Sacred and Roman History and passing
on thence to the affairs of his own country.

He is said to have written also an " Ogygia Christiana,"
but this is not forthcoming ; there also remains a
chronographical description of West Connacht from
his hand.   He suffered in his own person all the miseries
inflicted on the country during the Cromwellian period.
Though he was a minor at the time, he was deprived
of his paternal estate at Moycullen, and the Act of

* The original edition was published in 1685.   It was imper-
fectly translated into English by Rev. James Hely in 1793.
In 1775 Dr. Charles O'Conor published a vindication of
O'Flaherty's work in twenty-one Chapters, the last of which
was left unfinished.

Settlement of 1662 did not restore his property.   By two law-suits, in 1653 and 1677, he recovered a small part, but the heavy taxation and general poverty of the country made it of little use to him.   When Edward Lhuyd, of Oxford, visited him in 1700 he found him in a miserable condition of distress.   He describes him as " affable and learned," but says that " the late revolutions in Ireland had reduced him to great poverty and destroyed his books and papers."   In April, 1709, Sir Thomas Molyneux saw him living in a miserable condition at Parke, some three hours west of Galway. " I expected," he says, " to have seen here some old Irish manuscripts, but his ill-fortune had stripped him of these as well as his other goods, so that he has now nothing left but some pieces of his own writing, and a few old books of history, printed."   He was then in his eightieth year.   He died on April 8th, 1718, and was buried at Parke.   He was married and had one son and some daughters.   The son died an officer in the Austrian service.

The O'Clerys.—The learned family of the O'Clerys belonged originally to the south-eastern portion of Co. Galway, but they were driven from their home after the Anglo-Norman invasion.   One of them, named Cormac, came, sometime before 1382, to Donegal, and married the daughter of the hereditary " Ollamh " of the O'Donnell's, by whom he had a son.   It is from this ancestor that **Lugaidh (Lewy) O'Clery** and his two sons were descended.   Lugaidh was chief bard of Tirconnell about the beginning of the seventeenth century, and he died before 1632.   He took part in the celebrated bardic contest called *Iomarbháidh na bhfiledh*, or the " Contention of the Bards," himself contributing four poems, amounting to 1,520 verses.   But his most important work is his Life of Hugh Roe O'Donnell, which was written down from his dictation by his sons, Cucogry or Peregrine and Cairbre O'Clery.   The original manuscript, written in a beautifully clear hand, is in the Royal Irish Academy.

Cucogry (or Peregrine) O'Clery (d. 1664), son of Lugaidh, was born at Kilbarron, Co. Donegal.   He owned land from the Earl of Annandale, but was dispossessed of it in **1632** after an inquisition taken at Lifford, his little property being forfeit to the Crown because he was a " meere Irishman, and not of English or British descent or surname."   He was obliged to migrate to Co. Mayo, carrying with him his manuscripts and books, which in his will, written in Irish and preserved in the Royal Irish Academy, he styles affectionately " the property the most dear to me that ever I possessed in this world."   He bequeathed them to his sons, Dermot and John, before his death in **1664**, and they were passed on as a sacred inheritance from father to son, until they came down to Patrick (or John ?) O'Clery, who brought them to Dublin in 1817.

The joint work of these two scribes, father and son, is their **Life of Hugh Roe O'Donnell**, Prince of Tyrconnell (1572-1602).   This very interesting piece of contemporary history relates in a spirited manner and with plentiful detail the adventurous life of the last of the independent princes of Tyrconnell.   Lugaidh O'Clery must himself have witnessed many of the stirring scenes which he so graphically describes, and his work was naturally in large part incorporated into

the Annals of the Four Masters for the years with which
it deals. The Life of Red Hugh is of the deepest
interest ; as a youth he was twice confined in Dublin
Castle, and with other young princes of the North he
made his escape across the Dublin mountains. Once
he was recaptured and more severely confined ; the
second time the youths made their way in the depth
of winter and in blinding snow, without food and with
insufficient clothing, to Glenmalure, where they had
friends. Art O'Neill succumbed to the cold, and
Hugh Roe himself lost two of his toes through frost-bite.
His subsequent determined stand against the English,
his remarkable power in combining the native chiefs,
and the success that attended their arms, are matters
of general knowledge ; had it not been for the defection
of Nial Garbh "Neill the Rough," it seemed at one
moment as though the English forces would be driven
out of the West and North. After the fatal battle
of Kinsale, O'Donnell set out for Spain to try and
induce the King to send further troops, but he died there,
it is said by poison, on September 10th, 1602. He was
not yet thirty years of age when he died.

The life of Hugh Roe affords a good example of the
familiarity of the whole nation with the old legends, down
to the time of its dispersal, and of the persistence of the
native tradition. Here in a modern historical tract the
country bears its old mythological names, just as it
does in the semi-legendary tales of the Early Kings.
A district in Galway is spoken of as "the ancient
province of Sreng, son of Srengan" (i.e., one of the
chiefs of the Firbolgs) ; Ulster is called "the province
of Conor mac Nessa ;" the strand near Dundalk is
Tragh Baile mic Buain. Art Kavenagh is a "certain

famous hero of the Lagenians (Leinstermen) of the race of Cathair mór," and Morann, son of Maen, whose mythical collar was supposed to tighten round the neck of anyone who uttered a falsehood, is quoted as author of the proverb : " There has not been found, nor will there be found, a more truthful judge than the battle-field."

In spite of the rigorously historic nature of the work, the author indulges in an occasional lapse into the old rhetorical style of description.   In the report of the gloom that prevailed among the Irish when Hugh Roe was recaptured by the Council, he says, " There were many princesses and great ladies and noble white-breasted maidens sorrowing and lamenting on his account.   There were many high-born nobles clapping their hands and weeping in secret for him, etc."   The account of the Battle of the Curlew Mountains, in which Sir Conyers Clifford was mortally wounded and the English forces driven back, might have been taken direct from the Battle of Magh Rath ; it exhibits the same lists of alliterative adjectives and the same high-flown method of description.   So also in the description of Hugh O'Donnell, father of the hero, the old man is compared in a pompous passage to Lugaidh, son of Cian (*i.e.*, Lugh Lamhfada), and Troilus, son of Priam ; to the " hound of the artificer " (*i.e.*, Cuchulain) and to Achilles, son of Peleus ; with other classical and Gaelic heroes.

In spite of the patriotic ardour of the piece, justice is done to those among the English leaders who showed a fair spirit towards their adversaries.   Sir Conyers Clifford's death is lamented as warmly by the Irish as by his own party, and the author speaks of him as

" a knight famous by repute, noble by blood, and a man who bestowed jewels and wealth." In relating his fall in battle it is generously added : " Great was the grief for him who fell there, sad was the fate that befel him, and the Irish of the province were not pleased at his death, for he never told them a lie and he was a bestower of treasures and wealth among them." Not only in this biography but generally in the annals there is shown a desire for fairness and a freedom from recrimination which compares favourably not only with the mediæval English reports of the Irish leaders, but with much modern history on both sides.

But the most remarkable member of this family of scholars was **Michael O'Clery** (1575-1643), a distant cousin of Cucogry, who was perhaps the most voluminous writer and compiler that Ireland has ever produced. He was born in 1575 at Kilbarron on Donegal Bay, and was baptized Tadhg ; he was commonly known as Tadhg an tSleibhe, or " Teigue of the Mountain," until on his entrance into the Franciscan Order he took the name of Michael. His elder brother, Maelmuire, who afterwards became his ecclesiastical superior, took the name of Bernardin. It is under these names that we find the brothers entered in the inscription prefacing the Annals of the Four Masters, of whom Michael was head and chief, while Bernardin was superior or guardian of the Monastery of Donegal during the time that the Annals were being compiled within its walls. Michael, like his contemporary, Keating, received his early education in East Munster, and he was already esteemed one of the first Irish antiquarians of his day when he entered the Franciscan convent at Louvain, at that time the refuge of many Irishmen of learning. The guardian

I

of the convent, Aedh mac an Bhaird, or Hugh Ward, also a native of Donegal, was himself an ardent enthusiast for Irish studies, and he recognised the learning of Michael O'Clery. About the year 1620 he sent him to collect all the lives of the early Irish Saints that he could find, with other material bearing on the early religious history of the country. For fifteen years O'Clery wandered about in Ireland collecting and transcribing all the important literature relating to the early traditions of the country which he could procure. In the preface which his friend and contemporary, Father John Colgan, attached to the edition of the " Lives of the Saints," published at Louvain in 1645, for the materials of which he was so largely indebted to O'Clery's labours, O'Clery is said to have " laboured with indefatigable industry for about fifteen years : in the meantime copying many lives of saints from very ancient documents in the language of the country, genealogies, three or four different and ancient martyrologies, and many other monuments of great antiquity which he transmitted hither. At length, by the charge of the superiors deputed to this work, he devoted his mind to clearing and arranging, in a better method and order, the other sacred and profane histories of his country, from which, with the assistance of three other distinguished antiquarians whom he employed as colleagues, he compiled, or with more truth (since they had been composed by ancient authors), he cleared up, digested and composed three tracts of remote antiquity, by comparing many ancient documents." The three tracts here spoken of are (1) the *Reim Rioghraidhe*, or " Royal List " of the Kings and Saints of Ireland, with their pedigrees and the dues accruing to the former from their subjects and from dependent states ; (2) the *Martyrologium Sanctorum Hiberniæ*, a complete calendar of the Irish Saints, with their genealogies and some quotations in verse ; and (3) the *Leabhar Gabhála*, or Book of Invasions, giving an account of the early semi-mythical conquests of Ireland from the time of the Flood, and bringing down the history to the year 1171. The first of these was finished with the assistance of his three able co-editors in the " Annals of the Four Masters," at Athlone, in 1630.   The Leabhar Gabhála was written immediately afterwards (1630-31), at the Convent of Lisgoole, Co. Fermanagh, with the aid of the same scholars and under the encouragement of Brian Maguire, Lord Enniskillen, who lent him his own scribe to aid in the work.

In January of the following year, 1632, we find O'Clery settled in the Franciscan Monastery of Donegal, engaged on the great work of his life, the compilation of the *Annals of the Four Masters ;* and in the same year in which this vast undertaking was completed (1636) he produced his *Martyrologium*, which was doubtless the result of his earliest studies in Irish antiquities. In 1643 we find him back at Louvain, where he printed a glossary of difficult Irish words, entitled *Focloir no Sanasán Nuadh*, dedicated to the Bishop of Elphin, a book which was already rare in 1686.   O'Clery's heavy labours closed at Louvain in 1643.   He died as he had lived, poor and modest, a scribe who laboured unweariedly to rescue from oblivion the records of his native land, whose chiefs and saints he praises who never praised himself, and whose sorrows and ruin he mourned who never dreamed of mourning his own poverty and struggles.   If O'Clery did little work which can be called original, we owe to him the preservation of much valuable material which would otherwise have been irreparably lost to us.

It will be necessary to give a separate account of some of his compilations.

Leabhar Gabhala, or Book of the Conquest of Ireland, commonly called the " Book of Invasions." This book seems to have been known in very early times in Ireland, and from it Keating and the Annalists drew the material for their accounts of the early semi-mythical settlements of the followers of Partholan and of Neimheadh, and of the coming of their successors, the Tuatha Dé Danann and the Milesians, to the country. We find a fragment of it, one page only, standing at the beginning of the Book of the Dun (L.U.) and a larger portion, in prose and verse, occupies the opening folios of the Book of Leinster.   No doubt, the whole tract was once to be found in the Book of the Dun, for O'Clery, in his preface to the reader, mentions a copy of it as one of the authorities from which he wrote. He says : " These are the books of Conquest we had at hand when writing this Invasion of Ireland.   The Book of Bally Mulconry, which Maurice, son of Paidín O'Mulconry copied from the Book of the Dun Cow. The Book of Bally O'Clery, written in the time of Maelsechlainn the Great, son of Donnell.   The Book of the People of Dugenan of Seancuach, known as the Book of Glendalough. The Book of the Uacongbháil. Together with other books of conquest and history besides."

There is considerable variation in the manner in which the old writers opened their story.   A brief re-capitulation of the earlier chapters of the Book of Genesis prepares the way in the Book of Leinster for the introduction of a hero named Gaedel Glas, who is said to have formed the Gaelic tongue out of the seventy-two languages then spoken in the world, an explanation which satisfactorily accounts for any difficulties that may be met with by students of Irish. It then proceeds with the account of the arrival of Cessair, grand-daughter of Noah, who fled to Ireland to escape the Deluge, and with the settlements in the usual order, carrying the history down to the coming of Christianity to Ireland, with a brief supplementary list of the later kings, concluding at the date of the writer in the time of King Dermot mac Morrough of Leinster, 1166. O'Clery, however, decides in his opening paragraph that the Biblical part of the story is best discussed by theologians, and dismissing summarily the history of the first four ages of the world, he proceeds directly to the history of the invasions of Ireland. His version ends with the reign of Maelsechlainn the Great, " the last King of Ireland within her unopposed," at which point one, at least, of his authorities deserted him. It is uncertain whether the book which he calls the Book of Glendalough is the Book of Leinster or not ; some of the poems quoted from it, and many of the prose pieces, are undoubtedly the same as those quoted in the Book of Leinster, but it is possible that they were both copied from another MS. This recension, by Michael O'Clery, finished in 1631 in the Convent of Donegal, was made with great care and with the assistance of those learned historians who afterwards aided him in the compilation of the Annals of the Four Masters. O'Clery does not profess to write the Leabhar Gabhála,

transferred thither, with many of the other manuscripts originally belonging to Colgan at Louvain, from its earlier resting-place at the College of St. Isidore, at Rome. In a copy transcribed by Richard Tipper in 1728, and now in the Royal Irish Academy, Dublin, is found an additional preface, added in 1644, the year after O'Clery's death, by another Franciscan friar, Paul O'Colla, writing in the house of Conall Mageoghegan of Westmeath, the translator of the Annals of Clonmacnoise. This preface attempts to give a list of the authorities from which O'Clery and his companions compiled their work, but it is not accurate. O'Curry is evidently mistaken in ascribing this preface to O'Clery himself.

The **Martyrology of Donegal** was so-called because it was " begun and finished " in the Franciscan Convent of Donegal, 19th April, 1630. O'Clery tells us that he had been for ten years engaged in its compilation. Two autograph copies are among the Colgan manuscripts at Brussels, the shorter of the two having been written by the author in Douay in 1629, a year before the complete copy was finished. The Donegal copy has no preface. O'Clery gives as his authorities the Felire of Angus ; the Martyrology of Tallaght ; the Calendar of Cashel (not now existing) ; and the Martyrology of Maelmuire O'Gorman (composed 1167), taken from the Felire or Martyrology of Tallaght. O'Clery's compilation is peculiarly valuable from the number of legends of saints, poems and hymns that it contains. It records the names of a large number of Scottish Saints.

CHAPTER X.

The Annals of the Four Masters.

It was no doubt the feeling that if the collection and compilation of the annals and traditions of Ireland were not undertaken at once the time for doing so would have passed for ever that brought to the front the many laborious and erudite annalists whose work we are now considering. The dispersal and loss of manuscripts and old records was going on rapidly, and it was necessary, if the historical and ecclesiastical memorials were not to be for ever lost, to collect such records as remained and to transfer them into large books deposited under safe keeping for the benefit of posterity. It was this collection and transcription of material which gives its special character to the prose work of the seventeenth century. The spirit in which it was undertaken may best be gathered from O'Clery's own words, in the prefaces to his various writings. In his account of his search for manuscripts for his first work, the Reim Rioghraidhe, or Roll of the Kings, which included the genealogies of the Saints, he says, writing of himself in the third person : " Upon the arrival of the aforesaid friar, he sought and searched through every part of Erin in which he heard that there was a good or even a corrupt Irish manuscript, so that he spent four full years in transcribing and procuring the matters that related to the Saints of Erin. However, though great his labour and his hardships, he was

able to find but a few out of the many of them, because
strangers had carried off the principal books of Erin
into remote and unknown foreign countries and nations,
so that they have left her but an insignificant part
of her books."

If in his day there was difficulty in procuring the tribal
Annals, how much greater it would have been had it
been postponed to a later period is shown by the list of
authorities given in his preface as having been used
by him in the compilation of the " Annals of the Four
Masters." The larger number of these authorities have
since been lost.

The loss of the records was not the only difficulty
that such men as O'Clery were obliged to face. They
were forced to find patrons for their work ; and this,
in the fallen state of the fortunes of the Irish chiefs,
it was not easy to do. For the great compilation
known as the Annals of the Four Masters a patron was
at length found in the person of Ferral O'Gara, Prince
of Coolavin, Co. Sligo, and in looking at the splendid
work fostered by his care and carried through by the
industry of the little group of learned Franciscans and
their friends who actually accomplished the laborious
task, we feel that the warm tribute conveyed to O'Gara
in O'Clery's simple and modest dedication of the completed volumes is well deserved.*

We can only give an extract :—" I, Michael O'Clery,
a poor friar of the Order of St. Francis, . . . have
come before you, O noble Fearghal O'Gara. . . .

---

* O'Gara's interest in the work, and the friendship of the
compilers with him, is the more creditable to both from the
circumstance that he was an Anglican, and had been educated
at the then recently established Trinity College, Dublin.

I explained to you that I thought I could get the
assistance of the chroniclers for whom I had most esteem
in writing a book of Annals . . . and that should
the writing of them be neglected at present they would
not again be found to be put on record or commemorated,
even to the end of the world.   There were collected
by me all the best and most copious books of Annals
that I could find throughout all Ireland (though it was
difficult for me to collect them into one place), to write
this book in your name and to your honour, for it was
you that gave the reward of their labours to the
chroniclers by whom it was written ; and it was the
friars of the convent of Donegal that supplied them
with food and attendance in like manner.''

The ruined Franciscan monastery, in a cottage within
whose precincts the devoted brethren worked, stands
at the head of the beautiful Bay of Donegal.   It had
been built in the year 1474 by the Lady Nuala, daughter
of one of the Leinster O'Conor Falys, who had married
an O'Donnell of Donegal.   At her wish, enforced by
the unexpected appearance of the lady herself with a
troop of attendant gallowglass in the midst of the
deliberations of a provincial Franciscan Chapter near
her old home, a number of friars followed her to the
North and established a new house within the borders
of her husband's territory.   Looking out now upon
the still waters of Donegal Bay from the grassy pathway
which alone divides the monastic precincts from the
sea, no scene could be more peaceful, more mournfully
tender in its desolation.   Even the small bustle of the
market-town does not reach so far.   But in the half-
century preceding the date of the compilation of the
Annals, no spot in Ireland had been the centre of more

constant wars and tumults than these now silent shores. The passing and re-passing of Red Hugh's troops in his sudden and vigorous descents into Connacht, the trampling of English armies and the occasional arrival of a band of mercenaries from Scotland or of a war vessel from Spain to the aid of O'Donnell, kept the friars in perpetual peril. Twice they had been forced to fly, once when the Sheriffs of Fitzwilliam swooped down on Donegal at dead of night and occupied the monastery as a garrison ; once again, when in 1601, Nial Garbh, traitorously uniting with the English against his own brother-in-law, took possession of the monastery in Hugh Roe's absence, and the brethren were forced to take refuge in the woods or on board a vessel in the harbour. The accidental blowing up of the powder stored within the walls, which exploded with a terrific crash and involved the building itself and all that it contained in a common ruin, brought to an end the history of the monastery, and the flight of Rory O'Donnell, brother to Red Hugh, to Rome in 1607 left the friars without a protector. A few old friars passed the residue of their lives beneath the ruined walls or among the surrounding glens and mountains, but no young members were henceforth permitted to join the community.

Here, from January 22nd, 1632, to August 10th, 1636, Michael O'Clery worked uninterruptedly, chiefly upon the materials collected by himself in his wanderings through Ireland. He was assisted for longer or shorter periods by his relatives, Cucogry and Conaire O'Clery, by two members of the family of O'Mulconry from Co. Roscommon, Torna and Ferfeasa, and by Cucogry or Peregrine O'Duigenan of the family of the hereditary historians of the Mac Dermotts and Mac Donaghs in the same county. The true title of the famous Annals compiled during these four years of assiduous labour is the *Annales Dungallenses* (Annals of Donegal), or *Annala Rioghachta Eireann* (Annals of the Kingdom of Ireland). The name by which they are popularly known was bestowed upon them by Rev. John Colgan, author of the " Acta Sanctorum," in affectionate memory of the four chief out of the six compilers who had a share in the work. Among the books still existing to which the annalists refer in their address to the reader, are the Annals of Clonmacnois, the Annals of Ulster, the Book of the O'Duigenans of Kilronan (possibly that now known as the Annals of Loch Cé) and the Book of Lecan, but there are several others now unknown.

The first entry dates from the age of the world, 2242, " forty days before the flood," at which point is placed the arrival of the first inhabitant to Ireland, and we are given an uninterrupted narrative of events from that ancient date onward to the year 1616 A.D. The entries begin, like all national records, with legend and tradition, and as the Septuagint chronology for the date of the Deluge is adopted, there is a vast space of time to be filled up by occasional entries of events drawn from the stories of the successive invasions by different bands of pre-historic settlers, or from the traditions of the ancient kings ; long stretches of time being accounted for by a few brief entries. The annalists do not allow themselves to insert, as Keating does, the picturesque legends found in the Romances of the early Kings of Tara, nor yet the lives and traditions of the saints. For ecclesiastical affairs the Annals of

Ulster are more full and reliable ; the chronology of the Four Masters has also to be corrected from other sources for the first eight or nine centuries of the Christian era, being generally from three to five years earlier than the true date. The entries become fuller as the history proceeds, and they end with the detailed account of times quite near the date of compilation. Taken as they are from earlier records, these annals may seem in large part a dreary repetition of tribal raids and petty wars, burnings of churches, monasteries and territories belonging to neighbouring chieftains, drivings of cattle, and deaths of chiefs, learned men or ecclesiastical personages. But if these pages lack variety and large interest, we must remember that such was, in fact, the internal history of Ireland during many centuries.

Fortunately for the future church historian, and for the history of art, the building of a large church, the destruction of a monastery or tower, the carving of a stone cross, or the construction of a hand-bell or the metal cover for a crozier, and the loss of a valuable manuscript, were matters that were thought as worthy of mention as the raids or wars of chieftains. To reconstruct the history out of these isolated entries requires care and close investigation ; but as we watch the progress of events from year to year, we are able to follow the life of any particular personage of note, or to unravel the social and political condition of any special district much as the detached and uncoloured jottings in a diary might be studied.

The question of the general reliability of the Irish Annals after we arrive at the historical period is one of great importance in consideration of the fact that they endeavour to push the date of actual history much

further back than the records of the other portions
of the British Isles would take us.   The English
chronicle does not carry us back beyond the period
of the Roman occupation, and its entries, up to the
time of the coming of the Saxons, are few and inter-
mittent.   The Annales Cambriæ begin near the close
of the fifth century, and though the Historia Britonum
ascribed to Nennius carries us further back, it deals
rather with the traditions respecting the origin and
settlements of the different races inhabiting Britain
than with actual pre-Christian history.   The regular
entries of facts, however, begin about the time of the
departure of the Romans from Britain.   The Pictish
Chronicles present us in the earlier portions with
traditions of the origin of the Picts and with long bare
lists of names of kings.   The value of these tracts dealing
with the history of the sister countries was, nevertheless,
early recognised in Ireland.   Several short tracts on
the Picts and Scots are preserved in Irish manuscripts,
and we have numerous versions of the Historia Britonum,
the earliest of which is found in the Leabhar na h-
Uidhre, the oldest existing Irish manuscript.   It would
seem that in the Welsh and Scottish Annals earlier Irish
records have been largely drawn upon ; events relating
to Irish hagiology, such as the deaths of St. Patrick
and St. Brigit, the birth of Columcille and his departure
for Hi or Iona, the obits of SS. Ciaran and Brendan
of Birr, and the journey of St. Gildas in Ireland make
up a large portion of the scant entries in the early
portions of the Annales Cambriæ.   They are evidently
taken from an Irish original, and remind us of the close
connection that existed between these countries in the
early Christian period, drawn together as they were

by a common belief and by a church system almost identical.

It is plain that we can only test the reliability of the Irish records when we get to events of which the historical remains of other countries also retain a record with which they may be compared.   One of the first historical events that we can test by the light of contemporary evidence is the passing over of Fergus Mór and his clan to Scotland, and the settlement of the Kingdom of Scottish Dalriada in Argyleshire. This settlement of the Irish Dalriads is one of the best-marked and most certain points in the early history of these islands.   From Fergus mór the Scottish kings traced their descent, and the name of Loarn, one of the chiefs who accompanied him, is still retained in the house of the Dukes of Argyle as the title of the eldest son.   This event happened about 506 A.D., and the history of its fortunes, as told in the Irish records and by Adamnan, may be accepted as a simple record of fact.

But we can push our historical ground further back than this.   The reign of Niall of the Nine Hostages, and that of his predecessor, Crimthann, are said in the Annals to have been marked by important foreign wars in Alba, Britain and Armorica (Brittany). Crimthann, during his short reign, is supposed to have over-run these countries, and Niall is said to have died while conducting an army into Gaul by the treachery of one of his own followers. Besides this, Niall is said to have taken a great army into Alba, to strengthen the Irish settlers in the south-western districts, who already, before the time of Fergus, had made small settlements there.   Now these foreign raids and wars date about 366 A.D., and the

following half-century.   This was the period of those
terrific descents of the Picts and Scots from the North
and West which it tried all the power of the Roman
armies in Britain to arrest and hold back.   The Picts
were the inhabitants of Scotland or Alba ; the Scots
the Irish of Ireland, and the western coasts of Scotland.
The inhabitants of Ireland were called Scots until long
after this period.   It was only when the Irish settlers
in Scottish Dalriada gave their own name in affectionate
memory of the old country to their new possessions,
that the title passed away from Ireland and gradually
became the common name of the whole land of the
Picts.   It was probably about this time that the
western districts of Scotland began to bear the name
of Scotia Minor, in distinction to Scotia Major, or
Ireland, but it was not until the Kingdom of Scotland
was firmly established in the reign of Kenneth mac
Alpin that the old country finally abandoned a name
that had become confusing.   Abroad, Ireland was
known by the name of Scotia, and her people as Scots,
up to the fifteenth century.   The ravages made by
the Picts and Scots on the North and West of Britain,
and the efforts made by the Romans to stem the
advancing tide of conquest are familiar to every reader
of English or Roman history.   About 386 A.D., twenty
years after the time to which the conquests of Crimthann are ascribed, the Scots and their allies had
made such progress that they were driven back from
the gates of London by the Emperor Theodosius.

The Britons appealed for aid to Rome, and in 396
A.D. the able General Stilicho was sent to repel the
invaders.   The difficulty of his task is proved by the
rapturous praise bestowed on Stilicho by Claudian

on the successful General's return.   " The Scot "
(*i.e.*, the Irish), he exclaims, " moved all Ierne against
us and the sea foamed under his hostile oars."   It was
probably against Niall of the Nine Hostages that
Stilicho fought.

When the Roman troops were again withdrawn, in
402 A.D., the Picts and Scots once more swept over the
country, and again the Romans sent aid.   It was in
407 A.D., two years after the death of Niall, that Con-
stantine withdrew the Roman troops for the last time
to resist the invasions of the Goths who were threatening
to overwhelm Rome.

When we reach Christian times, the points of communication are numerous, and the records can be tested
at various points.   The great plague which swept over
Britain and passed on to Ireland, mowing down in the
path of its triumphant progress scholars of the schools,
abbots of monasteries, and even more than one Ard-
Righ of Tara ; the British and foreign men of note
who sought scholarship in Ireland ; the efforts of
Adamnan on behalf of the Irish captives carried as
prisoners to Northumbria by King Egbert (Bede, Book
IV., Chap. xxvi.), the many historical notices in Adamnan's Life of Columcille, such as the Battle of Magh
Rath or Moyra (called in Scotland Bella Roth), the
reigns of Eochy Buidhe and Aiden, etc., are all capable of
proof alike from the Irish and the British and Scotch
contemporary chronicles, and these elucidate each other.
Moreover, the whole history of the Celtic Church, on
either side of the Irish Sea, is closely connected, and the
history of the one cannot be understood without constant
reference to that of the other.

When we reach the period of the Norsemen, the Irish

records become invaluable.   At a time when Norse history proper contains little else but myths of the gods, the doings of the race in these western Isles, their incursions, their leaders, and their settlements are fully detailed in the Irish Annals.   Norse history begins with Harold Fairhair in the ninth century; before that all is mythical.   But in Ireland we are, in the ninth century, in the full career of certain history, and behind lies an indefinite period, filled up with what the mediæval Irishman took equally for positive fact, and which we to-day, in the light of modern criticism, cannot afford to throw entirely overboard. The more we examine these documents in connection with those of other nations the more, I think, we shall become convinced of their substantial accuracy.   Perhaps the greatest misfortune that befel them was when, under Biblical influence and in Christian times, the dates were pushed backward and made to correspond with the Jewish chronicles from the time of the Flood, thereby introducing a confusion that we shall never be able to rectify; but even allowing for this, and for the large romance element that the early history has undoubtedly incorporated, a mass of material remains, which, if we cannot vouch for its exactitude, may be taken as substantially accurate from about the fifth century onward, and which demands even for an earlier epoch to be treated with greater seriousness and openness of mind than is usually accorded to it.

CHAPTER XI.

Annals and Historical Tracts.

Annals of Tighernach.—The Annals of the Four Masters are only the most important of a large series of Annals, the earliest existing of which, the Annals of Tighernach, a learned ecclesiastic who died in 1088, are in mixed Latin and Irish, the foreign events being entered in Latin and those relating to Ireland in Irish. Up to the Christian era the larger part of the entries refer to foreign events, and a feature of these Annals is the preference given to the Provincial dynasty of Ulster over that of the Monarchs of Tara. The Hebrew chronology is used instead of that of the Septuagint, which is employed in the Annals of the Four Masters and the Annals of Ulster. These Annals are among the most reliable of the Irish records, as well as being the oldest. The Abbot Tighernach O'Braein, the compiler, belonged to a family of religious rather than of literary men, but his Annals show learning, accuracy and discrimination. He quotes from Bæda, Josephus, Eusebius and other early Christian writers, and shows an acquaintance remarkable for his time with general history. The Annals were written at the Abbey of Clonmacnois, of which Tighernach was Abbot. After his death, in 1088, the chronicles were continued by Augustine mac Gradoigh (Grady) who carried them on to 1405, and another scribe made some subsequent entries. Several copies of these Annals remain, but they are all fragmentary.

The Annals of Ulster.—So named by Ussher on

account of the prominence given in these chronicles to the affairs of Ulster ; but originally known as the " Book of Shanad of Mac Manus in Loch Erne," Shanad being the old name for the Island of Belleisle in Upper L. Erne, Co. Fermanagh.   The book is referred to by O'Clery as one of the volumes used by the Four Masters.   The MS. in T.C.D. states at the year 1498 that Cathal mac Manus was the author of the volume.   He was the head of a junior branch of the sept of Maguire, a Canon-choral of Armagh, and Dean over Loch Erne, and a magnificent eulogy is pronounced over him in the Annals on his death, in 1498.   This copy is continued down to the year 1504 ; but the MS. in the Bodleian Library carries on the Annals to 1541.   At the head of the Annals, which omit the early legendary history and open with the mission of Palladius to Ireland, in 431, stand the words " Jesus, mine it is to begin, Thine it is to finish."   These Annals, though not so full as those of the Four Masters, preserve for us many details, especially of ecclesiastical affairs, omitted by them.

O'Donovan justly praises their " extreme veracious simplicity."

Chronicum Scotorum —There are two good copies of these Annals in existence, one in the fine handwriting of Dugald mac Firbis, about 1650, in Trinity College, Dublin, and the other transcribed in France by Rev. John Connery about a century later, in the Royal Irish Academy.   Like most of the Irish Annals the entries in the earlier portions are scant, and Mac Firbis explains the omissions in his copy as being made by him " to avoid tediousness," for which reason he made " only a short abstract and compendium of the history of the Scots (*i.e.* Irish) in this copy, omitting the lengthened details of the historical books." The chronicle extends to 1136, with a supplement, carrying it down from 1141-1150. Mac Firbis seems to have undertaken the task of transcription unwillingly, for a note on one of the early pages says: " Ye have heard from me, O readers, that I do not like to have the labour of writing this copy, and it is therefore that I beseech you through true friendship not to reproach me for it (if you understand what it is that causes me to be so) ; for it is certain that the Mac Firbises are not in fault."

O'Curry thought that the Chronicum Scotorum was a compilation of Mac Firbis' own, but the above words seem to show that he was copying from some older manuscript against his inclination and at the desire of some other person. Probably Sir James Ware, who employed Dugald on many laborious tasks for which he made scant acknowledgment, required the material for some purpose of his own. Hennessy considers that he copied from a chronicle compiled in the monastery of Clonmacnois, possibly the " Book of Clonmacnois," mentioned by the Four Masters as one of their sources of information. Bishop O'Brien, who possessed O'Flaherty's copy, calls it " Chronicum Scotorum Cluanense." At the year 718 Mac Firbis says in a note " A front of two leaves of the old book out of which I write this is wanting." As a matter of fact there is no history between the years 718-804, about which period a break also occurs in the Annals of Tighernach, written in the same monastery. An inscription in the MS. copy at the Royal Irish Academy ascribes its authorship to Gillachrist O'Maeileoin, Abbot of Clonmacnois, who, according to these Annals, died in 1123 (=1127). The chronology is incorrect, and the author dismisses the account of the early invasions with the impatient remark " I pass to another time, and He who Is will bless it."   He then goes on to the birth of St. Patrick.

The Annals of Innisfallen.—These Annals have never been published. They are named from the Island of Innisfallen in the Lower Lake of Killarney, in which they were compiled. Remains of the ancient monastery, said to have been founded by St. Finan the Leper in the sixth century, may still be seen among the trees with which the island is thickly covered. The compilation of these chronicles has been ascribed with much probability to Maelsuthan O'Carroll, a powerful chief of the neighbouring tribes of the Killarney district, who had been educated in this monastery and retired there again at the close of an eventful life. He is described in the Annals of the Four Masters as the " Chief Doctor of the Western World ; " he seems also to have been an ecclesiastic, and was confessor and tutor to the famous King of Munster, Brian Boru, whom he accompanied in his royal progress through Ireland after his assumption of the throne of Tara. His inscription, entered in the Book of Armagh as Calvus Perennis (an incorrect Latin translation of his name Maelsuthan), is a lasting memorial of the King's visit to that city, for he says that he wrote it " in the sight of Brian, Emperor of the Scots."

In the British Museum are two poor copies with translation, the best of which begins in the Irish portion at the year 250 A.D. and ends at 1064, though the translation, very badly and roughly written, goes down to 1320. The Bodleian copy of the Annals comes down to the year 1319, but it is not known who continued them after Maelsuthan's death.

The history of the early kings is given at considerable length, and there are some entries differing from the other Annals.

Annals of Loch Cé (Loch Key), or Annals of Kilronan, usually known by the former name, because the single existing MS. from which it was edited* belonged to its part-compiler, Brian mac Dermot, of M'Dermot's Castle, who lived on a small island in the Southern corner of the beautiful lake of that name near Boyle, Co. Roscommon. On the death of its owner, in 1592, the MS. passed into other hands. It was bought in 1766 by Dr. Thomas Leland, who deposited it in Trinity College, Dublin, where it now lies. At this time and down to 1836 it was known as a continuation of the Annals of Tighernach, and was lettered on the back " Tigernachi Continuator," but in 1836, Dr. O'Donovan pronounced it to be the lost Book of the O'Duigenans of Kilronan, Co. Roscommon. O'Curry disputes this opinion, but the editor, Mr. William Hennessy, shows that there is good reason for believing O'Donovan to be correct, and that such portions as remain of the true Annals of Loch Cé are contained in another MS. in Trinity College, sometimes called the Annals of Innisfallen (F. 1. 18). The Annals edited by Hennessy open abruptly with a description of the Battle of Clontarf in 1014 and are carried down to 1590, having been completed by Brian mac Dermot, who brought them down to within two years of his own death. The

* Marked H. 1. 19, T.C.D.

tract originally began at an earlier date, for the Four Masters used its entries for the years between 900-1563 A.D. Besides the loss of these opening leaves, several other gaps occur in the MS., especially between the year 1138-1170 and 1316-1462. A fragment of the MS. was found in the British Museum, which the editor has used for the years 1577-1590. He has supplied part of the gap occurring between the years 1316-1413 from some Annals known as the Annals of Connacht (T.C.D., H. 1. 1-2), which agree so closely with the present work that they would appear to be independent copies of a common original. The scribes who copied these Annals seem often to have been obliged to stop their work from fatigue and exhaustion. " I am fatigued from Brian mac Dermot's book," says one of them. Another excuses himself because " his pulse has shrunk through excess of labour." More pathetic still is the brief note, " I cease from want of a dinner."

The Annals of Connacht.—There are two manuscript copies of these Annals in existence,* both written by Maurice O'Gorman, a busy but inaccurate scribe who copied them in 1764 and 1783. In their present condition they begin at the year 1224 and close at 1562. They closely resemble the Annals of Loch Cé, and the years 1394-1397 are missing in both.

The Annals of Clonmacnois.—There is no special reason why these Annals should have received the name they bear, except the prominence they give to the history of those parts of the country bordering on the Shannon, and their detailed account of St. Ciaran, the

* One at the R.I.A. (marked No. 25, 4-5), and one at T.C.D. (marked Class H., 1, 1-2). See above, " Annals of Loch Cé."

founder of the monastery of Clonmacnois, and of the
events of his time.   It is uncertain whether the book
mentioned by the Four Masters as one of their authorities
is the same which now goes under this name.   The
author, " a great Latinist and schollar " and a " worthy
Prelate of the Church, who would say nothing but the
truth," was so good an Irishman that he " could not get
his penn to name the Kings of England or other foreigne
countryes by their proper names, but by such Irish
names as he pleased to devise out of his own head,"
a habit which Englishmen using Irish names have not
failed to copy.   No manuscript of the original remains
to us, but we possess three copies of an English
translation made in 1627 in the quaint tongue of
Elizabeth's day by Conall or Conla Mageoghagan, of
Lismoyne, Co. Westmeath, whom O'Clery calls " the
industrious collecting Bee of everything that belongs
to the honour and history of the descendants of Milesius
and of Lewy, son of Ith, both lay and ecclesiastical,
so far as he could find them."   Mageoghagan tells us
that " the ould Irish book which he was translating "
had many leaves lost or stolen out of it ; and " by longe
lying shutt and unused " there were many parts which
he could hardly read, for they " were altogether grown
illegible and put out," so that he was obliged to omit
them.

These Annals begin with the Creation and end at
the year 1408.   The author tells us that he has made
use of Eusebius and of the Venerable Bede, as well as
of the works of several Irish Saints and Chroniclers.

The Annals of Clonmacnois are much fuller for the
earlier portions than the Annals of Ulster or those
of the Four Masters.   They embody a number of the

legends of the early kings and saints, and in particular give a lengthy account of the founding of Clonmacnois and the subsequent fall of Tara which is elsewhere found only in the historical tales ; also of the history of the unhappy Queen Gormliath, wife of King Niall Glundubh, whose matrimonial alliances rivalled those of her more notorious namesake in the time of Brian Boru. Occasionally the writer indulges in general reflections, as in his lament over the troubles brought upon the country through the Danish wars, or in his excursus on the limits of Magh-Breagh.   The quaintness of the language, as well as the freedom of style and fulness of the information given, make these Annals peculiarly interesting.   The chronology should, however, be corrected by that of the Annals of Ulster ; in some places the difference between them amounts to six or seven years.   But the Annals of Ulster are themselves antedated by one year up to 1014 A.D.

Annals of Boyle.—The original manuscript of these only partly published Annals is in the British Museum.   O'Curry seems to consider them to be the Annals of Loch Cé.   They contain numerous entries and marginal notes referring to the neighbourhood of Boyle, Co. Roscommon, where they were written, and extended originally from the Creation (the early leaves are now lost) to the year 1300 A.D.   A few passages phonetically spelled show that the peculiarities of Irish pronunciation in the district in which they were written are the same to-day as they were in the fourteenth century.

The **Leabhar Oiris** or Book of Chronicles (called also *Seancha Muimhneach*), a Munster Chronicle which has been sometimes ascribed to Mac Liag, bard of

Brian Boru, is mainly an account of the battles of that king from the accession of Maelseachlain in 979. The entries are carried on to 1027 A.D. where they end abruptly. It is written by a partisan of Brian, but probably not by Mac Liag, who is mentioned by name in the course of the history. Several of his long poems are included in the narrative.

It remains to mention the Irish versions of the British History of Nennius (so called), in Irish, **Leabhar Breathnach** or **Breathnochas**. It seems to have been at least as well known in Ireland as in Britain to judge by the Irish manuscripts that remain of it. These differ a good deal among themselves, some containing whole sections not found in other copies. The origin of these chronicles has always been obscure. The work may be described as a common-place book into which records of all sorts, British, Pictish and Irish, have found their way. The large number of Irish entries of saints in the early sections seems to show that the chronicles of Ireland were familiar to the writers of the earlier portions.

In some Latin copies a tract on the Wonders of Ireland follows the sections on the Wonders of Britain and of the Isle of Man, but this is omitted in the Irish copies.

Contemporary Records.—We have yet to deal with some other records of a more independent type than the genealogies, successions of kings, and Annals to which we have already referred. These are separate histories of special periods, of which by far the most important is the history of the Norse invasions known as " **The Wars of the Gaedhil and Gaill**," or of the Irish and the

Foreigners. There is no author given for this important piece, nor is the date of its compilation known.   It has been thought, like the *Leabhar Oiris*, to be the work of Mac Liag (d. 1016), the chief poet of Brian Boromhe (Boru) whose rise to power and wars with the Norse, ending in the fatal battle of Clontarf on Good Friday, 1014, it so affectionately describes ; but there is no absolute proof of this.   It is in any case probably the work of a contemporary of Brian, and of one attached to his house and family, as it sets his actions in the best light, and deals (in the larger part of the book) with the part played by Munster, and by Brian's clan, the Dal Cais or Dalcassians, in the events of the day.   The work opens with a general account of the arrival of the Northmen at various points round the coast and of their endeavour to effect settlements inland.   Even here, the south of Ireland comes in for the largest share of attention, and the details about Munster are the most explicit.   In this part of the work, which is necessarily a compilation from earlier sources, as it deals with events before the writer's own day, the matter is entered in a confused manner, the same events being frequently repeated and whole paragraphs being misplaced.   The narrative must, therefore, be used with care, the repetitions being frequent and confusing.   It is nevertheless an invaluable record of an important period, and without it our knowledge of the course of events during the Norse occupation would be much less precise than it is. The interludes by the author, too, are interesting as indicative of the general feeling in his time about the Northmen and their oppressions.   When we arrive at the second portion of the history, which is probably the original work of the author, and which deals exclusively with the family of Brian of the Tributes, the style becomes much more diffuse, and the events are narrated with all the detail of personal knowledge backed by the influence of clan and provincial feeling.

Hardly less important is a piece dealing with a later period called **The Triumphs of Torlough** [O'Brien] written by John Mac Rory Magrath, hereditary historian to the Lords of Dal Cais, probably about 1459 A.D.   This piece is a valuable record of the Anglo-Norman period.   It falls into two parts, the first containing the wars of Torlough O'Brien and Thomas de Clare, 1275-1285, and the second the wars between Mortough O'Brien and Richard de Clare, 1310-1318. An Introduction to the first part relates how the Sovereignty of Ireland passed to the English, and describes the attempts made by Donough Cairbrech, Conor na Lindaine and his sons, Teigue and Brian, to maintain their independence (1194-1275).   The preface to the second part tells how the prosperous Kingdom of Torlough, established after the death of Thomas de Clare, was disturbed and broken up under the rule of his son, Donough (1287-1310).   A brief continuation brings the story down to 1355.   The history, so far as Munster is concerned, is given in great detail and the piece fills an important gap.   It contains twenty-three poems in Rosg metre.*

* This piece has not yet been published, but an edition is in course of preparation for the Cambridge Press by Standish Hayes O'Grady.   The oldest known copy is in T.C.D., and is dated 1509 ; Andrew mac Curtin's copy, made in 1721, from a MS. of 1459, is in the same Library, and another copy made in 1608 exists in the R.I. Academy.   Two translations, purporting to have been made by Peter O'Connell, are to be found in the British Museum.

The Norse wars in Ireland gave rise to the composition of an unusually large number of pieces the foundation of which is historical, but which are related under the form of romantic tales.   There are, for instance, numerous versions of the Battle of Clontarf and the circumstances that led up to it, and there is a valuable and dramatic tract dealing with the wars of the turbulent King Cellachan of Cashel, a Munster Prince whose career is therein preserved.   Of great importance also for the history of this period are some Annals copied by Dugald mac Firbis from a vellum in possession of the Mac Egans, of Ormond, describing the Danish wars in Ossory and Leinster, of which unfortunately only a fragment has been preserved.   These separate historical pieces are full of passages of picturesque and dramatic description, and though the exaggerated and rhapsodical passages that they contain make it difficult to distinguish what is historical fact from what is poetical romance, the general truthfulness of their details can be tested from other sources.   The local colour they contain, the vividness with which historical events are pictured, and the knowledge they give us of the temper and habits of their day are of a special value owing to the meagreness with which such details are treated in the longer Annals.   Nothing could well be more dramatic, if it were stripped of some of the cumbrous circumlocution which to a certain extent detracts from the picturesqueness of all this mediæval literature, than the account of the capture of Cellachan of Cashel by the Danes of Dublin, and his lament over the slaughter of the friends who were trying to rescue him and whose gory heads were exhibited to him one by one on the green of the fort where he was imprisoned ;* or again, of his being tied to the mast of Sitric's ship in sight of the army sent to his rescue in the harbour of Dundalk, and the terrific sea-fight that preceded his deliverance. Cellachan was not altogether a prince who did honour to his country ; during the early years of his life he showed no hesitation in joining with the enemies of his nation to gain his own ends, and he was more occupied during the greater part of his reign in wasting Meath and Connacht in conjunction with the foreigners than in driving them out of the land. The Annals of Clonmacnois call him " that unruly Kinge of Mounster that partaked with the Danes." His career, however, is one of the most dramatic of all those of the Norse period.

Poetry in the Annals.—These romantic settings of historic tales contain much poetry. Just as in the pure romances long dialogues in verse, songs and laments, break the tedium of the prose narrative, so in the historic tales there are to be found numerous long poems which usually repeat in verse the substance of the prose matter. These are specially numerous in the career of Cellachan of Cashel and in the Wars of the Gaedhill and Gaill, the latter being frequently in the form of dialogues between the chieftains.

Even some of the Annals contain snatches of verse. It will be remembered that the original custom was to enshrine all matter of public importance in verse, and portions of these old poems are incorporated in the Annals of Tighernach and those of the Four Masters.

---

* Now College Green, Dublin. The poem uttered on this occasion is an evident imitation of the " Lay of the Heads," sung by Emer and Conall Cernach after the " Red Rout," made by the latter to avenge Cuchulain's death.

They are naturally more common in the earlier portions of the Annals than among the later entries. Even a trivial subject is sometimes invested with a surprising dignity in the quatrain devoted to its preservation, while events of importance are often enhanced by their poetic setting.   In the account of the terribly destructive Battle of Sligo, fought in 546 (537, Four Masters) in which Eoghan Bel, King of Connacht, was slain, these fine lines occur : " The Battle of Hy Fiachrach is fought with fury of edges over the border.   The kine of the foemen bellowed against the spears ; unto Crinder was the battle spread out.   The River (Sligo) carried off to the great sea the flesh and blood of men.   They utter pæans over Eba round the head of Eoghan Bél."

Again, in the entry on the slaying of one Dóir, son of Aedh Allen, in 623, there is a grim thought expressed in the verse put into the mouth of the murderer.   " What profit to me is the slaying of Dóir, for I have not slain the little Dóir (his son) ? 'Tis then one has killed a chafer when the chaferling is killed."

The apostrophe to the mill in which the two sons of King Blathmac, son of Aedh Slaine, were barbarously ground to death by Mael Odran of Leinster, is worth repeating : " O Mill, though thou hast ground much wheat, this time 'twas not a grinding upon oats, 'twas on the grandsons of Cearbhal (Karval) thou grindest. The grain that the mill grinds is not oats ; red is the wheat it grinds.   Of the saplings of the mighty tree is the feed of Mael Odran's Mill."   All these verses are found both in Tighernach's Annals and in those of the Four Masters.   They are either copied one from the other or they were well-known poems inserted from

a common tradition.   There is one quatrain that appears
in Tighernach only, and which is perhaps the most
poetic of all, indeed the most poetic description I have
ever met with, of the drowning of a man at sea.   The
entry runs : " (621 A.D.) The drowning of Conang,
son of Aedan, son of Gabhran. On it Ninine the poet
sang :—

" The sea's pure waves and the sun that pursued him, into his
    weak coracle they flung themselves together on Conang ;
" The woman that cast her white hair into his coracle against
    Conang, it is her smile that smiled to-day on Torta's tree."

The idea of the pursuit of the unfortunate youth
by the sun and waves, and of the sea-foam as a white-
haired woman flinging herself into his fragile bark and
smiling at her capture, are equally imaginative.

Two pieces of contemporary history remain to be
mentioned.   The first of these contains a description
of **The Flight of the Earls**, O'Neill and O'Donnell,
from Donegal, in 1607, written by their friend and companion, Teigue O'Keenan, who, with a large company
of other retainers, accompanied their flight and subsequent wanderings. The book may be described as the
travelling diary of the party.   It recounts their
departure from Ireland and the perils of their voyage
to Havre de Grâce on the coast of Normandy, where
they landed, and commenced a series of leisurely
wanderings through France and the Netherlands,
ultimately arriving in Rome by way of Switzerland
and Northern Italy.   They were received with
distinction by the Archduke in the Low Countries and
by the Pope in Rome, in which city they settled and
ultimately died.   Their tombs are still pointed out

to visitors in the Church of S. Pietro in Montorio. It is unfortunate that so interesting a piece of contemporary history should have been regarded by its author rather in the light of a record of matters that were of curiosity to himself as a traveller than of those likely to be of importance to posterity or to the historian. He is more concerned to give a minute account of the cities, churches and pictures visited by the party, and of the legends related about them, than to place on record the leading events of the Earl's career and the social and political conditions of their time. The original autograph remains in the Library of the Franciscan Monastery, Merchants' Quay, Dublin, whence it was transferred from St. Isidore's Convent at Rome. No other copy of it appears to be in existence.*

Even more important is the work styled *Historiæ Catholicæ Iverniæ Compendium*, written in Latin by Philip O'Sullivan Beare, and first published in Lisbon in 1621. Philip had been sent for refuge into Spain in 1602, while yet a young boy, from the same port whence Red Hugh O'Donnell had sailed ten months before. He became a soldier, and in 1619 he is heard of on a squadron appointed to guard the Spanish treasure-fleet on its approach to Cape St. Vincent. His father and family after many sufferings had joined him in Spain. It was from the lips of his father and his companions that he heard many of the details recorded in his history, by far the most important portion of which deals with the Elizabethan Wars in the South and West of Ireland. The Siege of the Castle of Dunboy by Sir George Carew, in 1602, and his

* It is being edited for the Irish Texts Society by Miss A. O'Farrelly.

demolition of the castle and savage butchery of the inhabitants on Dursey Island, with the retreat of his uncle, Donall O'Sullivan Beare, the Lord of Dunboy, across the Shannon, are detailed with much minuteness, and a pathetic account is given of their sufferings on the way to Ulster, only a remnant of thirty-five men out of the thousand persons who had accompanied him at the start having arrived alive at the end of their journey.

The Lord of Dunboy took refuge in Spain on the accession of James I., and was created by him Earl of Bearehaven. He was assassinated in Madrid by an Anglo-Irish refugee, in 1618. Other parts of this history deal with the general state of Ireland, and especially with the condition of the Catholics under Henry VIII., and his successors ; the account is brought down to 1613. A long section is devoted to the report of a Spanish Knight, named Ramon, who visited St. Patrick's Purgatory in Donegal, and described to the author his experiences there.

Among a number of other Annals written in Latin or English and giving fragments of contemporary history important for the periods with which they deal may be mentioned the Annals of the Franciscans of Multifernan, Co. Westmeath. They are among the oldest Latin chronicles existing in Ireland, and terminate in 1274.

The Annales Hiberniæ which terminate at 1370, but contain entries by different hands up to 1539 ;

Annals of Ireland, by Friar John Clyn, particularly full and valuable from the Scottish invasion in 1315 to the plague in 1349, at which date they close ;

A Treatise of Ireland by John Dymnock, in English,

important for its account of events at the close of the sixteenth century, and especially in the year 1599, of which the writer was evidently an eye-witness ;

Annales breves Hiberniæ, by Thady Dowling, Chancellor of Leighlin up to his death in 1628.   His chronicles close at 1600.

Macariæ Excidum.   A secret history of the wars of the Revolution in Ireland, written under feigned names and purporting to be a history of the Destruction of Cyprus.   Compiled by Colonel Charles O'Kelly.

CHAPTER XII.

Geoffrey Keating (Seathrún Céitinn), 1570— died sometime later than 1646.

There is no name better known in the Annals of Irish Literature than that of Geoffrey Keating. Yet our knowledge of Keating's career is, considering his fame as a preacher and the respect in which he was held on account of his learning and writings, singularly scant and unsatisfactory. The dates both of his birth and of his death are uncertain, but the best authorities agree that he was born in 1570, in the village of Burgess, in Co. Tipperary, and that he belonged to a family whose ancestors were pioneer Norman settlers, probably bearing a name resembling Fitz-Stephen or Fils Etienne, Hibernicised into Mac Eitinn or Céitinn, as found in the manuscripts. The family legend goes that the name was derived from the Irish word *cead-teine* or " first-fire," from a fire lighted by the author's progenitor to direct the troops of Fitz-Stephen on his arrival in Ireland, and that the family motto, " fortis et fidelis," with the crest of a wild boar rampant, was reminiscent of a wild boar which had been aroused by the blaze and slain on the spot by the courageous pioneer. Keating's parents must have been in good circumstances,* for after his early education in the bardic schools of his own

* There is a record of a permit or " pardon " granted to Keating's father by the Crown, releasing him from penalties for recusancy. This may account for the comparative freedom of action enjoyed by the family.

district he was sent abroad to receive a classical and theological training at one of those excellent Irish Colleges which then flourished in France, Spain, Italy and Germany.   His name, " P. Geofroy Ketting, docteur en théologie, Vatterford," appears among a list of Irish priests who were protected and educated by the Archbishop of Bordeaux in that city between 1605-1621 ; and he is mentioned by an anonymous writer (probably David Rothe, Catholic Bishop of Ossory, and author of the " Analecta "), in a work protesting against the attempt of the Scottish Dempster to appropriate the Irish Saints to Scotland, as an Irishman of singular distinction in Literature and Doctor of either Toulouse or Bordeaux.*

He seems to have returned to Ireland about the year 1610, early in the reign of James I., and was appointed curate to the Very Rev. Eugene Duhy in Tubrid, a village distant only a few miles from his native place. Here he laboured for several years, his fame as a preacher spreading through the country, so that he went hither and thither to minister to large and often fashionable congregations.   Together he and his vicar built the little church, beneath the shade of which both afterwards found a resting-place.   An inscription over the door of the ruined church, bearing the date 1644, contains the words in Latin, " Pray for the souls of the Rev. Fr. Eugene Duhy, Vicar of Tubrid, and the D. Doctoris Galfridii Keating, founders of this church, and also for those of all others, whether lay or clerical,

* The College of Bordeaux was founded in or about 1603 by Father Dermott M'Carthy, of Inniskerry, under the patronage of Card. Francis de Savodia.   Keating was the seventeenth student admitted to the College.

whose bodies are therein interred." One of his latest poems, probably the last he ever wrote, " Múscail do mhisneach, a Bhanbha," is dated in the body of the poem itself, 1646 A.D. We may therefore conclude that his death took place later than that date.*

Keating had already begun to write poetry when he was in France, whence he dictated a charming poetical epistle to Ireland, " Mo bheannacht leat, a scríbhinn," and he continued throughout his life to give expression to his feelings in verse. At least eighteen poems are certainly of his authorship, and several others are attributed to his hand.

To this early period, 1615, belongs also his theological treatise, *Eochair-scaith an Aifrinn*, or " The Explanatory Defence (or Apologia) of the Mass " ; his other large theological work, *Trí bior-ghaethe an Bháis*, or " Three Shafts of Death," being the production of a later period (about 1625).

Dr. Keating lived in troublous times for the Catholic clergy, for the exercise of their calling was always liable to be interrupted, and there were enemies constantly on the watch to report them to the Government. Soon after his return, his name, along with that of sundry other priests and friars, was noted in a report containing the names of ecclesiastics coming into Ireland from abroad, whom it was desirable to keep under observation. Nevertheless he laboured for many years

* An Irish note on a manuscript of Keating's History, recently in the possession of the late Mr. David Comyn, stated that Archbishop O'Brennan, of Cashel, who died in 1692, was buried at his own request in the grave of Geoffrey Keating at Tubrid. The statement was originally made by Tadhg O'Neachtan. This is testimony to the fact that the historian was interred in this church.

without very serious interference, and when at length his parochial and literary labours at Tubrid were brought to an abrupt conclusion, it was by the private action of a lady of his congregation who, incensed at a sermon which she believed to be directed against herself, addressed a complaint to the President of Munster, a personal friend of her own, and persuaded him to put into force the Conformity Act, which had hitherto lain in abeyance so far as Tubrid was concerned. In consequence, " orders were immediately issued for horse and foot to go in quest of our preacher, as obnoxious to the laws provided against seminary priests," and Keating was forced to fly.* He took refuge in a cave called Poll Granda, some seven miles west of Cahir, in the Glen of Atherlow, a spot long remembered by the peasantry as the place of his retreat. This lovely valley, lying at the base of the Galtees, had been a favourite haunt of " rebels " in the days of Elizabeth, but it had been " cleared " by order of Carew, who, in the ruthless record of the day, is stated to have left behind " neither man nor beast, neither corn nor cattle." It was while in hiding in this solitary spot that Keating planned and began to write his most famous work, the Forus Feasa ar Eirinn, or " Foundations of Knowledge of Ireland," commonly known as his " History of Ireland." The watch kept upon him cannot have been very close, for when his own manuscripts were exhausted he wandered in disguise through every part of Ireland accumulating materials for his work. It would have been easy to apprehend a man who remained for considerable periods in one place copying and collecting manuscripts, but the petty

* Clanricarde's Memoirs, Preface, Lond., 1722.

revenge of personal spite having been attained by his removal from Tubrid, he seems to have been left unmolested. We read that the Protestant gentry as well as the Catholics, who possessed manuscripts likely to be of service to Keating, everywhere received the learned and enthusiastic priest with honour and passed him on from place to place in safety. The chief difficulty he seems to have met with was from the Irish of Ulster and Connacht, who distrusted him on account of his Norman origin, and who were inclined to believe that a Munsterman would do scant justice to the records of the North. The enormous number of books and manuscripts, Irish, English, and Classical, from which Keating quotes, or which are alluded to as his authorities, show that he must not only have consulted many collections of books during his wanderings, but that he must himself have been possessed of a considerable library. Had he been continually hunted from place to place, as tradition states, this would hardly have been possible. The Díonbhrollach or Preface to his work was written in 1629, and the whole history was completed before 1634. The earliest existing copy is the important manuscript in the Franciscan Monastery, Dublin, which was written before 1640.* It seems to have been written in the Convent of Kildare and afterwards to have belonged to the Monastery of Donegal, whence it was carried to Louvain by the learned author of the " Lives of the Saints," Rev. John Colgan. It is described as one of the books " found in the chamber

* There is a condensed version of the work in MS. in the British Museum written by one of the family of the O'Duigenans, and dated 1638 (Egerton, 107), which would point to a still earlier date.

of our Father Colgan " after his death.   The other chief contemporary manuscripts of the Forus Feasa are those transcribed by his friends, the O'Mulconrys, one of whom was engaged at the same period in assisting the O'Clerys in their compilation of the Annals of the Four Masters.   They were a Connacht family of scribes whom he probably visited during his wanderings.   It is possible also that he met Michael O'Clery there, for there is a tradition that O'Clery visited Roscommon about this time, and even the manuscripts which O'Clery had collected for his edition of the *Leabhar Gabhála* seem to have been made use of by Keating for his own work.   Possibly he may himself have visited the Convent of Donegal where the learned confrères were engaged in compiling the Annals from 1632-1636.

During the war of 1641, Dr. Keating's sympathies were warmly enlisted in favour of the " Old Irish " party under Owen Roe O'Neill.   He, however, seems to have felt some personal liking for the Butler family, to whom several of his poems are addressed.   Several of his poetical efforts are laments on the deaths of his friends, some of whom fell in battle during the war.

We must now pass to the consideration of his literary work.   By far the most noted of his writings is his History of Ireland (*Forus feasa ar Eirinn*).   Though Keating's History was compiled at the same period as the Annals of the Four Masters, the design and execution of his work is quite unlike theirs.   The compilers of the Annals arranged and incorporated in chronological order the various existing chronicles which their diligence had managed to collect together.   They did not seek to edit or expand their material or to construct out of it a connected and readable history of the country. Their compilation, a monument of industry and an invaluable though frequently a bare record of events, appeals to the scholar rather than to the public or the general reader. They retain to a large extent the archaic spelling of the manuscripts from which they copied, and their only object is the preservation of the records. Keating, using much the same materials, attempts to construct out of them a consecutive narrative to suit the taste of the great mass of his Irish fellow-countrymen. His history was the first, and it remains the only important effort to write a history of Ireland in Irish and for the Irish people. It immediately became popular, and it continued to be one of the best-known Irish manuscripts * until after the famine of 1846, which gave the final death-blow to the native language and literature. After an elaborate preface in which he disputes with much spirit, but with, occasionally, an unfortunate lack of historical accuracy, the adverse opinions of English writers upon Ireland, he proceeds to give an interesting list of the authorities upon which he has drawn for his materials ; they include not only the traditional records and annals, but those romantic tales in which most of the old historical tradition is enshrined. It is in the use that he makes of these romances that Keating's History differs from the Annals ; they merely mention the supposed historic kernel of events, but he introduces the tale out of which the annalists have extracted the central fact. His history gains in this way in interest and poetry, but he

---

* There are no less than ten transcripts of Keating's History in the British Museum alone, written between the date of its compilation and 1703.

makes no attempt to separate history from romance. He opens with a lengthy account of the early settlements of Ireland, incorporating large portions of the " Book of Invasions," upon which he has copiously drawn. Romance and legend and ecclesiastical materials are all made use of, and his energy has collected and preserved for posterity a number of stories which are otherwise unknown.   In critical capacity Keating cannot be said to rise above the mediæval level.   He is diffuse and rambling, and many of his dissertations and chronological calculations might well have been spared.

His great claim to permanent study arises from his admirable and chaste use of the Irish tongue, and his works will always remain a standard of Irish at its best period, before it fell into decay.   It is free alike from the archaisms of the genealogists and bards and from the inevitable corruptions which the want of a written standard brought about at a later day.   It represents the current tongue of the Irish scholar writing when his native language possessed its full vigour and retained its purity of use as the natural method of his literary expression.

Dr. Keating's most important theological work is his " Three sharp-pointed Shafts of Death " (*Trí Bior-ghaethe an Bháis*), which treats in a mystical and symbolical manner of corporeal and spiritual death, with warnings and exhortations growing out of the consideration of these subjects.   The mournful topic is worked out in thirty-six chapters divided into three books, and is elaborated with the wealth of illustration and allegorical interpretation usual in mediæval treatises on death and the after-life.   Even apart from the grave and dignified style in which it is written, the work is interesting

as proving the wide range of the author's reading
and the enormous mass of examples that he had at his
command.   He draws in rapid succession upon Biblical
and Apocryphal literature, on Josephus and the Fathers
of the Church ; upon classical authors and facts from
ancient and mediæval history.   Occasionally, as in
his chapter on the advisability of holding " Grief-feasts "
or " Wakes " (Bk. iii., ch. vii.), or in that in which he
treats of various methods of burial among pagan and
Christian nations (Bk. iii., ch. viii.), he draws, among
other sources, upon native Irish customs for his illustrations ; more rarely still, he introduces a modern
incident drawn from personal knowledge or hearsay
(cf. Bk. ii., ch. vii.).

The work is a model of scholarly Irish in its best
period.   Besides this treatise, Keating wrote " The
' Key-shield,' or Defence of the Mass " (*Eochair-sciath
an Aifrinn*), a didactic and controversial work, and a
short tract on the Rosary or *Coróin Mhuire.*

Keating's poems are partly didactic and religious,
and partly laments over deceased friends or over the
state of the country and the departure of the native
gentry, a mournful theme which has inspired hundreds
of Irish poems by authors known and unknown.   Perhaps the best of Keating's poems on this subject is the
one beginning : "Óm sceol ar árd-mhagh Fáil ní chodlaim
oidhche," written after the Flight of the Earls to France
and Italy.   Among his laments for personal friends
is a poem of considerable length on the death, in 1640,
of Lord Dunboyne, beginning, " Druididh suas, a chuaine
an chaointe," which relates the virtues of the departed
chief in over three hundred lines.   Other laments are
those on the death of Lord James Butler, written before

1620, on Shawn Oge mac Gerald, Lord of the Decies (d. 1626), and that on the death of the two sons of Lord Dunboyne, who fell in battle in 1646.

Keating uses with considerable skill a great variety of the old metres ; yet his verse is rather the work of a cultivated prose-writer, wielding a form of expression not equally familiar to him, than that of a spontaneous poet. Some of his poems, however, show grace and ease of style. Among the best are his lines in praise of the Irish tongue, " Milis an teanga an Ghaedhealg," and his poetic epistle to Ireland " Mo Bheannacht leat, a scríbhinn," both of which are very charming, and his religious verses, " Caoin thú féin, a Dhuine Bhoicht." His spirited poem beginning, " Múscail do mhisneach, a Bhanbha," was written in 1646.

But besides these personal satires, the outcome of
private or petty spite, there are remaining several
longer pieces, of different periods, that stand on a quite
different plane, and in which matters of public interest
are treated in humorous prose or verse, or whole classes
of persons are held up to ridicule, and there are besides
large numbers of pure burlesques, stories recited purely
to excite the merriment of the hearers, and not having
any further intention beyond the entertainment of the
passing hour. Some of the serious satires are of sufficient
importance to be treated separately. One of the most
humorous is a piece in which the ancient bards and
satirists themselves are held up to ridicule, and their
numbers and methods, their dishonest extortions and
the obscurity of their language are exaggerated and
made ridiculous. This is a piece entitled "**The Proceedings of the Great Bardic Institution.**" The
main purpose of this extravaganza is to explain how the
story of the Táin bó Cuailnge was recovered after its
supposed loss, but this is preceded by a long prose satire,
describing the visit of one of the ancient bardic companies, headed by Seanchan, chief poet of the period,
to King Guaire, of Connaught, and the terror inspired
in the neighbourhood by the absurd and impossible
demands made by each member of the huge company in
turn. "They went not to bed any night without wanting
something, and they arose not a day without some one
of them having longing desires for things that were
extraordinary, wonderful, rare and difficult of procure-
ment." If they did not receive their most extravagant
demands within twenty-four hours satires and maledic-
tions were threatened. An abject terror of them seizes
upon their hosts. King Guaire is found on his knees

imploring God that he might die ere he should hear himself satirized and defamed by the great Bardic Association, and in another portion of the story when another bard, Dallan, the predecessor of Seanchan, tells King Hugh, of Oirgiall, that he will satirize him, the king exclaims, " The powers and miracles of the King of Heaven and Earth be on my side to save and protect me against thee." Though this bardic company includes only two-thirds of its whole number, because Seanchan remembers that the province is poor and that they might eat up all the land if they came in their full strength, yet his followers number thrice fifty professors, thrice fifty students, and an equal number each of male and female attendants, of hounds, and of every class of craftsman. Magnificent preparations are made for their reception, but all is defeated by their unreasonable behaviour. Although the subject and style of this piece make it appear heavy and antiquated to the modern reader, it is written with a good deal of humour and it gives some hard hits at the traditional extravagances of the bards.*

A satire worked out with more conscious art and of a far higher literary quality is the piece known as " **The Vision of Mac Conglinne**," which its editor, Dr. Kuno Meyer, considers to have been composed at least as early as the twelfth century. In the condition in which we have it the tale, which is partly in prose and partly in verse, has probably been pieced together out of two ancient tales which ran on somewhat different lines, for the narrative is confused and frequently repeats itself. The main theme of this curious

* Imtheacht na Tromdháimhe. Trs. of the Ossianic Society, Vol. V., 1857.

and powerful mock-heroic piece is the curing by a poor scholar of a King of Munster, Cathal mac Finguine (d. 737 A.D.), who was afflicted with a voracious appetite which no amount of food could appease, and which was supposed to be caused by " a demon of gluttony " which had taken possession of him. The main object of the piece seems to be a broad Rabelaisian satire on the monks and clergy of the day, but its most interesting feature is the vision of Mac Conglinne, the poor scholar, who undergoes many sufferings in his efforts to rescue Cathal from his affliction, and who relates for this purpose a vision which he had seen of a fortress or palace composed entirely of viands and set in a sea of milk. This curious poem seems to have suggested passages in " The Land of Cokaigne." It begins as follows :—

> " An apparition wonderful,
> A vision most delectable,
>   I tell to thee ;
> In coracles of lard we break
> Out of the port of New-milk Lake
>   To sail the World's smooth sea."

The loading and starting of the ship is then described, and the sailors reach an island made entirely of food :

> " The fort we reached was beautiful
> Out-works of custards plentiful,
>   Beyond the loch were laid ;
> The bridge in front new butter bright,
> The rubble dyke was wheat most white
>   Bacon the palisade.

> "Smooth pillars of ripe cheese were seen,
> With sappy bacon props between
>   Alternately displayed ;
> Of mellow cream the roof-tree beams
> The rafters of white curd, meseems,
>   The house from falling stayed, etc."

The viands mentioned in this piece are of the simplest pastoral kind, and include varieties of oaten and wheaten cakes, cheeses, curds, and butter, honey and porridge, with bacon, lard, eggs and broth, and meats of different sorts. Tripe and salmon are mentioned and of vegetables, kale, carrots, leeks, onions and apples. Ale and wine are also spoken of, but are not much insisted upon. Indeed, when, having reckoned up innumerable sorts of food, the Wizard Doctor who appears to Mac Conglinne in his vision comes to order him his " drop of drink," it is a drink of milk he gives. " A tiny little measure for thee, Mac Conglinne, not too large, only as much as twenty men will drink, on the top of those viands ; of very thick milk, of milk of great strength, of milk of medium strength, of yellow bubbling milk, milk that makes a snoring bleat like a ram as it rushes down the throat, so that the first draught says to the last draught : ' I vow, thou mangy cur, that if thou comest down, I'll go up, for a pair of dogs like us cannot fit at once in this treasure-house.' " There are exceedingly curious notices of old customs introduced incidentally into this piece.

As examples of mock-heroic poems of a more recent date, we may take two poems composed respectively early in the eighteenth century, and later on in the same century, the poem called " The Adventures of a Luckless Fellow " (*Eachtra ghiolla an ámarain*) by Donagh Rua Macnamara, and that called " The Midnight Court " (*Cuirt an mheadhoin oidhche*), by Brian Merriman.

Macnamara, or, to give him his Irish name, Donnchadh Ruadh mac Conmara, was born at Cratloe in Co. Clare, about the beginning of the eighteenth century. It was hoped by his parents that he would enter the priesthood and he was sent to Rome to finish his education and to receive Holy Orders. But his ungovernable character showed itself even at this early age, and he was expelled from the college and returned home to Ireland, where he followed, in the intervals of wilder courses, the profession of school-master at Slieve Gua in Co. Waterford, and other places in the same district. He did not stay long anywhere, for his evil ways made him feared and disliked in every village in which he chanced to plant himself, and he finally left the Decies country and spent the latter part of his life between the mountains of Comeragh and the River Suir. In 1745 he paid a visit to Newfoundland (*Talamh-an-éisc*, or the " Land of Fish"), which probably suggested the poem on his " Adventures." Macnamara was a man of considerable learning, but his method of life brought him into the lowest depths of misery, and in 1764 we find him appealing for help to a gentleman named James Ducket, who seems to have responded to his petition, for the bard remained for many years under his patronage at White's-town. In his last days he is found teaching the three sons of James Power in the same neighbourhood. He died about 1814. The first part of his " Adventures of a Luckless Fellow," or the " Mock Æneid," as it is often called, gives a humorous description of his determination to give up his miserable life at home and his start to try and retrieve his fortunes in America. His friends, probably glad to be rid of a worthless neighbour, loaded him with gifts, and he set sail from Waterford. He is relating the sudden state of misery into which he and his fellow-emigrants were thrown by the rise of a squall, shortly after they sailed out of the harbour, when, overcome by sickness, he sinks into a swoon, and the vision, which is the main subject of the poem, begins.   Part II. opens with the appearance of a gentle lady, the Fairy Princess Aoibhill, or Evall, of Craiglea, who places her cool hand on his forehead and draws him away into a wilderness, out of which opens a dismal cave which leads them down to the River Styx or Acheron, over which, as in Virgil's Æneid, the shades of the dead are being ferried.

But Mac Conmara has his own ideas about the conditions in the under world, and they differ considerably from those of Virgil.   He gives his Hades a specially Irish complexion.   Conan of the Fianna, and not Charon, is the boatman, and the hosts he ferries across are not persons who, as in Virgil, have not been duly buried in this world, but those who have caroused and drunk away their earnings and have not even left themselves a halfpenny to pay to the ferry-man, "unless one is given to them in charity."   Like Mac Conmara himself, who spoke little English, Conan will speak nothing but Irish or Latin, nor will he take any Saxon over the ferry without a bright sixpence.   In one place the poet sees, close beside the valiant men of Troy and Greece, the Tuatha Dé Danann being routed by the men of Fenius Fearsa, and in another "Hugh Mac Curtin from Erin" is sitting close beside Juvenal, "versifying melodiously in Irish."   He is suddenly awakened from his vision of the underworld by cries of "all hands aloft" from the deck, and is shortly afterwards plunged with the rest of the crew into a hand to hand fight with the crew of a French frigate which has borne down on them. They capture the French vessel and return with their booty to Ireland, where our hero lands with severe wounds on his body and an heroic resolve that never again in his life would he put foot on a ship unless he were dragged on board by ropes and cords.

It is singular that it is from the hand of the author of this rollicking comedy that we get one of the most beautiful and refined of Irish lyrics, the exquisite song called " The Fair Hills of Holy Ireland " (*Bánchnoic Eireann óigh.*")

Brian Merriman's poem, " The Midnight Court," stands on quite a different plane to that of the Mock Æneid. Although from the nature of its subject and treatment it can never be widely read, and is quite unsuitable to the young, it is undoubtedly a piece of sustained power, and is wrought with artistic skill of the highest order. The author, whose name is sometimes written in Irish " Brian mac Giolla-meidhre,"* was born in the middle of the eighteenth century in the parish of Clondagach, Co. Clare, where his father was a small land owner. He was a wild and pleasure-seeking youth, but an accomplished performer on the violin.   For thirty years he was school-master in the parish of Feakle in the Barony of Tulla Upper.   He died in Limerick in 1808.

His chief poem, " The Midnight Court," written in 1780-1, is a witty but broad satire on social conditions, written under the usual form of a vision or Aisling. On a beautiful morning in July the poet wanders out into the wild and mountainous region of Loch Gréine, in Clare, and takes shelter from the heat of the day

* Mr. S. H. O'Grady thinks that this is only a translation from the English form of the name, and states that he is always spoken of in his own district of Co. Clare as Merriman. (See Cat. of MSS. in the Brit. Mus., p. 493*n.*)

in a shady nook, where he flings himself down on the grass and falls asleep. Short was his sleep before there appeared to him a gigantic woman from fairyland, a terrific and grotesque figure, who bore in her hand a brass-mounted mighty wand of office. She called on him peremptorily to arise and follow her to a grand conclave that was even then being held under the presidency of the same Fairy Queen Evall, of Craiglea, who had appeared to Macnamara, and who was apparently always close at hand when any Munster bard happened to fall asleep in the open air, during a couple of centuries at least. The questions under debate were the needs, the depopulation and the misfortunes of Ireland, and how these evils might be remedied so far as Thomond was concerned. Into the midst of this debate the bard is precipitated. He hears the arguments on both sides, and at the close of them the summing up of the Fairy Queen, who gives it as her opinion, among other things, that as there is a general complaint from the women that the young men of Ireland are too slow to marry, every youth of twenty-one who is still unwed is to be handed over to the weaker sex to be chastised as they shall see fit, while every old bachelor is to be put to death with such tortures as they may please to devise. At this moment they observe Brian, who is still unmarried, and these " advanced " women, while solemnly entering the date of their glorious emancipation in a volume prepared for the purpose, determine to carry out their new resolutions upon him as the nearest victim. In a cold sweat of terror Brian awakes, and the vision vanishes away.

In spite of its unpleasant subject-matter and often coarse language, the mastery of form and speech shown in this poem give it a rank far above that of the rhetorical and often imitative and insipid verse of many of Merriman's contemporaries. It is an original work, wrought with conscious art and skill. The long sustained rhythm, with the use of double rhyme in many lines and the careful employment of alliterative vowels and words, combine to produce a poem of real power. The opening passage describing the, to him, familiar shores of Loch Gréine, is one of the most beautiful in Irish literature. Literally, it runs as follows :—

> " Full often I strolled by the brink of the river
> On the green-sward fresh, 'mid the heavy dew,
> Skirting the woods, or in mountain recesses,
> No care in my soul, in the full light of day.
> My heart would light up when I saw Loch Gréine,
> The heaven's expanse o'er the country I loved ;
> Delightful and soft was the lie of the mountains
> Peak beckoning to peak o'er the ridges between.
> The heart glowed with joy that erewhile had been withered,
> Spent of its vigour and wearied with pain ;
> The weakling, embittered by want or by exile,
> Might well gaze awhile on the green forest's crests.
> Wild ducks sailed in flocks o'er the bay's mistless waters
> Among them the swans gliding gracefully through,
> The fish in their jollity flung themselves upwards
> I saw the gay perch with its manifold hues ;
> I saw the loch's azure, the blue of its ripples,
> Which [one day would] thunder its weight on the shore,
> Bright birds in the trees made a melody mirthful,
> While hard by the doe bounded off to the wood,
> With winding of horns flashed the huntsmen upon me,
> Brave Reynard in front and the hounds on his heels."*

Three satires which became well-known in the South of Ireland are called the Parliament of Clan Thomas,

* The original of the first lines runs—
> Ba gnáth mé ag siúbhal le ciumhais na h-abhann
> Ar bháinsigh úir 's an drúcht go trom ;
> Anaice na g-coillteadh a g-coim an t-sléibhe
> Gan mhairg, gan mhoill, ar shoillse an lae.

the Adventures of Clan Thomas, and the Adventures of Tadhg Dubh.   The last is by Egan O'Rahilly, a Munster poet of the close of the seventeenth and beginning of the eighteenth centuries, and from their similarity in thought and structure the two former are believed to be from the same pen.   They are fierce social and political satires, ridiculing in often coarse and brutal language the habits and modes of life and thought of the Cromwellian settlers of low origin and of the Irish who imitated them and assisted them to oppress their own countrymen.   The pride and avarice of these men, their low morals and gluttony, and the brawls, disunion and treachery in which they engage are depicted in strong colours and with minute details.

CHAPTER XIV.

The Later Bards.

Towards the beginning of the seventeenth century a sudden and remarkable outburst of energy brought the bards once more into prominence.

Though the bardic schools had continued to turn out their annual quota of youths trained for the bardic profession throughout the previous hundred years, there is an unusual paucity of great names among the poets from about the middle of the fifteenth until towards the close of the sixteenth century.

Bardic Profession Hereditary.—The fact that the profession was hereditary in certain families and seldom admitted outsiders into its ranks, however well qualified as poets they might otherwise be, tended to destroy originality in a calling which could not attract to itself spontaneous genius from outside. From century to century some representative of each bardic family occupied the honourable position of his ancestors, even though he might not be well qualified by nature or disposition for the duties of his office. Thus, of the great family of the O'Dalys, the most famous bardic race in Ireland, there are thirty-six entries made in the Annals of the Four Masters between the years 1139-1589, and the family continued to flourish till well into the seventeenth century.

The same authority gives twenty-two entries of members of the family of Mac-an-Bhaird, or Mac Ward, hereditary poets to the O'Donnells of Donegal between the years 1173-1609. These flourished until the close of the seventeenth century. They gave their name to the wild district known as Lettermacaward, or the "country-side of the bards' sons." Of the O'Higgins of the neighbouring district in Sligo and Fermanagh there are thirty-three entries up to 1536, and other families, such as the Mac Brodins, O'Coffeys, and Mac Craiths or Magraths, produced equally long lines of family bards. They lived on the hereditary estates assigned to them by the chiefs to whose persons they were attached, and they were sustained by the ample fees bestowed upon them for their compositions.

In no country did the professional poet fare so well as in Ireland. It has been computed that in the petty princedom of Tyrconnel or Donegal, the real estate allocated to the maintenance of the *literati* amounted in value to £2,000 a year of our present currency; and we find Daire mac Brodin, poet to the Fourth Earl of Thomond (about 1570-1650), residing still on his own patrimonial estate in the Castle of Dunogan, Barony of Ibrican, in the west of Co. Clare.

Bardic Fees.—As to the fees or rewards of the later bards for their performances, we have the testimony of Tadhg Dall O'Higgin, or " Blind Teigue," in a poem describing a festive night spent in the house of Maelmora mac Sweeney.* After describing the great concourse of poets gathered round Mac Sweeney and the pledging of the host† from " golden goblets and from beakers

---

* He was slain by Scottish mercenaries at the instance of Captain Malby, titular English Governor of Connacht in 1581.

† Though *uisge beathadh*, Anglicised " whisky," was at this period drunk in the country, neither poets nor tale-tellers appear from their poems to have condescended to it; they speak only of ale, wine, and mead.

of horn," the poem relates that they went to rest shortly before dawn ; before they fell asleep Teigue promised them a story " for a price." The rewards given on this occasion were " a dappled horse, one of the very best in Ireland," from Maelmora, and from three chief bards who were present, " a wolf-dog that might be matched against any," a little book that was " a well brimful of the very stream of knowledge," and a harp belonging to Conor O'Higgin, minstrel-in-chief of the Mac William-Burkes. This was not bad payment for a story ; perhaps the ale from the golden beakers had taken effect upon the listeners.

The bards seem to have been very punctilious in demanding their full rights, and their complaints were loud and bitter if any unauthorised person usurped their authority with their chief or tendered him advice which they held it to be their own prerogative to give. O'Hosey or O'Hussey, poet of the Maguires, on being appointed ollave or poet-in-chief, reminded his patron in his laureate ode that the ollave ranked in all ways as an equal with a king and bishop.

" To him is due the warmth of loving-kindness, the primest of all largesse, the initiative in counsel ; the seat closest to the prince and a share of his bed, with payment whether ' in wood ' or ' in sanctuary.' "

He gave Maguire clearly to understand that he would lose no time in taking steps towards the assertion of an ollave's rights. He insisted that at his command Maguire was bound to harry one district or to protect another, and that no one was entitled to give him counsel before himself ; nay, even a chieftain might not stand higher with his master than he. He demands a dwelling close beside the chief's house and his share of " imperishable patrimonial soil."

" To every man of us ollaves the highest species of estate is a piece of land close to the chief and blessed with equal facilities for grazing or for tillage, as with resort to the bordering pasture mountain."

The very security and comparative affluence of their position must have tended among the less gifted bards to indolence of mind, and their professional duties, which consisted in producing laudatory poems on the births and deaths of their lords or on the coming of age of his heir and other similar opportune occasions, tended to become in their very nature mere mechanical productions.

Lack of Detail.—The value for historical purposes of the larger number of these compositions is much lessened by their vagueness of expression ; the bards seldom condescend to explicit details as to the actual conditions, feelings, and events of their own time ; they find it easier to indulge in poetic generalities formed closely on the models of their predecessors and wanting in that local colour which would have otherwise made of these panegyrics, composed to record intimate family events, a record of peculiar value.

Insincerity.—Again, we cannot but feel that much of this poetry is radically insincere. Whether the actual performances of their lord met with their approval or not, the poem in his praise had to be forthcoming at the required moment, at risk of the loss of their emoluments or place. Even a chief devoted to the English cause received his due measure of laudation, though we must imagine that on such occasions the bardic pen did not flow with its customary ease.   For instance, Tadhg mac Daire mac Brodin, or " Mac Dary," as he is commonly called, chief bard of the Earls of Thomond, says prudently in an early poem addressed to the Fourth Earl on his succession in 1580, that though he can now point out to him his duties (which he proceeds to do at some length), praise must be deferred until the Earl shall have deserved it by performance. We can scarcely believe that the Earl's devotion to Elizabeth's cause is the sort of performance contemplated by the bard, nevertheless on his death in 1624 his loss is bewailed by Mac Dary as an irreparable one to Munster.

Again, this same poet, in one of the poems contributed by him to the Contention of the Bards, after another panegyric of the same Earl and of the old-English families of the Bourkes, Barrys, Butlers, Roches, and Geraldines, exclaims of Clanricarde, who gained his order of knighthood for the wounds he received in fighting against Tyrone's army in the Battle of Kinsale, December, 1601, and who went over to London expressly to tender his duty to Elizabeth in 1602, " Had we but Ricarde, gallant chief, in yew-abundant Ireland now ; what other forest boughs than he (*i.e.*, young princes of the Gael) could be found more excellent as tested in the service of the fair extent of Ireland ? "   These services to Ireland were such as those he rendered in the army of Sir George Carew in 1601, when he " would not suffer any man to make prisoners of any of the Irish, but bade them kill the rebels."   " No man," we read, " did bloody his sword more than his lordship did that day." *

* Pac. Hib. Bk. II., Ch. xxi.

The sense of the perfunctoriness of many of these bardic poems is a great drawback to any pleasure we might otherwise derive from them.

More satisfactory, because we feel sure of its honesty, is such a piece as that by Loghlin Oge O'Daly, written about the time of the first plantations of Ulster, describing the violent uprooting of old customs and the introduction of a new and distasteful order of things. The fighting men of the four Provinces, he says, are driven to take foreign service in distant countries, and in their place " a conceited and impure swarm of foreigners " have settled down upon the lands. He sees with dismay the tillage of the new proprietors encroaching on the wild uncultivated pasture-lands, hitherto used only for cattle.

" This, the land of noble Niall's posterity (*i.e.*, Ulster), they portion out among themselves without leaving a jot of Flann's milk-yielding Plain but we find it cut up into acres. We have lived to see, heavy the affliction, the tribal places of convention emptied; the wealth of fishes perished out of the stream; dark thickets of the chase turned into streets. In the House of Saints we find a congregation of boors, and the true service of God carried on meanwhile under a rude shelter of boughs of trees; the night-coverings of minstrels used to litter cattle; the mountain broken up into fenced fields." (O'Grady's Cat. of MSS. p. 375.)

This is a good example of much anti-English poetry of the period. The forcible seizure of the tribal lands by planters from over seas and the expatriation of the old owners was hard enough to bear, but to the bard, who was the natural conservator of the old order, it became more difficult still when it was attended with the break up of the old system of life, on the maintenance of which his position and his very existence depended. The tillage of the old pasture and forest lands and the building of commercial and manufacturing towns on the northern water-ways was to him but an outward symbol of the reversal of the entire social régime with which it was everywhere accompanied. The bitterness of spirit with which the changes were regarded by the bards comes out in a multitude of poems of this period. Here is a specimen from a poem by Mahon O'Heffernan, written probably about the same date as the above, caustically bidding his descendants to forsake an art no longer useful to its patrons, or bidding them satirically to praise the young English gallants who have replaced the old Gael and who alone have now the means to reward them for their poems.

" My son, cultivate not the poetic art, forsake utterly the calling of thine ancestors ; though to poetry first of all honour is rightly due, she is henceforth but a portent of misery. To the worst of all trades cleave not, nor fashion any more thine Irish lay ; better than any well-turned poem, perfect in sound and science, is now esteemed obscurity, new-fangled and unknown. A vulgar doggrel, ' soft ' vocables that barely need to be of even length, plainly concoct such, without excess of involution, and from that poor literary form shall thy promotion be the greater. Praise no man, nor any satirize—but, and if thou praise, laud not a Gael ; to him who might perchance seek to do so, to him the panegyric of a Gael means odium earned. . . . The good that hath been, heed it not ; the good that now is, dwell on that ; flatter the English gallants' reputation, since to have fellowship with them is now the likelier. . . . Fling to oblivion the memory of their munificence, of old the poets treasure—kingly Gerald's blood that never warmed to love of self, no poem ponder thou in praise of them. If, nowadays, none care for fair accomplishments or for the understanding of instruction (far different this from fencing-in of arable lands), what profits it to make a poem ? " *

Metres.—The compression necessitated by the metres

* Eg. 111. Art. 71, B. Museum, and cf. O'Grady's Catalogue of MSS. p. 393.

employed must also have tended to destroy originality of thought. Where the whole ingenuity of the mind was fixed upon the stringent rules under which alone bardic composition was permitted, only men of strong original power and complete mastery over their difficult art could rise above the consideration of the mere technique to the production of verses of real poetic quality.

The rules of the Irish Classic Metres (which went under the generic name of *Dán Díreach* or " Straight Verse ") required a break or suspension of the sense at the end of every second line, while each idea or thought of the poet must be completed within the quatrain. Hence there could be no carrying over of the sense from one stanza to another. Within these narrow limits the laws governing the construction of the verse were extraordinarily complicated, alliteration, rhyme, and number of syllables being all governed by precise laws. The result of this close attention to metrical exactitude is that a great number of the poems produced under this system are unimpassioned, sententious and mechanical. It would have been impossible for them to be otherwise; the wonder is, that they ever rise into true poetry at all. O'Gnive calls the poets the " Schoolmen of condensed speech," and the Scottish bard, Mac Vurich, speaks of Teig Dall O'Higgin as putting into less than a half rann what others would take a whole crooked stanza to express.*

Yet, in spite of all these difficulties, there are many examples of bardic poetry not only pure and stately in diction and elevated in style, but stirred by true and

* Reliquæ Celticæ, Vol. II., p. 297 ; Hyde, Literary History, p. 537.

deep feeling.   The master-bards wielded their pon-
derous and complicated canons of art with consummate
facility.   However the obligations of the bards to
their own chief and Province may have tended on the
whole to perpetuate jealousy and feuds between the
lords of rival houses, we find here and there a poem
which shows that some among them wrought hard for
the union of the chiefs and were not unconscious of
aspirations towards a national ideal.   They were,
perhaps, the only class to whom such a conception was
possible at all.   Their journeyings from province to
province to carry the messages of their patrons, their
occasional expeditions out of the country,* and their
opportunities of intercourse with other members of the
bardic community must have helped to give them a view
of things larger than the limits of their own province
or sept.   Their education also tended to widen their
sympathies and interests.   They seldom resorted in
their youth to the bardic schools of their own immediate
neighbourhood ; they preferred to take their education
in a different province, so that no interference of friends
or relatives might be allowed to disturb the course of
their studies.   The connection with the bardic families
of other districts, begun thus in youth, must have
cultivated their sense of being members of a race of
men whose learning and influence should not be confined
strictly within the limits of one family or even of one
Province.

Bardic Schools.—The Bardic Schools seem still to

* Thus, when Shane O'Neill went at Elizabeth's command
to London, in 1562, his chief bard, O'Gnive, was one of his
train of attendants.

have been in full operation at the beginning of the seventeenth century. Dr. Keating was educated in one in his own district near Clonmel, and during the first two years of his retirement he passed the larger portion of his time either in the schools or homes of different bards in Munster, employing his enforced leisure in making a collection from their manuscripts of the stories and legends which he afterwards threw together to form the earlier portions of his history. In a dissertation prefixed to Clanricarde's memoirs, published in 1744, we have an interesting account of the later seminaries, which lingered on until the writer's time in a degraded condition, though he tells us that since the beginning of the wars of 1641, the old bardic schools had died out, and not one in the country had been frequented since that date. His description, therefore, applies only to the later survivals, but these probably continued the system of the earlier schools so far as altered circumstances and reduced means allowed them to do so. The writer tells us that they were exclusively reserved for youths who were descended from poets and had the bardic calling in view for themselves. He says: "The qualifications first required were reading well, writing the mother-tongue and a strong memory. It was also necessary that the place should be in the solitary recess of a garden or within an inclosure far out of the reach of any noise. The structure was a snug, low hut, and beds in it at convenient distances, each within a small division, without much furniture of any kind, save only a table, some seats, and an arrangement for clothes to hang upon. No window to let in the day, nor any light at all used but that of candles, and these brought in at a proper season only."

stirred a truer note than usual and brought forth a number of poems of exceptionally fine quality. The second cause was a sudden flaring up of the old contention for superiority between the North and the South, in which various bards espoused the side with which they were in sympathy and produced in support of their arguments a quantity of poems which became known under the general title of the " Contention of the Bards."

Poems on the O'Neills and O'Donnells.—Among the most popular of the poems that were inspired by the downfall and death of the Northern chiefs or by the condition of the country after their departure from Ireland may be named the following :—A long anonymous poem called " The Roman Apparition " or " Vision " (1650), supposed to be written in Rome beside the graves of the two Irish Princes. As he is resting there, the poet sees a vision of a maiden coming over the hill, who breaks into a passionate lament for the unhappy condition of Ireland. In the course of the poem, the history of the English monarchs from Henry VIII. to Charles I. and Cromwell, and of the Irish leaders, especially of Owen Roe O'Neill, is recounted, and the chiefs of the old families are called upon to forget their internal dissensions which have helped to bring about the miseries of the country, and to unite for her salvation.

Even more familiar, through Mangan's fine version of it, beginning " O Woman, of the piercing wail," is the lament addressed to Nuala, sister of O'Donnell, who is pictured as weeping alone over her brother's tomb in Rome.   The bard, Owen Roe mac Ward (d. 1609), chief bard of the O'Donnells, tells the solitary mourner that had her brother been laid in a tomb in the North of Ireland, she would have had trains of mourners to share her grief. He bids her remember the deeds of valour achieved by those now dead, and calls on her to reflect that ere long she, too, will follow them.

> " For God's sake, thy weighty sorrow banish away, O daughter of O'Donnell! Short time till thou in self-same guise must tread the way ; the same path's weariness awaits thee. . . . Think on the cross that stands beside thee, and, in lieu of thy vain sorrowing, from off the sepulchre lift up thine arm, and bid thy grief begone."

Nuala was younger daughter of Black Hugh, and married her cousin, Niall Garbh, but her husband having gone over to the English side, she joined her brother in his flight. Her husband was rewarded for his services to the English by being shut up in the Tower of London, where he and his elder son both died in 1626.

The poem begins *A bhean fuair faill air an bfeart*— " O Woman, that hast found the tomb all lonely."

Poems with a similar subject are Flann Magrath's poem upon " Ireland's Shepherdless Condition," a bitter complaint, designed to call forth new leaders, and Andrew mac Marcus' verses, *Anocht as uaigneach Eire*, " To-night is Ireland desolate," in which, the Earls being gone, the bard sees a pall settle down on Ireland ; all gaiety and mirth are at an end ; music is choked, the Irish language chained, and even tales and poems are no longer called for. These are only specimens of a large and interesting group of poems suggested by events of national importance.

Contention of the Bards (*Iomarbhaidh na bhfiledh*), or the "Contention between the North and South" (*Iomarbhaidh leithe Chuinn agus Mogha*). This poetic controversy, which flared up with such energy in the beginning of the seventeenth century, and which engaged the pens of several leading poets of the time, was only the final expression in a contest for precedence that had been carried on for centuries between the North and South of Ireland. According to the ancient traditions, the country had been divided on the arrival of the Gael in Ireland into two parts (poetically styled Leith Cuinn and Leith Mogha), Eber or Heber, the eldest son of Milesius, becoming master of the Southern Provinces, and Eremon or Heremon, the younger, of the Northern half. From age to age the bards of both districts had kept up a dispute (which in later times became purely sentimental), as to which was the leading Province, the Southern poets claiming precedence by right of seniority, and those of the North contending that it was theirs by right of their more brilliant achievements. The controversy was unexpectedly renewed by Tadhg mac Daire mac Brodin, or Brody, familiarly known as Teigue mac Daire. Citing as his text two poems supposed by the bards to be ancient, and ascribed by them to Torna Eigeas, a poet who lived in the early part of the fifth century, Mac Daire sets out to combat their assertions in a long poem of his own. These supposed poems of Torna, who was poet to Niall of the Nine Hostages (sl. 405), state that the Southern Prince of Cashel was obliged to submit to Niall and pay him a heavy tribute, besides offering eight hostages of rank, among them his own son, Cairbre, thus bringing Munster under the súzerainty by an appeal to the annals of their race and their pride in the deeds of their ancestors. The attempt was pathetic, for the time when such appeals could avail had passed away, and the uselessness of the effort to revive a vanished state of things is only too well summed up in an epigram on the " Contention of the Bards " found in an MS. in the British Museum (Eg. 161), " Lugaid O'Clery, Teigue mac Brody and Tórna Eigeas, the excellent ollaves of our land : dogs they are, endowed with much learning, that wrangle over an empty kennel," *i.e.*, as dogs quarrelling when the pups of both are stolen, so the poets wrangled about the claims of the North and South when the cause of either was lost for ever.

Teigue mac Daire mac Brodin.—Teigue mac Daire's efforts were not confined to his contributions to the " Contention of the Bards." He wrote a fine inauguration ode to his patron, Donogh O'Brien, the fourth Earl of Thomond (1580-1624), admonishing him with many wise counsels how a prince should rule his people, and also five quatrains summing up briefly the same maxims, with other verses to members of the houses of Clanricarde and Thomond. Donogh O'Brien had been bred at the Courts of Elizabeth and James I., and he returned to his own country determined to enforce English laws and ideas upon Munster. It is curious, therefore, to find his bard, not only welcoming him with ardour, and admonishing him in the old style, but apparently accepting changes which made a revolution in the whole system of his native province without disapproval. It appears to have been the success of this O'Brien, who was appointed President of Munster in 1605, that inflamed his ardour and led to his poetic effort to reinstate his Southern Province in the position of pre-eminence which he believed it ought to hold. His eulogy on Earl Donogh's death declares in the usual bardic style of panegyric that his loss to Munster is one that cannot be repaired.

The position of the bards was, indeed, a difficult one at this time ; to keep their posts they must produce the usual tribute of laudatory verse, even to a patron whose acts they disapproved, and whose career was spent in breaking down the system of things on the continuance of which their own existence was staked.* Some were bought over, like Angus of the Satires, to abuse their own race ; others were put to the rack, like Cuchonnacht O'Cianain, or Kennan, to extort " voluntary confessions " about their chiefs' plans and actions, and others, like Mac Daire and Tadhg Dall O'Higgin fared no better at the hands of their native lords.   Mac Daire, it would appear, retained the patrimony and castle of his ancestors in the Barony of Ibrican, in the West of Co. Clare, but the Earl's patronage had been more in name than in deed.   A contemporary writer states that he had seen with his own eyes Teigue going about without a car or coach, except when some rustic would give him a lift in his cart. Though he was head of his family, the garment that he wore on making a journey would not be worth ten florins. †

This poet's end was a melancholy one.

* " In 1572, the [then] Earl of Thomond enforced the law against the bards and hanged three distinguished poets, for which abominable and treacherous act the Earl was satirized and denounced." (Ann. : IV. Masters).   A timid bard might be excused for thinking his weapon of satire insufficient protection against the hangman's rope.

† Solisbaci, 1672, pp. 124-5.

When he was an old man his estate was granted to a soldier in the Cromwellian army.   In 1652, when Mac Daire was over eighty years of age, the new owner, coming down to take possession, found him still living in his old home and prepared to dispute his claims. Calling out in Irish, *Abair do rainn anois, fhir bhig,* " Say your rann now, little man," the brutal soldier, an Irishman, alas! flung him over the cliff.   Thus perished the last of the hereditary bards of Thomond.

Collections of Family Poems.—Besides the poems connected with the O'Neills and O'Donnells, there are several other great groups of family poems, most of them produced about this time, and many of them referring to the public events in which the subjects of the verses took part.   In some manuscripts we find these poems belonging to a single house collected together.   Such a family collection is the " Book of the O'Byrnes," which contains over sixty poems in honour of the great Wicklow house of that name, written for the most part by bards attached to the family, the Mac Craiths, O'Coffeys, Mac Keoghs, O'Husseys, and others.   Hardly less valuable is a collection of poems chiefly addressed to the house of the Maguires of Fermanagh, which belongs to the King's Library of Copenhagen.*   Many of them are by Feargal óg mac an Bhaird, or Ward, and Eochaid O'Hosey, or Hussey, two fine poets, many of whose productions are still extant, others by two of the O'Clerys, Irial and John O'Higgin, Conor O'Daly, Maolin O'Cainte, and others.   Most of these poems were written to

* Edited by Dr. Ch. Stern in Zeit. für Celt. Phil. II., pp. 323-372.

Cuchonnacht Maguire, who died in 1589, and to his two sons, Hugh and Cuchonnacht óg Maguire. The latter followed in the train of O'Neill to Italy, and fell ill at Genoa of a fever which also prostrated Tyrone and Tyrconnel, and died there is 1608. His half-brother, Hugh, married a daughter of Hugh O'Neill, and succeeded his father, Cuchonnacht, in the chieftaincy in 1589, in direct opposition to old Irish customs of tanistry, by which a senior kinsman claimed possession. Hugh's connection with the powerful O'Donnells through his mother, Nuala, however, secured his elevation. Let us take as a specimen of the intimate internal knowledge we sometimes get of family history through the poems of the bards, the poems written by Eochaid O'Hosey, or Hussey, on this young Hugh Maguire.

Eochaid O'Hosey, or Hussey.—We have a poem by O'Hussey written on the occasion of Hugh Maguire's inauguration as chief, full of exaltation at his accession, and another, probably written immediately afterwards, on his own elevation to be chief poet or ollave to the new chief.*

Next comes a poem commemorating a winter campaign of the young lord in alliance with Hugh O'Neill in Munster in 1599-1600, undertaken by O'Neill for the purpose, as Fynes Moryson tells us, of setting " as great a combustion as he could " in that Province.† The poet, sitting at home in Fermanagh, bewails the intense cold and the great hardships that he feels sure are being

---

* For quotations from this poem see p. 156, *supra*.

† Moryson says that O'Neill entered Munster with 2,500 foot and 200 horse under the religious pretence of visiting the sacred relic at Holy Cross in Co. Tipperary.—Bk. II.

endured by the chief and his followers in the open camps during the winter season.

> Too cold for Hugh I deem this night, the drops so heavily downpouring are a cause for sadness ; biting is this night's cold—woe is me that such is our companion's lot.
>
> In the cloud's bosoms the water-gates of heaven are flung open ; small pools are turned by it to seas ; all its destructiveness hath the firmament spewed out.

> A pain to me that Hugh Maguire, to-night, lies in a stranger's land,
> 'Neath lurid glow of lightning-bolts, and angry armed clouds' clamour ;
> A woe to us that in the Province of Clann Daire,* our well-beloved is couched
> Betwixt a coarse cold-wet and grass-clad ditch and the impetuous fury of the heavens.

The poet comforts himself with the assurance that (and this not for the first time †) Maguire will warm himself and his followers by setting the whole country in a blaze, and that the burning cinders made by the conflagration of the mansions and courts of Munster will thaw the pellets of the frost and warm the manacles of ice that bind the taper fingers of their hands.

This poem is well-known in Mangan's free version of it :

"Where is my chief, my master, this black night ? movrone."

* *i.e.,* the District of Curoi mac Daire, who, according to the legends, was a king of S.W. Munster in the time of Cuchulain.

† "The mischief is not new," says the poet.   Perhaps he was thinking of the act of Maguire two years before (1597), on which occasion he went to punish the town of Mullingar, when "they left not any property of gold, silver, copper, of iron armour or of over-sea wares, or any other thing that could be carried or driven from the town, but they took away with them ; when they came back they set the town in a crimsoned blaze and conflagration, and so returned safely to their homes." (IV. Masters.)

But the original is in strict Deibhide metre, the most difficult and scientific of all the Classical forms of verse.

It would seem to have been during this descent into Munster, or one not much later, that Hugh was slain in a sudden and unexpected attack made by him near the town of Cork on Sir Warham St. Leger and his party. Sir Warham discharged his pistol at Maguire's head at the same moment as the latter struck at St. Leger with his horseman's staff, both of them dying the same night of their wounds.* O'Hosey wrote a lament on his death, but he omits all mention of the circumstances. He likens Maguire's career and end in an elaborate allegory to that of the pelican, who gives her heart's blood to feed her young and endeavours to protect them from venomous serpents which hang about the nest, seeking to harm the fledglings. The snakes represent the English, who are on the watch to destroy the " race of Conn," or the tribes of the North. His two other poems to the same patron are a lament on hearing that he has had his hand wounded in some fray at an earlier stage in his career, and a humorously-worded appeal to Hugh that in dispensing his favours to other bards he will not overlook his own chief poet, O'Hosey himself.

Angus of the Satires.—Two other poets of note in this period claim a separate notice. Angus the Red O'Daly, called Angus *na naor* " of the Satires," or Bard Ruadh, the " Red Bard " (d. 1617). Of all the literary class in Ireland, he it was who most shamefully sold his art and his position to revile his country for the benefit of his country's foes. He was employed

* Pac. Hib. Bk. I., Ch. 2 ; IV. Masters, at 1600 A.D.

by Sir George Carew and Lord Mountjoy to use his dreaded weapon of bardic satire against the native Gaelic families in the kingdom, as well as the " old English " or Anglo-Normans who held to their side. For this purpose he travelled up and down the country, staying at the various houses of the gentry, whose generosity he rewarded by holding them and their hospitalities up to ridicule in a lengthy satire of the most abusive and scurrilous type. The only families that escaped his pen were the Mac Canns of the Upper Bann, because he could find no evil to say of them, and the O'Donnells of Donegal, here called Clann Dalaigh, or Daly, from the name óf an ancestor, because, as he openly says, he is afraid of their vengeance. " If I lampoon the Clann Daly, the [whole remainder] of old Adam's race were no protection to me ; if the Clann Daly protect me, I may lampoon the [whole remainder] of Adam's race." Vengeance did overtake the satirist, however, though not from the hands of the O'Donnells. Angus appeared one day at a banquet at Ikerrin in Co. Tipperary, at the table of the O'Meaghers, on the poverty of whose mansion he had made some scurrilous remark. During the banquet, and at the command of his host, a servant stabbed him to the heart. Before he died he gave vent to one more of his punning quatrains, retracting all he had formerly said :

> Every false judgment ever I made
> On the good men (nobles) of Munster, I make good ;
> The meagre youth of grey Meagher has made
> As good a false judgment now upon me." *

> * ᵹᴀċ ᴀ⠀ ċuᵹᴀ⠀ ᴠ'ᴀ⠀n�⠀⠀ᴇᴀċᴀ⠀ᴃ ⠀⠀ᴀ⠀
> ᴀ⠀ ⠀ᴀ⠀ċ⠀ᴃ ᴍu⠀ᴀn, ⠀ᴀ⠀ċ⠀⠀ ⠀ᴀᴠ;
> ᴅo ⠀uᵹ óᵹᴀnᴀċ ⠀ᴇᴀcᴀ⠀ ⠀ᴇ⠀ċ, ⠀om,
> ᴀn o⠀⠀eᴀᴠ ⠀'ᴀ⠀nᴃ⠀eᴀċᴀ⠀ᴃ o⠀m !

There seems no doubt that the object which Angus' employers had in mind was to stir up angry passions among the native gentlemen, of which they might reap the advantage. The encouragement given to the native cause by the odes of the bards was always a source of annoyance to the English leaders, and we find even so good an Irishman as Florence MacCarthy (elected MacCarthy More by Hugh O'Neill) advising the English Government, while he was himself confined in the Tower, to bribe the bards to bring over the Irish gentry to the English interest. He wrote this advice in 1602, and it may have been in consequence of it that the services of Angus were retained. How much heart the Red Bard had in his disgraceful task we cannot tell, but the fact that he was cited before the Lord President and Council in this very year, 1602, for making offers to Owen O'Sullivan on behalf of the " rebels," to persuade him to combine with them, seems to show that he endeavoured to serve both parties at once. He received from both his just reward. (Pac. Hib. iii., ch. 3).

Angus O'Daly lived at Ballyorrone on the S.W. of Co. Cork. When a large part of Cork was made over to Sir George Carew he was permitted to remain on condition of becoming a " rimer and chronicler " to Carew and his successors. He appears to have been ready to obey their commands.

Teigue Dall O'Higgin.—The poet who occupies the most conspicuous place in the literary history of this epoch is Teigue O'Higgin, whose blindness gained him the sobriquet of Dall " the blind." He belonged to Co. Sligo, and his poems are addressed to the neighbouring lords, such as the Maguires, O'Neills, O'Conor-

Sligos, and O'Rourkes. Teigue Dall rises far above his contemporaries in the clearness and brilliancy of the pictures which his poems convey of the actual social conditions in which he finds himself, as well as in the directness and easy flow of the language in which these pictures are conveyed to the reader. Almost alone among the poets of his day, he eschews generalities and gives us a sharp and detailed impression of the scenes which called forth his verse. We seem to be actually present at the banquet in Mac Sweeney's house ; we hear about us all the bustle of the courtyard of Cúchonnacht Oge Maguire, crowded as it is with fighting men, artificers and poets, with baying dogs returning from the chase, and wounded sufferers being tended by the leech, while on the lake a fine flotilla rides at anchor ; we feel keenly interested in the result of his stirring appeals to Maguire or O'Rourke. That he himself was held in esteem in his lifetime is shown by the gifts presented to him by poets holding positions as honourable as his own, the bards of O'Neill, Mac William of Clanricarde, and Mac William-Burke, as well as by the cordiality extended to him at all times by Cathal O'Conor-Sligo, who, as he says in one of his poems, ever shared with him his innermost councils, and secured for him both respect and due rewards from those neighbouring chiefs to whom he had offered poems. Teigue, however, seems at one time to have fallen into disgrace with Cathal's brother, Donall, on account of a poem addressed to him, and for a year or more he was a wanderer in the country, afraid to show his face at home ; finally, he appealed to Donall's wife to intercede for him, and comically bids her to mope before her husband and to refuse him any assistance

O

Teigue does not often fall into the exaggerations common to most of the contemporary poetry, but a notable exception is his address to Turlough Luineach O'Neill (a prince to whom a multitude of poems are extant)* in which he and his fellow chiefs are said to be " not men at all but Angels in human body," with other equally preposterous comparisons.

Teigue is fond of introducing into his poems illustrations taken from fables or legends ; these often occupy a great portion of the poem and it is not always easy to see how the moral fits in with the main subject ; he seldom condescends to satire, and is on the whole serious and dignified in style. He lost his life in a melancholy way. Six men of the O'Haras passing one day by his house, and driven by hunger, entered and ate up all they could find to lay hands on. Stung by anger, Teigue on this occasion poured out his feelings in a stinging satire, accusing them of being a lot of ragged, lazy loons and no gentlemen, which they so resented that they returned, murdered his wife and child, cut out his tongue, and so ill-used him that he died shortly afterwards. The actual date is uncertain, but his murderers were attainted of his murder in June, 1617, and their lands were forfeited to the king. He thus describes the O'Haras, feigning to have mistaken them for a troop of kerne or common foot soldiers, an insult not to be forgiven by members of an old Irish family.

" The first man that we saw and the best-harnessed of the kerne was a young fellow whom for his whole get up a groat

* He succeeded Shane O'Neill, to whom as representative of the senior line he was bitterly opposed. He died in 1595. He was a prominent figure in the Ireland of his day.

CHAPTER XV.

The Jacobite Poets.

A remarkable outburst of poetry greeted the close of the seventeenth and the opening of the eighteenth centuries. At this epoch modern Irish poetry may be said to have begun. Unlike the older bardic poetry, it sprang not from a professional class but from the people themselves; it was democratic alike in origin and in tone. The bards who produced it were men of the people, and they reflected in their songs, as the aristocratic poets had never been able to do, the dreams, the hopes and the sufferings of the class to which they belonged. Their very method of expression changed; and instead of the strict syllabic forms of the classical school of poets, we have simple lyric songs in a great variety of metres. Poetry had left the courts of chieftains and the schools of the bards; it sprang at last spontaneously from the cottages of the poor. It is, when at its best, warm with a tenderness and pathos, or strong with a passion of revolt that the bards in happier times rarely felt, or that the means at their disposal seldom permitted them to express.

The new poetry is partly social, made up of love songs, drinking songs, religious verse, and verse on personal topics; and partly political, voicing the feeling of the country for the house of Stuart.

It sprang out of the changed conditions in Ireland in the period which gave it birth, and to understand it, it is necessary briefly to summarise the political events which brought about the state of things which we find reflected in the poetry.

At the close of Elizabeth's reign Munster lay waste, stricken with the plague and famine consequent on the devastations which followed the suppression of the rebellions of Desmond and Tyrone. It seemed natural that the hopes of the Irish should concentrate themselves upon the accession of the first of the Stuarts to the throne of England. James I. was son of Mary Queen of Scots, and he had been educated as a Catholic ; when he ascended the throne it was believed that the Catholic churches and schools would be re-opened, and that liberty of worship and equal rights would be restored all over the country. But James pursued in his Plantation of Ulster the same policy as Mary had carried out in Leix and Offally, and Elizabeth in Munster ; and so far was he from framing means of relief for the Catholics that he revived and enforced with fresh energy the Acts of Uniformity and Supremacy, which had fallen very much into disuse towards the close of Elizabeth's reign. Priests were banned, churches closed, and schools and colleges suppressed even more rigorously than before.

Trinity College, Dublin, which had been founded in 1591, was strongly Protestant and Puritan, and it was largely in order to counteract its influence that many of the Catholic colleges and schools had been recently resuscitated by the energy of the Jesuits, and were in a flourishing condition at the beginning of James' reign. But this was not to last, In Galway, a public school kept by Alexander Lynch, probably the father of John Lynch, the learned author of " Cambrensis Eversus," which attracted pupils from all parts of Ireland, was

ordered to be closed after the visitation of 1615.   At
Waterford, whose schools were said to be " more like
universities than schools," the educational establishments,
though they lingered on in an unobtrusive fashion till
1632, lost their most celebrated scholars and teachers
about the same time. A great exodus of learned men went
out from Ireland to adorn positions in foreign universities.
The Irish Minorite Convent at Louvain was founded
in 1616, and the Irish College of St. Isidore's at Rome
by Rev. Luke Wadding in 1618.   These, in addition
to the already existing Irish Colleges in Spain, received
and benefited by the exclusion of the Catholic scholars
from their native country.   Among those who went
abroad were the Jesuit, Stephen White, who became
Professor of Scholastic Theology at Ingoldstadt and
Rector of Cassel College, and Rev. Luke Wadding, who
went from Waterford to Louvain and thence to Rome
to found the Irish College of St. Isidore's. At Louvain
we find Rev. John Colgan, who was carrying on his great
collection of the lives of the Irish Saints under the
general direction of Rev. Hugh Ward of Donegal,
Guardian of the Convent at Louvain, and who was
assisted in his work by the researches of the Irishmen,
Stephen White and Patrick Fleming abroad, and by
Michael O'Clery, Br. Brendan O'Connor and others in
Ireland.   The interest awakened at this juncture in
the history and antiquities of the mother country was
quite unprecedented, and was shared alike by Catholics
and Protestants.   Archbishop Ussher brought the
prodigious resources of his learning to bear upon the
ecclesiastical traditions of Ireland, and Sir James Ware,
Lynch, O'Flaherty and Mac Firbis in various ways
illustrated its secular history ; while at the very same

period the O'Clerys and their companions were compiling in Donegal the native records and Annals. As a result of a similarity of tastes, a kindly personal feeling seems to have existed between these men which, in their private relations, transcended the bitterness of party strife or of religious differences. A correspondence was kept up between them and they mutually furnished each other with materials for their respective labours.

The stern rule of Strafford was followed by the Rebellion of 1641, and from 1649-1652 Cromwell's army swept over the country. In the confiscations and sale of lands that followed most of the remaining gentry of both Anglo-Irish and old native race were dispossessed and their lands given instead of pay to Cromwellian soldiers, or sold wholesale to "adventurers," who frequently purchased in London properties which they had never seen, and upon which the old owners were still living. Many of these owners were reduced to becoming tenants upon their own lands under the heel of the new possessors, while in some districts, especially in the wilder parts of Kerry, the younger men, instead of sinking into small farmers, or vacating the district in which they had lived, formed themselves into armed bands of marauders who took shelter in the mountain fastnesses and swooped down upon the "new English," as they were called, who had settled upon their lands. These men were known in the records of their day as "Tories" and "Rapparees." They became a terror to the neighbourhoods in which they congregated, especially in Kerry, where the stronghold of the O'Donoghues of the Glen became the headquarters of a strong party known as the "Rapps of Glenflesk."

The country was swarming with spies and adventurers in search for lands, and with outlaws driven from their possessions. To the majority of the Catholic population every avenue of respectability and every post of trust in the State, the army, the law or any learned profession whatever was closed, and the life and liberty of every Catholic proprietor or peasant was at the mercy of any ill-disposed or designing neighbour. It would be impossible to over-rate the miseries, anxieties and degradation caused by the condition of the country and destined to be aggravated to intensity by the Penal legislation.

James II., whose accession to the throne in 1685 had once more raised the hopes of the depressed people, had fled before the Battle of the Boyne (1690) was well over, and secured the safety of his own person in France, leaving his troops under Colonel Talbot, whom he had created Earl of Tyrconnell, and Sarsfield, to struggle against hopeless odds. The terrible defeat of Aughrim in 1691, and the fall of Limerick which followed, compelled Sarsfield to surrender. Twenty thousand of his soldiers, the best blood of the nation, followed him to France. Their departure, which was the symbol of the extinction of all national hopes, is known to posterity as the "Flight of the Wild Geese." Green, the historian, who is never inclined to favour the Irish cause, says at this point, "When the wild cry of the women who stood watching their departure was hushed, a silence as of death settled down upon Ireland. For a hundred years the country remained at peace, but it was the peace of despair. The most terrible legal tyranny under which a nation has ever groaned avenged the rising under Tyrconnell."

It was out of this silence of despair that the democratic poetry of the eighteenth century arose, and it cannot be understood without recalling the circumstances which gave it birth.   Unlike the poetry of the bards, it was not produced to order ; it was the spontaneous expression of the people's hopes and griefs.   Its note is gloomy, often despairing ; it is at times satirical, fierce and vindictive ; it is limited in the range of its ideas, full of repetitions and often careless in style, yet, with all its faults, it cannot be read unmoved.

Centre in Munster.—The centre of this new out-burst of song was in Munster ; poets of Clare, Kerry, Cork and Waterford chiefly contributed to it.   No doubt this prominence of Munster is largely due to the fact that the language lingered for a longer time over large portions of the Southern Province than elsewhere. Not only was poetry freely produced and fostered there, but it was handed down to later times in numberless hand-written collections of verse usually copied and possessed by village schoolmasters, and it was cherished and preserved in the memories of the Irish-speaking peasants, to whom even at the present day many of the songs of Tadhg Gaedhealach O'Sullivan and other bards are familiar.   Owing to this preservation of the language, the loss of manuscripts has not been so great in the South as in other parts of Ireland.   Though much poetry was produced in Leinster and Ulster and Connacht, less of it survives to the present day ; it is no longer possible to recover, as it is from Munster, the larger portion of the output of whole groups of verse-writers.

Change of Style.—Simultaneously with the out-

burst of democratic song, there came into existence
a completely new method of versification, which helped
to free the poetry from the close restraints under which
the older bards had worked, and made it a more flexible
and simple instrument of expression for an unlearned
class of writers.   With the closing of the schools of
the bards and the extinction of the system of things
under which the bards had flourished, the opportunity
for the study of the old classic metres passed away.
The poets of Munster in the eighteenth century underwent no such strict discipline in the acquirement of
their art as was given in the old bardic schools.   Most
of them were schoolmasters themselves, or they pursued
the profession of teaching in the intervals of irregular
work of other kinds, harvesting, potato digging, or
peddling from village to village.   But the hedge-schools
in which they taught were very different from the
old-established schools of the ollaves or from the later
founded colleges which gave such a fine classical
education that the gentlemen in Ireland in the sixteenth
and early seventeenth century could use Latin freely
in conversation and writing, and, as a rule, did use it
in their communications with those Englishmen who
did not understand the native tongue.   It was no longer
possible to obtain this broad education in Ireland, and
only the few had the means to seek it abroad in foreign
universities.   Hence, though one or two of the later
poets, like Seaghan Claragh mac Donnell and the wild
Donagh Roe mac Conmara, were educated men, both
having been designated for the priesthood in early
life, the larger number were obliged to pick up their
learning as best they might and to pass it on in rustic
cottage schools gathered hurriedly together in the

standing of their craft.   Many of the poems of the
seventeenth century bards voice this distaste and
contempt for verse produced in an irregular way and
in unauthorized metres.   It is evident from them that
poems in non-classical metres were composed even as
far back as about the beginning of the seventeenth
century.   A poem we have already quoted speaks of
the composition of " vulgar doggrels," which were
considered good enough to replace the " well-turned
poem, perfected in sound and science," if merely " the
lines should be of even length," and the sounds " soft,"
however poor and obscure the total effect.*   The author
seems here to point to the use of free metres and to the
employment of vowel-rhyme which was distinctive of
them.   Andrew Mac Curtin, again, a century later,
between 1718-1743, complains to James mac Donnell,
of Kilkee, that he has to fit himself for an evil fashion
never practised in Erin before, " and to frame a left-
handed awkward ditty of a thing " (i.e., a poem of the
new school), because the gentlemen of the country will
give more for it than for a well-made lay or poem.
More respect, he says, is accorded to a dry half-educated
boor, " who has no clear view of either alliteration or
poetry," than to the highly trained bard or man of
song.   He himself is now thought a fool if he composes
a lay in good taste, but he is not of this opinion, and he
protests that he will still continue to write after the
strict manner of his craft.†

It has been supposed that Ireland owed this revolution

* p. 160, from MS. Egerton III., cf. O'Grady's Cat. of MS.
in the British Museum, p. 393.
† cf. Brian O'Looney's " Collection of Poems written by Clare
bards," Dub., 1863.

in style to Scotland, where, as early as the close of the sixteenth century, poems by an old nurse * of the family of Mac Leod had been composed in a variety of free vowel metres. There is no doubt that the connection between Ireland and Scotland during the Jacobite period was of the closest possible kind, and that any literary change that affected the one country affected the other. They knew each other's poems, and sometimes closely imitated them. Yet it seems unnecessary to seek anywhere out of Ireland the source of the new movement. Varied metres, not included among the classical forms of the bardic system, had been in use in Ireland from the earliest times. We find songs interspersed in the old romances, such as the Táin bó Cuailnge, the Sick-bed of Cuchulain, the Death of the Sons of Usnach, that, careful as is their structure, remain independent of the fixed models. And we may imagine that although the special training in the schools of the bards rigidly preserved the authorized metric among the professional class, there must always have been singers among the uneducated peasants who produced and sang ballads and lyrics expressive of simple personal feeling in some free native form of verse. Naturally these rustic lays, so despised by the regular literary men, were not copied by them into their books and were therefore not preserved. It is quite possible that many of the exquisite folk songs of Ireland stretch further back into the past than their existing modern form would lead us to suppose.

The changes in the new poetry consisted (1) in the use of vowel-rhyme instead of consonantal rhyme, and

---

* She was Mary, d. of Alaster Rua mac Leod, born in the Island of Harris in 1569. Nine poems are ascribed to her.

(2) in the use of accent and stress instead of a certain number of syllables in each line. The new writers, in fact, broke utterly with the past and flung themselves at once into a modern and perfectly free style of verse, varied according to the requirements of the subject. The painful measuring of syllable by syllable, the involved system of alliteration, the difficult internal rhymes, the weighing of consonant against consonant, all that complex and laborious framework which it cost the aspirant so many years to acquire, and the proficient such terrible compression of thought to execute, was laid aside, and a perfectly free and flexible system took its place.   The greatest gain was undoubtedly the introduction of vowel-rhyme, for the Irish language is peculiarly rich in its vowel-sounds, and for the first time the full harmonious tones of the mother-tongue were brought into play.   The richness and profuseness of the language became, indeed, a snare to many of the Munster bards ; they revel in mere sound, and sacrifice to it both sense and dignity.   Poets like Owen Roe O'Sullivan are in constant danger of degrading their art from its natural and just use as a vehicle of expression for thought or feeling into mere sound-painting ; they attempt to produce music by words, regardless of the poverty of thought which this luxuriance of colour often only half conceals. Their unbridled use of alliteration became a jest among themselves, a mere feat of mental dexterity, entire poems or pages being formed of lists of alliterative adjectives strung together without care or reason. Nowhere does the copiousness of Munster Irish come out as it does in these poems of the eighteenth century, lists of adjectives which have in Irish some slight shade of difference of meaning having in English

perhaps only a single equivalent word. The fulness of the two languages lies in different directions ; in matters of description, in which the English method of expression is usually terse and simple, the Irish is profuse, and at its worst verbose. The richness of language in some of these Munster poems is extraordinary ; nothing like it is to be found in either earlier Irish or in Scottish poetry.

Poets of the Stuart Cause.—Both in Scotland and in Ireland the misfortunes of the Stuarts awoke a passion of sympathy which voiced itself in a remarkable outburst of lyric poetry. In Scotland the cause of the Jacobites was a national one, belonging to the heart and traditions of the people ; the Stuarts were their own princes, their own kith and kin, and all the strong clan attachment, strengthened by the pathos of misfortune, went into their feeling for the family. The note of the Scottish Jacobite lyrics is therefore the note of personal affection, especially in those addressed to Prince Charlie, whose romantic adventures called out the devoted and chivalrous warmth of the whole nation. He threw himself on their hospitality, and they rewarded him with a love like that of a mother for her son, as well as that of a clan for its tribal chief.

In Ireland the personal tie was wanting. Prince Charlie never set foot in Ireland ; and there was little of the excitement and energy of active events to arouse enthusiasm. The Stuart tradition there was not a happy one. In every way the hopes of their adherents was betrayed. Yet the loyalty to the house of Stuart survived all shocks. To them the people looked as their deliverers, the inaugurators of a happier age wherein Ireland should once more take her place

fair women, where they are not pure love songs, take
in Ireland a stereotyped form known as the *aisling*
or Vision.   *Aislingi* are as old as Irish poetry itself,
but in this period, instead of signifying in a general way
any imaginative subject called up before the mind of
the writer, these reveries became the standard poetic
framework within which the muse of the Munster
bards might expand into patriotic praise of their native
land and into hopes of a speedy deliverance from every
oppression through the coming of the Stuarts.   The
vision of a beautiful woman appears to the poet when,
either on his bed or beside some purling brook,
he falls asleep.   The charms of this lady are described
at great length, the beauty of her hair, in particular,
which is curled and twisted and plaited and waved
and branched and ringletted in a variety of ways for
which the English tongue can find no equivalents,
being dwelt upon with much prolixity of language.
She is, in a general way, a symbolical figure of Erin,
but in particular she is one of the local shee or fairy
princesses of Munster, generally Cliodna, the Tuatha
de Danann princess who died at Glandore Harbour
in Kerry, and who gave her name to Cliodna's Wave,
which wailed whenever a national calamity was immi-
nent ; or Aoibhill (Evall) the banshee of the Dalcassian
race, whose dwelling was at Craiglea, near Killaloe.

The poet, entranced at the vision, plies her with
questions, calling up the whole of his classical and
antiquarian resources in order to find out who she is.
Is she Emer, wife of Cuchulain, or Deirdre, wife of the
son of Usnach ; or is she Venus or Juno ? or Helen of
Troy or Isis ?   At the torrent of inquiries with which
she is assailed, the maiden usually takes flight ; but

the poet following her through the fairy haunts of Erin, she is finally re-discovered, and she then reveals herself as Ireland bereaved or unwedded, waiting for the return of her spouse.   Though in the hands of the later poets this convention is apt to become mechanical, some of the finest lyrics of the period are founded upon the theme.   There is something truly pathetic in the innumerable versions in which the changes are rung upon this well-worn and hopeless note.   Some of the noblest of Egan O'Rahilly's poems are *aislingi ;* such are his delicious *Gile na Gile*, " Whiteness of Whiteness," which is unsurpassed for subtlety of rhythm and mournful melody of sound ; or the grave and long-lined *Mac an Ceannuighe*, " The Merchant's Son," *i.e.*, the Old Pretender, a poem burdened with sorrow.   Profound affliction and deep pathos are felt through every line.

Before dealing with the three poets who best represent the Jacobite poetry of Ireland, it will be necessary to allude to one of the writers who immediately preceded them, and whose verse deals also largely with political themes.

David O'Bruadair, who was born in Limerick or Cork and began to write before the year 1650, stands midway between the old school of bards and the new school of Munster poets who were beginning to vary the old classic forms of verse by experiments in accented metres. He composed with vigour and facility in both kinds of verse.   He tells us that though he " had English," he was " seldom able to fetter his tongue to the point of speaking it," and one of his stanzas ridicules those who tried to converse in what he calls " the conceited and mouth-parching English."   A Jacobite by sympathy, he lived in the time of Sarsfield, and witnessed the stirring events that preceded and followed the surrender of Limerick in 1691. What gives his poems an unusual interest is that the larger number refer to the political and historic affairs which he saw with his own eyes. His admiration for Sarsfield was unbounded, and it is expressed in a poem written to him as Earl of Lucan in 1690, when he had routed the English at Ballineety, Co. Limerick, and burst the great cannon that they were bringing from Dublin to besiege Limerick with. It begins : " O King of the Round World, Who madest it and all things that on it created are, Redeem Ireland out of this war's extremity and knit her kindreds in love together."

He says that though he had never thought again " to yelp in jingling stanzas at any warrior's heels, yet for love of the bright deeds of him that remedies some part of their neglect he will proclaim aloud the lustre of Sarsfield's renown." One of his best-known poems is his spirited " Advice addressed to a trooper who was that day (October 13th, 1686), joining the army," to serve under Tyrconnel, a piece intended for the whole Irish army as well as for the particular soldier, one James Aherne, to whom it was sent. This, like several of O'Bruadair's political pieces, contains on the margin quaint explanations of the obscure allusions in the piece, the explanations being often hardly less obscure than the lines themselves. We find the same marginal notes in a curious piece supporting Sarsfield's party and bewailing the miseries of the common people and the cabals of the leaders during and after the siege of Limerick. It is called " Ireland's Hurly-burly " (*Longar Langar Eirenn*), and shows, according to the heading,

" how in this year, 1691, her own children's sins had turned Ireland topsy-turvy ; ' a kingdom divided against itself is brought to desolation.' "   The obscurities of his allusions, which made these marginal notes necessary even in his own time, the difficulties of his verse, and his frequent use of antiquated words and inflections have rendered his work almost unknown in our own day. Yet he is a vigorous, reflective and often humorous writer, with a great command of language both ancient and modern, and his poems have, as Mr. S. H. O'Grady remarks, " a lilt and swing that convey the idea of rapid extempore utterances." *   He has seemingly unlimited resources of versification and he so rarely repeats his images that he is always fresh.

Little is known of the poet's career, but a *ceangal* or binding stanza to " Ireland's Hurly-Burly " tells us that he had hoped in his old age to have found a comfortable post as steward to some gentleman remaining in the old country, but " since the end of it all is that I am come down to a pair of old brogues, here's an end to my scribbling about the men of Ireland."   He appears to have lived six or seven years after this date (1691), which would place his death somewhere about 1697-8.

Three Representative Jacobite Poets.—Three noteworthy poets represent on different sides what is best in Irish Jacobite poetry.   These are Egan O'Rahilly, John Clarach Mac Donnell and Owen Roe O'Sullivan. Though not very widely separated as to date, they witnessed successive stages of the fortunes of the House

* Cat. of MSS. in the British Museum, p. 577, *n*. 2.   Nineteen of his pieces are preserved in two MSS. in the Brit. Museum. Add. 29, 614, and Egerton, 154.

of Stuart. O'Rahilly was writing in the period of the Battle of the Boyne and the Fall of Limerick ; he knew of the flight of James II., and he heard the rumours of his proposed descent upon the west coast in 1708 ; but he was dead before the Young Pretender came into prominence. Owen Roe wrote when the Stuart cause was hopelessly lost ; the landing of Charles Edward in Scotland in 1745, and the final defeat at Culloden a year later must have been, if he remembered them at all, but vague traditions of his childhood. But John Claragh, who was born in the year of the Capitulation of Limerick (1691), and died in 1754, lived through the whole of the exciting time that preceded the arrival of the Young Pretender, he witnessed the eagerness of his adherents, and he sympathized with his hopes, his fears and his perils. To this difference of outlook we may partly ascribe the contrast in the tone of the poems of these three men. O'Rahilly's massive and splendid lamentations are a fit dirge for the sorrows of his native land. He writes with something of the tremendous solemnity of the Hebrew prophets of the exile, and his poem beginning " Woeful and bitter to me are the wounds of the land of Fodla (*i.e.*, Ireland) " seem to echo the spirit of the writer of the Book of Lamentations : " How doth the city sit solitary that was full of people."

In all his work there is a mournfulness, a brooding intensity, a vigour and simplicity of expression that place it far above that of any of his fellows in distinction and in a sense of grave reality. He writes elegies, lyrics and satires, tender and full of pathos when he speaks of friends, fierce and cruel when he lashes the vices and crimes of those who " in an hour of national crisis endeavoured to purchase a vulgar upstart nobility at the cost of honour and virtue."* He is happy only in recalling the opulence and the wide hospitalities of the old gentry, who were being dispossessed by newcomers hostile to the old inhabitants and to the ancient ways.

The date of Egan O'Rahilly's birth is unknown, but he probably composed his elegy on Diarmuid O'Leary of Killeen, one of his finest pieces, in 1696, and he was in the full tide of his powers at the close of the seventeenth century. He lived most of his life in the neighbourhood of Killarney, first at Stagmount, ten miles east of the town, and later, at Duinneacha, near the great cascade under the Tomies Mountain, the roaring of which in its impetuous descent he celebrates in a poem written on the night of his arrival. From these places he wandered about among the houses of the gentry, to several of whom he wrote poems or laments. He was deeply stirred by the attempts to displace the old landowners in favour of interested and selfish adventurers, and his sympathies were especially aroused in behalf of the family of Nicholas Brown, the Second Viscount Kenmare, who had been attainted for participation in the Jacobite war and whose estates it was sought to transfer into other hands. To the members of this family several of O'Rahilly's poems are addressed. His wedding-song on the marriage of Valentine, son and heir to Lord Kenmare, in 1720, voices the public joy at the reinstatement of their family fortunes.

O'Rahilly lived and died in great poverty. Though he was a man of some learning and evidently of force

* See Fr. Dinneen's Introduction to his Poems, Irish Texts Society, Vol. III., p. xxxvii.

and elevation of mind, he delighted to wander about the country, feigning himself to be a simpleton. A poetical letter, written on his death-bed, shows that he was reduced at the end of his life to the direst misery and want.

The structure of O'Rahilly's verse differs entirely from that of the older clan-poetry. He is master of a grave and composed rhythm, and some part of the serious effect he produces is due to his lengthened line and the extraordinary regularity of the rise and fall of the stressed vowel-sounds. He seldom used rhyme, and though this at first brings a sense of loss to the ear accustomed to English verse, the wonderful management of his vowel-sounds more than compensates for its lack ; it makes terminal rhyme sound cheap and thin. The Irish method of verse structure has, in O'Rahilly's hands, something of the effect of stately movement and freedom from restraint which is gained in English by the use of blank verse. Though O'Rahilly does not possess the variety of metres of some of his contemporaries, no Irish modern poet approaches him in majesty and impressiveness. His satires, whether personal or political, are generally fierce and often coarse and cruel.

John (Seaghan) Claragh Mac Donnell (1691-1754)

approaches in his verse more nearly to the Scottish type of Jacobite poetry than any of his fellows. His familiarity with the Northern songs is proved by his happy rendering into Irish Gaelic of " My Laddie can fight and my Laddie can sing," in which the Irish and Anglo-Scottish verses alternate. Other songs, evidently formed on the Scottish model, are the charming

"Seal do bíoṙ im ṁaiġdin ṙéiṁ," and the equally delightful " bím-ṙe buan aṙ buaidiṙc ġac ló," with its response, sometimes attributed to O'Tuomy, " A ṗioġán uaṙal ṙuaiṙc, 'ṙ a ṙcóiṙ."* The former song is written to the air " An Cnócá bán," known in Scotland as the " White Cockade," a familiar air in Munster in the eighteenth century or earlier. The White Cockade was originally a white favour worn by girls at weddings, and there are old songs celebrating it as such ; but in Jacobite times both the air and the symbol adopted a political significance and became Jacobite tokens.

Seaghan Claragh was a native of Charleville, Co. Cork. He was born in 1691, about the time that O'Rahilly began to write, and he died in 1754, twenty or more years later than O'Rahilly, and thirty years before Owen Roe. He was the undisputed head and chief of Munster poetry in his day, and he presided at the provincial poetic contests which were organised with a certain solemnity and which kept up and fed the poetic ardour of the local bards. In the days of Mac Donnell and his friend and successor, O'Tuomy, these annual contests became celebrated. Aspirants for admission to the bardic assemblies had to give proof of their ability by furnishing extempore poems. The members were given notice of the gatherings by ‧ " Warrants," half-serious and half-humorous, as were the meetings themselves. Many of these " Warrants " still exist. Poems produced were criticised and long discussions were carried on in verse ; but probably the chief object of the Assemblies was to form a centre

* The " ceangal " or final " binding " stanza is in any case O'Tuomy's.

of social and convivial intercourse heightened by a professional literary purpose. Mac Donnell was a man of education, for he had been trained for the priesthood, and probably took holy orders. He knew Latin and Greek well and even attempted to translate Homer into Irish verse. He was a good antiquary, and had made a valuable collection of manuscripts and papers with the intention of writing a history of Ireland. His residence abroad may have widened his interests, for he is one of the few poets of the time who seems to have been aware of the events passing outside his immediate neighbourhood. He wrote a fierce poem on Philip of Orleans, Regent of France, during the minority of Louis XV., and one on the European wars of 1740-48. Mac Donnell possessed to the full the Irish power of satire, and on one occasion the exercise of this faculty brought him into serious trouble. About the year 1738, he launched a satire of the most cutting and merciless kind on the death of a landed gentleman of the name of Colonel Dawson, of Atherlow, against whom O'Rahilly also composed a bitter elegy. Dawson probably fully merited the overwhelming denunciation ; nevertheless, it is not astonishing that on account of it, the family of the dead man hunted Mac Donnell out of the place. Mac Donnell seems to have been obliged for a time to take refuge out of the country,* but he returned and kept his position as leader of the bardic assemblies until his death in 1754. He was much respected and beloved by his contemporaries, and a quite unusual number of lays and elegies flowed forth on his death, testifying to the esteem in which he was

* O'Curry says for fourteen years, and he thinks that most of this time was passed in London and in Ireland.

held in his own neighbourhood.   He unfortunately wrote little, but the taste and delicacy of his language, which bears the mark of a refined and cultured mind, makes each of his lyrics a gem in its way, choice and graceful in thought and expression.   The chief blemish in his verse is that he sprinkles his poems with the usual classical allusions which, however it may have been in his case, do not necessitate any more extensive acquaintance with Greek and Latin authors than could be gleaned from any school reading-book.   The sun is always Phœbus, a singer or minstrel always Orpheus, and a fair lady is the spouse of Mars or Jupiter, or she is Venus or Helen of Troy.   Mac Donnell's fame is founded on a mere handful of poems ; either he wrote sparingly, or some of his pieces must have been lost.

Owen Roe O'Sullivan (1748 ? 1784) is a more popular and a more voluminous poet than Seaghan Claragh.   He has none of the self-restraint of his predecessor, but pours forth his verse in a torrent of language the luxuriance of which has probably never been equalled and which frequently degenerates into looseness and vagueness of expression.   He belonged to the same district as the O'Rahillys and the O'Scannells, and was born at Meentogues, seven miles east of Killarney. In his youth, dancing festivities and hurling matches were still kept up in the old style, and the school of Faha, which prepared students for the seminary at Killarney, fostered not only classical and general knowledge but also native song and music.   A friendly rivalry in the composition of poetry sprang up among the representatives of the different bardic families of the neighbourhood, and Owen early showed his dexterity in the management of rhyme as well as the vigour and humour of his mind.   But his restless temperament and the wildness of his character drove him into a wandering life.   He varied his pursuit of the profession of schoolmaster by excursions as a harvest-man and potato-digger, but, in the end, his misconduct obliged him to fly the country.   He enlisted in the British navy and took part in the great sea fight of Rodney against the French in 1782.   But though he was commended by his officers, and offered promotion by Rodney himself, to whom he sent a rude ode in English, complimenting him on his victory, he was eager to get back to Ireland.   Probably he thought to earn his freedom in reward for his panegyric, but as this failed, his captain saying that " they would not part with him for love or money," he drifted into the land forces, from which, by means of scheming, he at last got his discharge.   He returned to Knocknagree Cross, where he opened a school, but soon after, in June, 1784, he died of a wound received in a drunken brawl which arose out of a quarrel with the servants of a Colonel Cronin, of Park, near Killarney, whose master he had lampooned.

Eoghan Ruadh's songs had an immediate and immense popularity.   Throughout Munster he was known as " Owen of the Sweet Mouth " (Eoghan an bhéil bhinn), and from the extraordinary richness of his word-weaving and the melody of his verse, the title is well deserved. His fecundity in metres is remarkable, many of his pieces being fitted to old and well-known airs, to which they were sung by the peasants all over the South of Ireland.   He was emphatically the people's poet, though there is in his verse none of that simplicity of style and

meaning which we usually associate with the songs of
the folk.   But from a literary point of view his very
fecundity is a weakness ; his poetry is over-loaded
with adjectives, which, though they occasionally have
a certain torrential effect when used with a definite
purpose, are, when flung down pell-mell, as Owen Roe
uses them, often a mere trick to cover poverty of thought.
His alliteration, too, a legitimate and beautiful ornament of verse, when used with restraint and good feeling,
degenerates into mere childish rhetoric in many of
his lyrics.   A large number of his compound words
are coined by himself ; and that he delighted in exhi-
bitions of his cleverness in thus stringing together
adjectives beginning with the same consonant may be
judged from examples both in his prose and poetical
pieces.   The very profuseness of his power of expression
and the quickness of his ear for melodious combinations
of sounds tends, from his lack of restraint, to become
degraded into mere word-weaving devoid of meaning
and dignity.   Like most of his contemporaries he wrote
bitter and cruel satires, yet his enthusiasm and
vehemence, his pathos and music, give his poems a
place of importance in the literary output of his day.
His poems, more than those of any of his fellows, show
the wonderful fecundity and richness of the Gaelic
tongue.

CHAPTER XVI.

The Poets of the People.

The group of bards whom we have now to consider recalls us again to those local bardic assemblies which endeavoured in the eighteenth century to keep alive by friendly rivalry the composition of Gaelic poetry and the interest in the Irish tongue and the history and antiquities of the country. On the death of Seaghan Claragh MacDonnell, in 1754, his friend, JOHN O'TUOMY, succeeded him as chief of these assemblies, and became the acknowledged head of Munster poetry during his lifetime.

He was born at Croom in Co. Limerick, in 1706, or a couple of years later, and during his residence there he made the little town, which stands on the eastern bank of the R. Maigue, an intellectual centre for the surrounding district. He kept an inn at Croom during the earlier years of his married life, afterwards moving into Limerick, where he seems to have died in 1775. During O'Donnell's lifetime the bardic assemblies had been usually held half-yearly either at Charleville or Bruree, and in the open air. But under O'Tuomy's presidency they met at his tavern in Croom, a village which earned for itself the title of Croom " an t-súgha-chais " or " the merry," no doubt on account of the gatherings of these witty and pleasant companies of bardic associates. O'Tuomy was himself commonly known as " an ghrinn " or the jovial. A certain mock solemnity was attached to these assemblies, the " Warrants " issued being couched in the terms of English law, and officers called sheriffs being appointed to conduct the proceedings. But though they may have done something to preserve an interest in the composition and recitation of Irish verse, the results attained are not to be taken too seriously. They did not tend to the production of poems of a high level, and the mutual recriminations in verse into which the output of the assemblies often degenerated are unworthy of any sort of immortality.

Many of O'Tuomy's own poems are, however, exceptionally melodious. Such songs as "Ⱥ ċuiṗle nⱥ ḣ-éiꞃe, éiṗiꞃ ꞃuⱥꞃ," or his Aisling "1m ⱥonⱥꞃ ꞃeⱥl ⱥꞃ ṗóⱱⱥiⱱeⱥċṫ" are delightful; but he was, like most of his contemporaries, unequal in his work. He seems to have been a man of some education and respected both for his ability and wit and for the solid qualities of his character. Probably it was owing to his generosity to his fellow-bards that he fell into poverty and was forced for a time to accept a position as steward on the farm of a gentleman residing in Limerick. He seems in any case to have been in straitened circumstances at the time of his removal to that city. He is buried at Croom within sound of the waters of the River Maigue, whose charms are so often celebrated in the poems of this group of writers.

Among the bards who gathered around O'Tuomy the best known is ANDREW M'GRATH, called the "Mangaire Súgach" or Jolly Pedlar, not because he actually followed the trade of peddling, but from his roving and thriftless life.

Though closely associated with O'Tuomy in the bardic assemblies, and often taking advantage of his bounty, he was a man of very different character. Reckless, hot-tempered and dissolute, he was never long able to

keep steady to his profession of schoolmaster, and even
so good a friend as O'Tuomy suffered under the lash
of his caustic wit. The dates of his birth and death
are unknown, but he survived O'Tuomy, on whose
death he, like several other of their companions, wrote
an elegy. He was, however, an old man before O'Tuomy
died, and probably did not long survive him. At one
time, driven to any expedient by want, he thought to
gain employment by a pretended conversion to Protes-
tantism, but he was as little welcome in the Church
to which he offered himself as he had been in his own.
Denounced by his own priest and rejected by the
Protestant rector of Croom, he took advantage of the
occasion to write a humorous poem complaining of
his outcast position. Wild as he was, and rakish in
character as are several of his pieces, M'Grath had a
true gift of song. Several exquisite compositions are
from his hand. Of these one of the most touching is
his " Slán le Máig," bidding farewell to the River
which flowed through his native district, to which
O'Tuomy wrote a reply ; and the hardly less graceful
love song, " Cé faoa mé le haep an traogail."
A vigorous and forcible poem is his political " Duan
na raoirpe " or Song of Freedom, beginning, " 1r
faoa mé i g-cuma gan tnút le téapnam," which seems to
have been composed in the earlier period of the Seven
Years' War (1756-1763), an appeal in favour of the
exiled Stuarts and calling for vengeance on their enemies.
Among his remaining songs are two other Jacobite
poems, satires, drinking songs and amatory pieces.
There are also a number of pieces written in the form
of questions and replies with O'Tuomy. In several
of their songs, these writers adopted the Irish ornament

of binding the stanzas together by making the new verse begin with the same word as that which ended the verse before it.

Among the minor poets who gathered round Mac Donnell and O'Tuomy one of the best was WILLIAM O'HEFFERNAN, called William Dall or "the Blind," a native of Shronehill, Co. Tipperary. He was born sightless, and wandered about the county subsisting on bounty. He often contended in the bardic sessions of the Maigue. His poems are allegorical visions, written with a political and national purpose, elegies and love songs. Several of his lyrics are universal favourites. Such are his "Caitlín ní Uallacáin," his "Uaill-ġuṫ an aoiḃnir," and his charming song, "Bé n-Eiṁnn í." A familiar example of his allegorical poems is "Clioḋna na cappaiġe," sung to the Irish air, "Staca an Mhargaidh" or the "Market Stake."

Tadhg Gaedhealach O'Sullivan, d. 1795 ?—More remarkable than any of these poets is the religious writer whose devotional poems were familiar in every home in Munster so long as the Irish language was the natural vehicle of speech between man and man. They had the unusual good fortune to be printed in Limerick during O'Sullivan's lifetime, and so widely were they used and appreciated that they passed through several editions in the early years of the nineteenth century. Tadhg is believed to have died in 1795, and an edition printed in Cork in 1837 is marked "Eleventh Edition." It was commonly known as "The Pious Miscellany," * and in an edition brought out in 1819

* O'Daly used the Edition printed at Clonmel in 1816 in drawing up his own.

by Patrick Denn an appendix was added containing poems by the editor, also of a simple and devotional cast.

The devotional spirit of the people found expression in the passion of religious sentiment that breathes through O'Sullivan's verses. Father Dinneen says of them: " The poetry of Tadhg Gaedhealach reflects in the clearest manner the aspirations after virtue and holiness so remarkable in the lives of the majority of his contemporaries. . . . He spoke not merely for himself, he was the unconscious mouthpiece of the greater part of the populace. They found in his songs remedies to apply to their spiritual wounds, consolation in their trouble, and peace amid worldly strife. They found what oft they thought, but ne'er so well expressed."

Tadhg was born early in the eighteenth century and most of his life was spent in the neighbourhood of Youghal and Cappoquin, Co. Waterford, or in the east of the same county in the district known as the Powers' Country. He was naturally of a gay disposition, witty, and given to practical jokes, and possibly inclined to dissipation. But a time came when he withdrew from these early distractions and devoted himself to a life of ascetic piety. He abandoned the bardic assemblies and attached himself to a sort of confraternity at Dungarvan, dying at a good age, " worn-out," Fr. Dinneen tells us, " with fasting and penance, and ever-during prayers." His poems were everywhere known in his own country before his death, and their simplicity and fervour appealed powerfully to the hearts of the peasantry. They formed almost the entire printed literature of the Irish-speaking portion of the population of Munster for many years after his decease.

Their subjects are sin and penitence, verses in praise of piety and chastity, and on the terrors of the last day. There are tender hymns and carols to the Blessed Virgin Mary and to the Redeemer.   Besides these poems on strictly religious subjects, there are secular songs to friends, political ballads, love songs, and a farewell to Ireland ; the occasion which called forth the latter is unknown. Why Tadhg gained the title of Gaedhealach is also uncertain ; it is supposed to have been bestowed on him either from his rustic appearance, or on account of his Irish speech.

Other parts of the country besides the Southern districts of Munster produced about the same period groups of bards of more or less renown. In Mayo and Clare we have, besides MacNamara and Merriman, of whom we have already spoken, and who survived into the early years of the nineteenth century, an earlier group, which included Andrew MacCurtin and his cousin Hugh, Cormac Common, usually called Cormac Dall on account of his blindness, Michael Comyn, and a number of smaller writers. ANDREW MACCURTIN (d. 1749), who was ollave to the O'Briens of Thomond and hereditary bard of Clare, lived just when the transition from the old system of metric to the new was taking place, and he was much disturbed by the change. He had been trained in the severe methods of the regular bards, and in a poem addressed to Sorley MacDonnell of Kilkee he complains bitterly of the obligation to compose in metres "void of all rule or concord," instead of in the well-turned and correct style of older days. He seems to have been a proud and reclusive spirit, endeavouring to keep up, when it was no longer possible to do so, the old haughty prerogatives of the family ollaves.* He tells us that because he had not received invitations with due ceremony from Sorley MacDonnell inviting him to partake of the hospitalities of his house, he had withdrawn into the bleak hills of Ibrican, often wanting food, raiment and money, and never condescending to go down amongst the gentlemen and musicians of Kilkee where he could have been refreshed with food and music, games and pleasures. In his old age he begins to regret what he had missed, and his poem, which he calls " an insipid lazy lay, void of elegance, ill-woven and weak," because it was composed in the fashionable new style of writing verse, was presented in the hope of recovering the friendship of his patron. This it seems to have succeeded in doing, and in his latter days both the MacDonnells and O'Briens helped him in his difficulties.   Andrew lived chiefly on his family property at Maghglas in Ibrican, where he was born.   After the death of his parents, he sold part of the property in order to continue the antiquarian studies in which he was interested, and to support himself he was forced to become a teacher.   Among his poems are two laments on the death of Sir Donagh mac Conor O'Brien of Dromoland, Co. Clare (d. 1717), " the great Sir Donat," as he is called in his own country, and a semi-humorous address, written in 1733, to " Doun of the Sand Hills," a fairy potentate supposed to inhabit the sand hills on the Clare coast, begging him to take him under his protection now that he was neglected by the new gentry of his native district.

His cousin, HUGH " BOY " or BUIDHE MAC CURTIN, who succeeded him as ollave of Thomond, was a native of Kilmacreehy in the barony of Corcomroe, where he

* Chap. xv., p. 189.

lived and died.   He went abroad for his education, and through the efforts of Isabella O'Brien, wife of Sorley Mac Donnell of Kilkee, he was introduced to the Dauphin and was retained by him for seven years as tutor during his sojourn in France.   His interest in the Irish language and archæology had been fostered by his association with his cousin, and in 1717 a work vindicating the Antiquities of Ireland was published by him in Dublin.   His Irish grammar was published in Louvain in 1728, and his Irish dictionary and grammar in Paris in 1732.   His later works were left unpublished through lack of patronage in his own country.   On his return home he opened a small school in his native parish.   He died in 1755, and is buried at Kilmacreehy.

Among the minor poets of the same district are John Hore (d. 1780 ?), a blacksmith, who wrote a number of poems to the Mac Donnell family of Kilkee ; John Lloyd (d. 1757-8), a vagrant bard of·Upper Tulla, who wrote some mellifluent verse ; John Hartney (d. 1755), who lived and died at Kilkee ; and Thomas Meehan (d. after 1798), a native of Ennis, where he taught a literary school and was much esteemed by his neighbours.   More important than any of these is MICHAEL COMYN, b. at Kilcorcoran, Co. Clare, about 1688, whose Lay of Oisín in Tir na n-Og, or the Land of Youth, is well-known and studied as a classic.   It is probably founded on some earlier Ossianic legend known to the writer, and is full of brilliant description.   He is known also as the author of two prose tales, the " Adventures of Turlough, s. of Starn," and the " Adventures of Turlough's Three Sons," and of some minor poems.

At a slightly earlier period Meath and Louth produced an important group of poets.   Of these, one, Turlough

O'Carolan, has gained a world-wide fame, and we must speak of him at greater length.

Turlough Carolan or O'Carolan (1670-1738).— This famous man, who outlived the contemporaries of his youth, and has been rather erroneously called " the last of the Irish bards," was the son of James (or John) O'Carolan, and was born at Newtown, Co. Meath.   He came of people of good position, but soon after his birth, his father, who owned property in the county, was, with many of his fellow-countrymen, stripped of his possessions, and he was obliged to retire to the West, where he settled, with the help of his good friend, Lady St. George, at Carrick-on-Shannon, in Co. Leitrim.   Here he made the acquaintance of the family of M'Dermott Roe, of the County Roscommon, whose friendship and admiration for the bard formed one of the strongest ties of his life.   At their house he often lived, and it was to their home that he returned to die when he felt himself overcome by sickness.   He lies buried in their ancient burial-place at Kilronan Church. At the time of his father's retreat to Carrick, Turlough was a bright and engaging boy, and Mrs. M'Dermott frequently had him at her house and caused him to be instructed with her own children.   He learned to read in his native tongue, then universally taught ; but he also studied English, though not with a very satisfactory result, as his few attempts at writing English verse show.   But Carolan's lessons were suddenly cut short.   He was growing to manhood when he was seized with small-pox, and though he escaped with his life, it was with the total loss of his sight.   In this afflicted condition he was seized with a desire to learn the harp.

Mrs. M'Dermott not only had him instructed in the instrument, but provided him with a horse and a servant to attend him. It was in this way that Carolan drifted into what was known as the " idle trade," *i.e.*, that of wandering bard. He was never, however, regarded as a mere musician. His good birth and breeding, his amiable disposition, and his great natural genius caused his visits to be looked upon as a favour, and his welcome never failed wherever he chanced to wend his steps. There was often a contest between his friends as to who should next have the honour of entertaining him.

Wherever he went he poured forth songs in praise of members of these hospitable houses. The M'Dermotts, the family of his life-long friend, Denis O'Conor of Belanagere, and many others, shared the honour of being celebrated in his verse. His first effort in poetry was undertaken at the suggestion of his friend, Mr. Reynolds, of Letterfian, who proposed to him as a subject an imaginary battle between the " Good People," or the fairies, who were supposed to inhabit two hills in the neighbourhood and to be adverse to each other. " Perhaps, Carolan," said Mr. Reynolds to him, jocosely, " you might make a better hand of your tongue than of your fingers." It is difficult to tell which was Carolan's best " hand " henceforth ; beautiful airs and verses full of feeling and spirit flowed from him with apparently equal facility. His music was in the highest degree popular so long as Irish was spoken ; the airs suit well only Irish metres. About a hundred out of the two hundred airs he is said to have composed can be accounted for ; to most of them he wrote accompanying songs. He generally named his tunes and songs after the persons for whom they were composed.

Among his early songs we may name the following :—
" The Fairy Queens," beginning : " ιmρeαραn móρ
ταιnιc eιoιρ nα Rιჳτe." This was Carolan's first
composition, and gives a romantic picture of Fairy Strife.
" Planxty Reynolds,"* written to his friend, Mr.
Reynolds, of Letterfian. " Grace Nugent," beginning :
"1ρ mιαnn Leαm τρáċταὁ αιρ ὐláιτ nα ρinne," written
for the first cousin of Mr. Reynolds. " Bridget Cruise,"
beginning : " α ράċταιρ α'ρ α cuιρLe, ná τρέιჳ-ρι coὕce
me-ρι." This sweet song was one of several addressed
to his early love who, though she shared his attachment, was never united to him. It is a very beautiful
lyric, full of passion and tenderness. Another air and
song composed to the same girl, begins : α ὑριჳιὁ
ὑeuραċ ιρ ὁuιτ αn ὑéιρρe. It is said to have been sung
by him in a sort of dream or rapture after sitting for
hours listlessly in the sun upon a fairy rath to which he
was wont to retire for solitude. The memory of this
early love affair clung to him even to middle-age, and
O'Conor relates that he recognised his lost lady by the
touch of her fingers in helping her to step into the
ferry-boat going with pilgrims to Loch Derg in Co.
Donegal. Carolan married Mary Maguire, a young lady
of good family in Co. Fermanagh. Mr. Walker tells us
that she " proved a proud and extravagant dame." He
built for her a house on a small farm near Mohill in Co.
Leitrim. He wrote several songs to her, of which one
of the best-known begins :

" mo Léun 'ρ mo cρáὁ ჳαn mé 'ρ mo ჳρáὁ
α n-ჳLeαnnτán áLuιnn ρLéιὑe."

---

* A Planxty is a harp-tune of sportive and animated character ;
it usually moves in triplets with a $\frac{6}{8}$ measure like the Irish jig.

And his monody on her death is full of pathos and unaffected grief.

Among his numerous songs to ladies are his spirited " Wild Mabel Kelly," one of his finest pieces ; the " Ode to O'More's Fair Daughter," called " The Hawk of Ballyshannon ; " Bridget O'Malley, and Peggy Corcoran. Among his convivial songs, generally written in recognition of hospitalities extended to him, are " Planxty Kelly," written for Mr. Kelly of Cargin, Co. Roscommon ; " Planxty Stafford," called " Carolan's Receipt for Drinking," of which, however, only the first stanza is by him, the second having been added by his friend, Mac Cabe ; " Planxty Maguire," written at Tempo in Ulster ; and " The Cup of O'Hara," composed in recognition of the hospitality of a gentleman of the O'Hara family in Co. Sligo. Though Carolan wrote many convivial songs and enjoyed to the full the pleasures of a friendly feast, the stories of his reckless drinking appear to be quite untrue. He was, says his friend, Charles O'Conor, " moral and religious." In Mayo he wrote a great number of verses for the families of Lord Bourke, Lord Dillon, the Palmers, Costellos, and O'Donnells. In Roscommon, to Mrs. French, Nelly Plunket, the O'Conors and M'Dermotts ; in Sligo, to the Croftons, Colonel Irwin and Loftus Jones. A well-known and favourite poem is his Lament over the grave of his fellow-bard, Mac Cabe, written under a false impression of his death, conveyed to him in joke by the bard himself. He wandered much, chiefly in Connacht. In the year 1737 he fell ill while staying at Tempo, and hastily returned to the house of his old friend, Mrs. M'Dermott, of Alderford, bidding farewell to his friends on the journey. On his arrival he called

for his harp and sang to it his " Farewell to Music,"
a final effort.   He died on March 26th, 1738.

Carolan was the centre of a group of musicians and
song-writers, of whom Dall mac Cuairt, Cahir mac
Cabe, Patrick mac Alindon and Peter O'Durnan
all came from the Meath and Louth district.   They
poured forth songs on all occasions, a large number
being amatory ditties, drinking-songs, and satirical
and personal pieces.   None of them were men of education, and their verse is not of high merit, though occasionally a lament or a love-song of more than ordinary
beauty is to be found among their voluminous
productions.

A poet of quite a different stamp, who lived a
little later, is JOHN O'NEACHTAN, a Meath writer,
who flourished about the beginning of the eighteenth
century.   He was an educated man, and his poems rank
high for their pure and correct style and the simplicity of
their language.   Only a small portion of them have as yet
been published,* but among these is his delicate elegy
on the death of Mary d'Este, widow of James II. (d.
1718), and two charming laments on the death of his
own wife, beginning ᴀ τéᴀӡᴀıп 'ré m'éᴀӡ-ʀᴀ and
Cʜuӡ mé ʀeᴀпc mo cᴌéıʊ 'ʀ mo ӡпᴀʊ.   There is also
a sweet and simple lay calling on a young maiden
to come out and enjoy the beauties of nature, which
are recounted at length and with evident affection.
The best-known of his poems is the famous " Maggie
Laidir," describing with great spirit a convivial feast
at which the chairman is supposed to recite this poem.
In it Ireland is toasted under the poetic title of " Maggie
the Strong," and there follow toasts to the chief families

* Edited by Miss A. O'Farrelly for the Gaelic League.

of the four provinces, to the bishop and priests of his native district, and to the tribes of Ireland at large. After heartily wishing destruction to the enemies of his country and success to its friends he calls for a dance, and ends by enumerating the chief families of Erin, from all of whom he claims descent. This rollicking lay is one of the best of the many feasting songs composed about this time. It is a better piece even than " O'Rourke's Frolic," written in the same period by Hugh mac Gowran, of Leitrim, and translated into English verse by Dean Swift. A very amusing poem is O'Neachtan's " Battle of Bridget's Gap and Cross," a humorous account of a battle supposed to have been fought near Tallaght, in 1705, between the potatoes and the beans and peas, that is, between the farmers and the gardeners who supplied Dublin. The poet records the triumph of the potato over its inhospitable foe, the pulse. Some of his poems are written in imitation of Fenian tales, others are addressed to imprisoned priests, and there are penitential poems, satirical lines and occasional verses. His prose works include a treatise on geography, giving some curious particulars regarding Ireland and other countries, some fragments of Annals from 1167 to his own date, and prose tales, of which the best known are an extravaganza called the " Strong-armed Wrestler," and an allegorical tale ridiculing persons learning English, entitled the " History of Edmond O'Clery.* He translated several Latin verses into Irish. One of his poems was penned shortly after the Battle of the Boyne, when he was deprived of all his property by the marauding soldiers, except one small book in Irish which they could not read.

* Published in the Gaelic Journal, Vol. II.

Another O'Neachtan, Tadhg, who was alive in 1750, also wrote poems, twenty-five of which are mentioned by O'Reilly, besides some fragmentary prose works. He is, however, better remembered as the compiler, between the years 1734-39, of a voluminous Irish-English Dictionary, which has never been published. He lived chiefly in Dublin.

Characteristics of the Later Poetry.—It would not seem that the genius of Irish poetry lent itself to the ballad form, which was handled by the lowland Scotch with such weird force and solemnity; nor have we among the compositions of this period any of those long poems descriptive of natural scenery in which the Highland bards of the Jacobite period revelled. Outside the *aislingi* or Visions, expressive of the troubles and expectations of the country, of which we have already spoken, the themes of the Irish song-writers were local, love-songs, drinking-songs, satires and dirges being the staple of their craft. There are numberless poems written by one bard to another among the private circle of personal friends and companions. In general, the limitations of their subjects, as of their allusions and illustrations, is painfully clear, and there is an oppressive mass of verse thrown off without care or finish on the trivial suggestions of the moment. So little originality of thought and structure is shown that it is often difficult to distinguish the output of one bard from that of another. The vagrant and often disreputable lives led by many of these men, such as Magrath and MacNamara and Owen Roe O'Sullivan, and, for the first part of his life, Tadhg Gaedhealach O'Sullivan, could not fail to affect their poetical gifts and to narrow the circle of their ideas.

There is nothing universal in their poetry. It is the product of a special epoch and of the special circumstances that gave it birth, and it cannot with advantage be judged by outside standards. But its popularity with the people among whom it had its origin and the manner in which it was cherished and copied and sung so long as the native tongue was retained in familiar use, show that it was the true expression of their sentiments and feeling. There is no doubt that this poetry tended to foster and keep alive a spirit of revolt and disaffection which might otherwise have died down. " These ' heart home lays ' of their venerated bards," as Hardiman says, " the people treasured up in their memories, and, as it was treason to sing them openly, they were chanted at private meetings or by the cottage firesides throughout the land, with feelings little short of religious enthusiasm."

It is from this period, that is, the period of the seventeenth and eighteenth centuries, that the fixed melancholy of Irish poetry may be said to date. It is not a native note of the older Irish literature ; it began to make itself heard in the output of the bards during the despair and desolation of Elizabethan times, and it grew to be the definite mood and temper of the democratic and Jacobian poetry. It is, therefore, as regards the great bulk of the poems of any particular period, a modern rather than an ancient note. Yet at all times there was to be heard in the popular songs of the peasantry, as well as in their airs, the accent of a tender and passionate pathos, whether in the expression of the regrets and desires of love, or of the aspirations of religion, or in the poems inspired by affection for country or friend.

The true power of the Irish bards lay in the delicate manipulation of pure song and lyric. There is a wealth of tender and passionate songs of love and religion, of which the authorship can only occasionally be traced, but which is the common property of every Irish-speaking district. Most of them are wedded to airs, some of which may be older than the words to which they are sung, while others were composed at the same time as the song itself. Carolan frequently composed air and words together, but we find, both in Ireland and Scotland, more than one version of a song set to a familiar air, the air being sometimes slightly modified to suit the variations in the words. Similarly, it is said that Burns seldom set himself to write a lyric without humming to himself, or getting someone to play over to him, some favourite air which suggested the words. We thus have many songs written to the same air and many versions of the same song. There are different versions in Munster and Connacht of several songs well-known in both provinces. The community of airs between Ireland and Scotland is also interesting. No doubt the soldiers of the Jacobite period carried the old airs with them as they passed backward and forward, adding new words appropriate to their own circumstances. Wandering minstrels, also, carried the songs of their own district with them and sung them wherever they stopped for hospitality. Several famous harpers and minstrels are known to have passed over to Western Scotland and to have introduced there Irish compositions. One of these, O'Kane, is mentioned by Dr. Johnston in his " Journal of a Tour through the Hebrides," while at the beginning of the eighteenth century a brother of Thomas O'Connellan, a celebrated Irish composer, went over to Scotland, taking with him several of his more famous brother's airs. O'Connellan is said to have been a harper of great beauty and power, and he composed an immense number of tunes. It is to this circumstance that Hardiman ascribes the introduction into Scotland of the airs known in Ireland as " Planxty Davis " and the Prelude to the " Breach of Aughrim," known respectively in Scotland as " The Battle of Killicranky " and " Farewell to Lochaber." Several of the most beautiful old airs are common to both nations and have Irish and Scottish words set to them. The most familiar, perhaps, is Robin Adair, which is the sweet Irish song, " Eileen Aroon," while " Gramachree " or " Molly Astore," and " Cean Dubh Deelish " have sometimes been claimed, in the former case by Burns and in the latter by Corri (who published it under the name " Oran-Gaoil " in his collection), as Scotch. Another song usually supposed to be exclusively Scotch is that called " Kelvin Grove," which is to this day sung in Munster to the old Irish words of the " Sean Bhean Bhocht." Of the " White Cockade " or " Cnota Bán," we have already spoken. Another song about the origin of which there seems to be some doubt is that known as " Maggie Lauder," which is usually but doubtfully ascribed to a gentleman of Renfrewshire named Semple, who lived at the close of the seventeenth century and who claimed to have composed it and other well-known songs, whose authorship is equally open to question. The notorious woman to whom it was addressed lived near Dunbar at the time that Cromwell's army lay in the neighbourhood. But in Ireland, Maggie Laidir, " The Strong," represents Ireland. We have spoken of the spirited convivial song of this name written by John O'Neachtan.

The delicacy and tenderness of many of the songs of affection could not be surpassed. They are full of expressions showing that peculiar brilliancy of fancy which has always been a distinctive quality of the imaginative work of the Gael. What could be more beautiful than the description of the loved one as a " Star of Knowledge," going before and following after the one who loves, opening on every side of him a fresh vision of life and of its glory and beauty, so that it seemed only to be known for the first time or to be known in double measure through knowledge of the one woman who was loved. It is an expression that we find repeated again and again in the later love-poems. Here is one example of it, found by Dr. Hyde in a poem in Connacht, beginning " Ringleted Youth of my Love ;" it is from beginning to end an exquisite song :

> I thought ! O my love ! you were so—
>   As the moon is, or sun on a fountain,
> And I thought after that you were snow,
>   The cold snow on top of the mountain ;
> And I thought after that, you were more
>   Like God's lamp shining to find me,
> Or the bright star of knowledge before,
>   And the star of knowledge behind me.*

It is naturally among these well-known songs of love which were repeated all over the country that we find

---

* ᴀ'ᴘ ꝼᴀoɪʟ mé, ᴀ ᴘᴄóɪᴘín
  ᵹo mbᴜᴠ̇ ᵹᴇᴀʟᴀċ ᴀᵹᴜᴘ ᵹᴘɪᴀn ċᴜ,
ᴀ'ᴘ ꝼᴀoɪʟ mé 'nnᴀ ᴠ̇ɪᴀɪᵹ ᴘɪn
  ᵹo mbᴜᴠ̇ ᴘnᴇᴀċᴛᴀ ᴀᴘ ᴀn ᴄᴘʟɪᴀᴠ̇ ċᴜ,
ᴀ'ᴘ ꝼᴀoɪʟ mé 'nn ᴀ ᴠ̇ɪᴀɪᵹ ᴘɪn
  ᵹo mbᴜᴠ̇ ʟóċᴘᴀnn o ᴠ̇ɪᴀ ċᴜ
no ᵹᴜᴘ ᴀb ᴄᴜ ᴀn ᴘᴇᴜʟᴄ-ᴇóʟᴀɪᴘ
ᴀᵹ ᴠᴜʟ ᴘómᴀm ᴀ'ᴘ mo ᴠ̇ɪᴀɪᵹ ċᴜ.

the greatest number of variants.   Occasionally they
are different both in subject and metre, as in the version
given by Dr. Hyde in the Love Songs of Connacht of
the " Paisteen Finn," which is a totally different song
from that which goes usually under that name and
which has been printed in Hardiman's collection and
elsewhere.   Nor does Dr. Hyde's version contain the
curfa or chorus usually sung at the end of each verse.*

There are many different versions also of the sweet
and plaintive " Ɔʀᴀɪʒɴeᴀɴ Ɔoɴɴ," or " Dark Black
Thorn," which differs not only in Munster and Connacht but in different parts of the latter province,
sometimes only the first verse being similar ; or again,
of Ᵽn Ċúiʟ Ᵽɪoɴɴ, or the " Coolun," of which quite
different versions are given in Hardiman, in Mangan's
" Poets and Poetry of Munster," and in Dr. Hyde's
" Love Songs of Connacht."   The words of Hardiman's
version are attributed to Maurice O'Dugan, of Co.
Tyrone, about 1641 ; but probably words of some
sort were always sung to the beautiful and mournful
air of that name, which must be of great antiquity.
The word Coolun, " Cúl Fhionn," meaning " Fair Poll "
or " Tresses," is in these poems applied to a maiden with
fair locks or flowing hair, but it seems originally to
have been used for youths, who, in spite of laws and
edicts, persisted in wearing the hair long in Ireland.
Usually the songs that bear the same name are composed to the same airs, but this is not by any means

---

* These choruses, sung by the whole company, sometimes
had no connection with the song.   An example is the " curfa "
to the " Humours of Joyce's country."   The same chorus was
often used for several songs, and more than one chorus is sung
to the " Paisteen Finn."

uniformly the case. For instance, Raftery's version of Conoaé Ṁuıġ-eó, "County Mayo," is in a totally different metre to the popular song of that name. Frequently the authors and the date of these songs are unknown, but to a few of them at least a traditional origin is assigned. The original form of Eıḃlín a ṗúın, or "Eileen Aroon," is said to have been composed under the following circumstances. A brother of Donagh Mór O'Daly named Carroll, a man of position and an accomplished gentleman, paid his addresses to Eileen, daughter of Kavanagh. During his absence from home, she was persuaded by her relations to abandon him and to marry a rival. On the eve of the wedding, O'Daly returned and, disguised as a harper, he entered the wedding-gathering. Here he sang this appeal with such pathos that Eileen followed him that night. The last stanza is one of welcome. There is a more modern production by a Munster bard of the seventeenth century set to the same air.*

At least three well-known sets of words are attached to the tender old air, Uileacáin Dubh O ! or, "Oh the heavy lamentation," and of each the traditional origin

---

* Handel is said to have declared that he would rather have been the author of the air "Eileen Aroon," than of the most splendid of his own compositions. It is now best known as "Robin Adair" and is commonly supposed to be Scotch. It is, however, a very ancient Irish air. Hardiman states that Robin Adair was an Irishman living at Hollypark, Co. Wicklow, and a member of the Irish Parliament ; cf. his note in Vol. I., p. 328.

A rúin, anglicised "aroon," means "Secret One," and is, like *a stóir* "asthore," meaning "My Treasure," *Cuisle mo chroidhe,* or "Pulse of My Heart," and many other Irish words bearing a similar endearing signification, used as an expression of affection.

is known.   The oldest, dating from the beginning of
the seventeenth century, begins :

> Ɗá v-ɔiocɼá-ɼa liom-ɼa ʒo cúnɔaé liaɔɼoim
>   A uileacáin vuib, O !

" If thou wilt come with me to the County of Leitrim,"

and is said to be an invitation addressed by one of the
unfortunate landholders driven out of Ulster during
the plantation of James I., to his lady, praying her to
follow him into Connacht, in this version to Leitrim,
in another to Mayo.   It contains the exquisite lines :

> Conaiɼc mé aʒ ɔeaċɔ ċuʒam í ɔɼé láɼ an ɔ-ɼléibe,
>   Máɼ ɼéilɔion ɔɼív an ʒ-céov.

I saw her coming towards me o'er the face of the mountain,
Like a star glimmering through the mist.

The second form of the poem beginning :

> Iɼ ɼaiɼɼinʒ 'ɼ ɼáilɔeaċ an áiɔ vo beiċ a neiɼinn
>   uileacán vub O !

Wide-hearted and welcoming to all is this land of Erin
Uileacán Dubh O !

is said by Walsh to have been written by an Irish student
in one of the colleges of France to the same air.   It is
not a love-song, but an ardent and joyous description
of the richness and beauty of Ireland.   This must in
all probability be of about the same date, as it is the
period when most of the more promising youths were
sent abroad for their education.   It is over this poem
that Donnchad Ruadh MacNamara worked, when about
the year 1730 he produced his splendid version set to
the same air—

> beiɼ beannaċɔ ó'm ċɼoive ʒo ɔíɼ na h-Éiɼeann
>   bán ċnoic Eiɼeann óiʒ.

Take a blessing from my heart to the land of Erin,
.   The Fair Hills of Holy Ireland !

probably written while he was abroad.   This version
has been made familiar by Mangan's and Dr. Sigerson's
fine renderings in English, while the second version
has been well translated by Sir Samuel Ferguson.
Though Donnchad did not create the poem he added
to his original some noble lines.   Especially beautiful
are those with which he closes his last verse :

Τɑιτneɑṁ nɑ ȝréιne orrɑ, ɑoroɑ ɑr óȝ,
    Αr ὸɑnċnoιc Éιreɑnn óιȝ !

The glory of the sun shine on them all, young and old,
    On the Fair Hills of Holy Ireland.

Religious Poems.—Almost more beautiful, on account
of their extreme simplicity, are some of the short religious
songs floating among the people.   Dr. Hyde has collected
a number of these in the Province of Connacht, and
it were to be wished that the same could be done for
the other provinces, although some of those included
by Dr. Hyde are of Munster origin or are common to
both.   Many are charms, similar to those found on the
Western coasts of Scotland, and they probably come
down from equally remote ages.   Others are long poems,
generally in the form of arguments or debates between
death and the writer or some imaginary human being,
on the shortness of life and the transitoriness of earthly
happiness.   The " Dialogue between the Body and
the Soul,"* a discussion of this sort which was widely
spread on the Continent in the Middle Ages, was known
in Ireland, the Irish version being apparently a para-
phrase of the Latin.   This mediæval tract, which had
its counterpart in art in the pictures and plays of the

---

* It is found in the *opera minora* of Robert Grosseteste.
There are Anglo-Saxon, Anglo-Norman, French, Swedish,
German and Spanish versions of it.

" Dance of Death " or " Dance Macabre," no doubt
gave rise to the popular Irish poems on the subject.
A great number of these mournful religious dissertations
were composed in the seventeenth and eighteenth
centuries, called by such names as " Death and the
Sinner," or " Death and the Man," " The Final End of
Man," etc. Some of these pieces are humorous and
full of a shrewd worldly wisdom, as when Death argues
with the Sinner that it is dangerous and sinful to drink
in a tavern, and the Sinner replies that it is hard that
this should be brought up against him, " considering
the excellence of his heart in paying for his drink,
beyond the rest of them."

Other poems of the same sort contain confessions of
faith, or warnings of the danger of unrepentance.
They are, as a rule, lugubrious and mediæval in tone,
but even some of the dreariest contain occasional
passages that show the peculiar fine quality of vision
which is distinctively Irish. We give an example in Dr.
Hyde's rendering, which keeps close to the sense of the
original. In a fragmentary poem taken down from the
mouth of a Galway man named Martin Rua O'Gillarna,
the silence and unexpectedness of the coming of the
Day of Judgment is described as being like the pushing
up, noiselessly but irresistibly, of a blade of grass through
the ground.

> As a light comes over the rising moon,
> As a heat comes over the settled sun,
> As the grass steals up through the fields of the world,
>   The day of the judgment of God shall come.*

* In the original :

> Mᴀᵽ tᴉꞩ ꞅolᴀꞅ ᴀᵽ ᴀn n-ꞁeᴀlᴀᴉꞑ,
> Mᴀᵽ tᴉꞑeᴀꞅ teᴀꞅ ᴀᵽ ᴀn nꞡᵽéᴉn
> Mᴀᵽ tᴉꞑeᴀꞅ ᴀn ꝼéᴀᵽ tᵽíᴅ ᴀn tᴀlᴀ́ṁ
> Tᴉucꝼᴀᴉᴅ lᴀ́ bᵽeᴉꞇeᴀṁᴀᴉꞅ ᴅé.

It would be singular anywhere but in Ireland to find on the lips of a rude uneducated lad, so delicate a poem as ᴀ ṁuiṛe nᴀ nᵹṛᴀṛ, " O Mary of the Graces." No translation could transfer into another language the fine chasteness and melody of the original. It can best be compared to some of the Christmas cradle-songs existing among the peasants or to the extreme simplicity of the runes and prayers of the Western Highlands.

ᴀ ṁuiṛe nᴀ nᵹṛᴀṛ
  ᴀ ṁáṫᴀiṛ ṁic Ꝺé
ᵹo ᵹ-cuiṛiꝺ ṫú
  ᴀṛ mo leᴀṛ mé.

ᵹo ṛáḃálᴀiꝺ ṫú mé
  ᴀṛ ᵹᴀċ uile olc
ᵹo ṛáḃálᴀiꝺ ṫú mé
  ḟoiṛ ᴀnᴀm ᴀ'ṛ coṛp.

ᵹo ṛáḃálᴀiꝺ ṫu mé
  ᴀṛ muiṛ ᴀ'ṛ ᴀṛ ṫíṛ
ᵹo ṛáḃálᴀiꝺ ṫu mé
  ᴀṛ leic nᴀ bṛiᴀn.

ᵹáṛꝺᴀ nᴀ n-ᴀinᵹeᴀl
  Oṛ mo ċionn
Ꝺiᴀ ṛóṁᴀm
  ᴀᵹuṛ Ꝺiᴀ liom.*

In a similar metre and expressive of the same rare refinement and sincerity of feeling is the melodious and touching little song, got from an old woman of near a hundred years of age living in a hut in the midst of a bog in County Roscommon, which Dr. Hyde gives in his love-songs, and which, though so recently rescued,

* The guard of the angels above my head, God before me and God with me.

may be said already to have become a classic. It begins :

mo ḃ𝑟ón ᴀı𝑟 ᴀn ḃ𝑟ᴀı𝑟𝑟ᵹe
ı𝑟 é τᴀ́ mó𝑟
ı𝑟 é ᵹᴀḃᴀıl ıᴅı𝑟 mé
'S mo ṁíle 𝑟τó𝑟.

ᴅ' 𝑓ᴀ́ᵹᴀḃ '𝑟ᴀn mbᴀıle mé
ᴅeunᴀṁ ḃ𝑟óın
ᵹᴀn ᴀon τ𝑟úıl τᴀ𝑟 𝑟ᴀ́ıle lıom
Ċoıḃċe nᴀ ᵹo ᴅeó.

Translation.

" My grief on the sea
    How the waves of it roll !
For they heave between me
    And the love of my soul !

" Abandoned, forsaken,
    To grief and to care,
Will the sea ever waken
    Relief from despair ? "

In most of these songs, even those composed in the most recent periods, there is a fine art displayed in the management of the vowel-sounds ; a whole stanza or even the larger portions of an entire poem being often composed on one or two vowel sounds, interwoven and repeated with extraordinary care and complexity. Many poems, otherwise valueless, have a curious interest from the ingenuity with which they are built up on certain open or closed vowels.

Thus the poems of ANTHONY RAFTERY, the blind poet of Killeadan, Co. Mayo (about 1784-1835) which do not, as a rule, attain any great poetic dignity of thought or expression, are yet remarkable for their wonderful facility of verse structure.   Raftery led a wandering life in the neighbourhood of Gort, Co. Galway, and his verses are still alive among the people.   They had

more than a local celebrity, for Raftery was something
of a political and social force in his day, and his verses
were often directed to practical purposes during the
risings of the Whiteboys and in the Tithe War of 1830.
He loses no opportunity of exalting O'Connell and of
decrying Orangemen, Protestants and Englishmen.
Besides his political pieces and a long poem on the
history of Ireland, he wrote some good songs to women,
and a pathetic piece upon the loss of a boat-load of
people on Loch Corrib in 1828, bound for the fair of
Galway.   There is also a fine lament for Thomas O'Daly
which carries out with wonderful skill and with a most
melodious effect the vowel-rhyming system, the stress
of the voice falling repeatedly and at regular intervals
upon the same vowel-sound.   Raftery, like many of his
fellows, is anxious to make a display of classical or
historical knowledge in his verse, but it is not by these
efforts that he and the other peasant-poets of Ireland
will be judged, but by those simple lays, often thrown
off in the pressure of a moment's necessity, which
express in the simplest language the deepest and most
pathetic feelings of the soul.   None of Raftery's learned
poems can approach to the pathos of the three stanzas
composed, apparently without forethought, in response
to a man who heard him playing the fiddle and asked
him who he was.

> Miſe Raipteſſi an ſile,
> Lán ᴠóċaiſ aᵹuſ ᵹſáᴠ,
> Le ſúiliᴠ ᵹan ſoluſ
> Le ciúnaſ ᵹan cſáᴠ.
>
> Oul ſiaſ aſ m' aiſteaſ
> Le ſoluſ mo ċſoiᴠe,
> ſann aᵹuſ tuiſſeaċ
> ᵹo ᴠeiſeaᴠ mo ſliᵹe.

ⱲⱸⱯⱱ ⱯⱣⱭⱮ Ɱⱸ
ⱧⱬⱳⱲ Ɱ' ⱯⱬⱭⱱ ⱯⱲ ⱲⱯⱡⱡⱯ
Ɐⱬ ⱲⱸⱮⱮ ⱞⱸⱭⱮ
Ɒⱥ ⱬⱭⱮⱯⱮⱲ ⱲⱯⱡⱯⱞ.

Translation.

I am Raftery the poet,
Full of hope and love,
With eyes that have no light,
With gentleness that has no misery.

Going west upon my pilgrimage
By the light of my heart,
Feeble and tired
To the end of my road.

Behold me now,
And my face to a wall,
A-playing music
Unto empty pockets.

It is when we read these runes and prayers, or these love-songs and patriotic songs, with their soft and beguiling movement, that we feel that we have touched the very heart of the people. Even above and beyond the old romance of Ireland the old poems of the peasantry stir and touch us. The old romance, fine, vigorous and manly as it is, has in it elements of bombast, of huge and jocose exaggeration, of rude savagery, which set it apart from the world of thought in which we live to-day. We appreciate the old tales only by a distinct imaginative effort by means of which we set ourselves many centuries backward into regions of life and into conditions of primitive barbarism not familiar to our minds. But love-songs like " Ɐⱬ ⱤⱬⱲ ⱳⱸⱯⱡ ⱱⱰⱲ," or "CeⱯⱬⱬ ⱯⱱⱲ ⱱⱱⱡⱸⱯⱲ," "ⱧⱯⱳⱲⱯⱭⱡ, Ɐ ⱳⱲⱯⱱ," or "ⱲⱸⱯⱬ Ɐⱬ ⱲⱯⱬ ⱲⱯⱯⱯⱰ;" spirited patriotic lays like " ⱡⱯ ⱲⱱⱞⱬⱯⱭⱡ ⱯⱲⱭ ! " or the original form of Ⱨ҉ⱳⱯⱯⱨⱯⱬ ⱠⱯⱬ* need no such

---

* Dr. Sigerson gives a translation of this original poem in his " Bards of the Gael and Gall," p. 258.

effort.   They express a universal human language which is unchanging from century to century.   The old songs, often anonymous, often coming out of peat-browned cabins and from the lips of the poorest of the peasantry, are the best literary heritage of Ireland.   They are in most cases wedded to beautiful and still more ancient airs.   Both the melody of their rhythm and the delicacy of their sentiment surprise and delight us.   It is when we read these poems that we wonder most why Irishmen are content to be so ignorant of their own literature ; why they are so slow to rescue it from destruction, so careless as to whether or no it shall ever see the light in print, so little moved to desire that it should take its place among the recognised literatures of the world. To read them, too, is to supply ourselves with an argument, perhaps the strongest that could be urged, that the language in which these poems were composed should never be allowed to die.   For in no other language, except its own, could the poetical genius of the nation find a true and complete expression.   The idiom of a people's thought can only be adequately conveyed in the idiom of the language they have created to express their thought.   The difficulty of translating these poems into English verse without losing the colour, the intimate suggestiveness and the bewitching quality of the original, is very great ; it is yet greater when an attempt is made to reproduce the metre and the verse-structure of Irish poetry.   Thus, either to create such poems or to enjoy them, they must be handled and read and sung in the original.   The thought and the native expression of the thought cannot be divided.

I would conclude by recalling the words of one who, though not himself an Irishman, was ever ready to give his aid and his influence to the cause of Irish learning and to extending the knowledge of Irish literature, the late Professor York Powell, Regius Professor of Modern History at Oxford and first Chairman of the Irish Texts Society.   He says, in a protest on behalf of the Gaelic League, in whose linguistic and social work he was warmly interested : " I would willingly see much forgotten in Ireland that Irishmen choose to remember. . . . But for Irishmen to consent to forget what is best for them to remember, the cradle-song of their mothers, the hymn their grandmothers sang, the wise, quaint talk of the elders, the joyous verse and the sad mourning verse of their own poets, and the whole fabric of their folk-lore, their folk-wisdom, their own names and the names of the hills and rivers and rocks and woods that are so dear to them, seems to me incomprehensible." (Life I., p. 282).

LIST OF ABBREVIATIONS.

R.C.—Revue Celtique (Paris, 1870-1907).

Z. für Celt. Phil—Zeitschrift für Celtische Philologie.

Ir. T.—Irische Texte.

Sil. Gad.—Silva Gadelica (S. H. O'Grady).

Pub. Oss. Soc.—Publications of the Ossianic Society.

Pro. R.I.A.—Proceedings of the Royal Irish Academy.

Anec. Oxon.—Anecdota Oxoniensia.

Mans. Cust.—Manners and Customs of the Ancient Irish (E. O'Curry).

MS. Mat.—Manuscript Materials for Irish History (E. O'Curry).

NOTE.—The Chapters at the head of each division refer to the corresponding Chapters of the Text Book. The Editors' names are printed in brackets.

BIBLIOGRAPHY.

OLD ROMANCE AND MYTHOLOGY.

Vol. I., Chapter IV.

Táin bó Cuailnge.—*L.L.* Text, and Germ. Trans. (E. Windisch), 1905 ; Ferdiad Episode and Eng. Trans. (O'Curry) Mans. Cust. Appen. I. ; *L.U.* Text, Eriu, Vol. I., etc. (in progress) ; Eng. Trans. (Faraday), 1904 ; Eng. Trans. of portions, from Add. MS., 18748, Brit. Mus. (S. H. O'Grady) in Hull's " Cuchullin Saga."

Vol. I., Chapter V.

Tales introductory to the Táin.—Táin bó Dartada, Flidais, Regamain, Regamna (E. Windisch) Ir. T., Vol. II., Pt. 2 ; Táin bó Fraech (O'Beirne Crowe), R.I.A., Ir. MSS. Series, Vol. I., Pt. 1 ; Adventures of Nera (K. Meyer), R.C. x. ; Debility of the Ultonians (E. Windisch), *Gesellschaft der Wissenschaften Phil.—Hist. Classe,* 1884 ; Vision of Angus, E. Muller, R.C. iii. ; Dispute of the Swineherds (E. Windisch), Ir. T., III., Pt. 1 ; Recovery of the Táin, see " Proceedings of the Great Bardic Institution " (Connellan), Oss. Soc. Pub., Vol. V. ; Birth Story of King Conor (K. Meyer), R.C. vi. ; Birth Story of Cuchulain (L. Duvau), R.C. ix. ; Text only, Ir. T. I.

Vol. I., Chapters I., VI.-VIII.

(1) Second Battle of Moytura (Wh. Stokes), R.C. xii.

Fate of the Children of Lir ; Fate of the Children of Tuireann (E. O'Curry), Atlantis III., IV., and Soc. for the Pres. Irish Language.

Fate of the Sons of Usnach (O'Curry), Atlantis III., IV. ; (T. O'Flanagan), Gaelic Soc. Trans., 1808 ; (Wh. Stokes), Ir.

T., II., Pt. 2 ; and Soc. for the Pres. Ir. Language. Battle of Rosnaree (E. Hogan), R.I.A., Todd Lec. Series, IV., 1892 ; The Great Rout of Muirthemne (S. H. O'Grady), Trans. in Hull's " Cuchullin Saga " ; Cuchulain's Death (Wh. Stokes), R.C., iii. ; The Red Rout of Conall Cernach, Mod. Vers. (J. Lloyd), G.L. Publications ; Lay of the Heads, Reliquæ Celticæ, Vol. I. ; Phantom Chariot of Cuchulain (O'Beirne Crowe), *Jl. Kilkenny Arch. Soc.*, 1870-71 ; Destruction of Bruidhen Dá Choga (Wh. Stokes), R.C. xxi. ; Intoxication of the Ultonians (W. M. Hennessy), R.I.A., Todd Lecture Series, I. ; Tragical Death of Conlaech, Miss Brooke's " Reliques of Irish Poetry," 1789, Eriu, Vol. I., Pt. 1, two versions (K. Meyer and J. G. O'Keeffe), and Reliquæ Celt. I. ; Siege of Howth (Wh. Stokes), R.C., viii. ; Feast of Bricriu (E. Windisch), Ir. T., I. and (G. Henderson) Ir. Texts Soc., II. ; Violent Deaths of Goll and Garbh (Wh. Stokes), R.C. xiv. ; Bargain of the Strong Man (K. Meyer), R.C. xiv. ; Exile of the Sons of Doel Dermait, Ir. T., II., Pt. 1 ; Mac Datho's Boar and Hound (K. Meyer) *Hib. Minora.* Anec. Oxon. ; and Ir. T., I. ; Wooing of Emer (K. Meyer), R.C. xi., and *Arch. Rev.*, Vol. I. ; Sickbed of Cuchulain, Ir. T., I. ; (E. O'Curry) Atlantis I., II. ; Wooing of Ferb (E. Windisch), Ir. T., III., Pt. 2 ; Wooing of Etain, Ir. T., I. ; Story of Baile the Sweet-Spoken (O'Curry), MS. Mat., Appendix II., and (K. Meyer), R.C. xiii. ; The Martial Career of Congal Clairingneach (P. mac Sweeney), Ir. Texts Soc., V., 1904 ; Violent Deaths of Ulster Heroes (K. Meyer), Pro. R.I.A.

(2) The following contain translations of many of these tales without text : in English, Leahy, " Heroic Romances of Ireland," 2 vols., and " Wooing of Ferb " ; E. Hull, " The Cuchullin Saga in Irish Literature " ; in French, D'Arbois de Jubainville, " L'Epopée Celtique en Irlande " ; in German, R. Thurneysen, " Sagen aus dem Alten Irland."

(3) *Summaries of Tales.*—A. Nutt, " Voyage of Bran " and " Cuchulainn, the Irish Achilles."

(4) *Free Renderings.*—S. J. O'Grady, " History of Ireland " and " The Coming of Cuchulain " ; Lady Gregory's " Cuchulain " ; Mrs. Hutton's " Epic of the Táin."

OSSIANIC TALES AND VERSE.

VOL. II., CHAPTERS I.-VI.

(1) *Prose.*—The Six Volumes of the Ossianic Soc. Publications contain a great number of the Fenian Tales and Ballads ; others will be found in Rev. Celt., I., II., V., VII., XI., XII., XIII., XIV., etc. ; Eriu, I., etc. ; and in Silva Gadelica. '' The Colloquy with the Ancients '' will be found in Sil. Gad. I., pp. 94-233, II. pp. 101-265 (S. H. O'Grady), and in Ir. Texte, IV. (Wh. Stokes) ; The Battle of Ventry (K. Meyer) Anec. Oxon., 1885. The Pursuit of Diarmuid and Grainne (S. H. O'Grady) has been reprinted by the Soc. for the Pres. of the Ir. Language. The Gaelic League has printed '' The Naked Man of the Riffian Mountains '' ; the '' Enchanted Fort of the Quicken Trees,'' and other late romances. Others, such as the '' Flight of the Gilla Decair,'' and '' The Kerne of the Narrow Stripes,'' or '' Slender Swarthy Kerne,'' will be found in Silva Gadelica (S. H. O'Grady). For Collections of West Highland Tales, cf. (Campbell of Islay), Popular Tales, and Waifs and Strays of Celtic Tradition, 5 vols. ; for Mongan Legend, Nutt's Voyage of Bran, and K. Meyer in *Zeit. für Celt. Phil. II.*

(2) *Poetry and Ballads.*—Ossianic Soc. Pub. ; Miss Brooke's '' Reliques of Irish Poetry,'' 1789 ; Duanaire Finn (MacNeill), Ir. Texts Soc. vii. ; Poems of Oísin (Simpson), 1857 ; Leabhar na Feinne (J. F. Campbell), 1871 ; Reliquæ Celticæ (Cameron) ; Book of the Dean of Lismore (P. MacLauchlan) ; others in *Zeit. für Celt. Phil.*, The Gaelic Journal, etc.

(3) *Folk Tales.*—Larminie's West Irish Folk Tales, 1894 ; Curtin's Hero Tales, 1894, and Myths and Folk-lore of Ireland ; Hyde's '' Beside the Fire,'' and An Sgeuluidhe Gaodhalach, 2 Parts, 1895-7.

(4) *Free Renderings and Studies.*—Lady Gregory's '' Gods and Fighting Men '' ; S. J. O'Grady's '' Finn and his Companions '' ; A. Nutt, Ossian and the Ossianic Literature (Popular Studies) ; Mac Pherson's '' Ossian '' and '' Temora.''

LEGENDS OF THE KINGS.

Vol. I., Chapter X.

Destruction of the Bruidhen Dá Derga (Wh. Stokes), 1902 ; Battle of Magh Rath or Moira (J. O'Donovan), *Ir. Arch. Soc.*, Vol. VII., 1822 ; Battle of Magh Leana (E. O'Curry), *Celtic Soc.*, 1855 ; Battle of Crinna (S. H. O'Grady), Sil. Gad. ; Battle of Allen (Wh. Stokes), R.C., xxiv. ; Battle of Carn Conaill (Wh. Stokes), *Zeit. für Celt. Phil. III.* ; Destruction of Dind Righ (Wh. Stokes), *Zeit. für Celt., Phil. III.* ; Death of Murtough mac Erca, Story of Aedh Baclamh, Death of K. Dermot and Fall of Tara, Adventures of the Sons of Eochaid Muighmedóin, Panegyric of Cormac, Battle of Magh Mucramhe (S. H. O'Grady), Sil. Gad. ; Boromhean Tribute, *ibid.* and (Wh. Stokes) R.C. xxiii. ; Expulsion of the Deisi (K. Meyer), Eriu, Vol. III., Pt. 2.

Many of these tales will be found in Keating's History and O'Flaherty's Ogygia ; also outlines in the Prefaces to facsimilies of Irish MS., R.I.A., and to the Book of Fermoy, Ir. MS. Series, Vol. I., Pt. 1.

VOYAGE AND VISION LITERATURE.

Vol. I., Chapter XI.

Adventures of Connla (Windisch), *Kurzgefasste Irische Grammatik*, and (O'Beirne Crowe), *Kilkenny Arch. Jl.*, 1874-5 ; Bran, son of Febal (K. Meyer), in Nutt's " Voyage of Bran ; " Lay of Oísin, Michael Comyn (O'Flannery) ; Cormac's Adventure (Wh. Stokes), Ir. T., III., Pt. 1, and (S. H. O'Grady), *Pub. of the Oss. Soc.*, III. ; Voyage of Maelduin (Wh. Stokes), R.C., x., xi. ; Voyage of the Sons of O'Corra, *ibid.* xiv. ; Voyage of Snedgus and Mac Riagla, *ibid.* ix. ; Adventures of Columcille's Clerics, *ibid.* xxv.-xxvi. ; Voyage of Teigue, s. of Cian (S. H. O'Grady), Sil. Gad. ; Legend of St. Brendan (Wh. Stokes) in Lives of the Saints from the Book of Lismore * ; Vision of St. Adamnan

---

* The best introductions to the foreign versions of the Voyage of St. Brendan are—A Jubinal, *La Legende latine de S. Brandaines*, Paris, 1836 ; Carl Schröder, *Sanct. Brandan*, 1871 ; Schirmer, *Zur Brendan's Legende* ; English versions, Thomas Wright, Percy Soc., Vol. xiv., 1844 ; and cf. Zimmer's Study of the Legend in Keltische Beitrage, *Zeit. fur D. Alt.*, xxxiii.

(Wh. Stokes), Calcutta, 1870, and in Miss M. Stokes' " Forests of France " ; Second Vision of Adamnan (Wh. Stokes), R.C. xii. ; Two Sorrows of Heaven's Kingdom (Dottin), R.C. xxi. ; The Ever-new Tongue (Wh. Stokes), Eriu, Vol. II., Pt. 2 ; Tidings of Doomsday, R.C. iv. ;   Vision of Fersius,* *ibid.* xxv. ; Vision of Tundale (K. Meyer and V. Friedel), 1907.

Summaries of the tales in Nutt's " Voyage of Bran, s. of Febal."

* The Latin version will be found in Bæda, *Eccle. Hist.*, Bk. III., ch. xix.; and Count Ramon's Vision (Latin) in O'Sullivan Beare's *Hist. Catholicæ Iver. Compendium.* The Irish versions of the Vision of Owain Myles have not yet been published.   Turnbull and Laing have published early English versions (1837); and Turnbull a version of the Vision of Tundale, 1843.

ECCLESIASTICAL WRITINGS.

VOL. I., CHAPTER XII.

Glosses : Three Irish Glossaries and Goidelica (Wh. Stokes) ; by Stokes and Strachan, Thesaurus Palæohibernicus (1901-3) ; by Zeuss, Grammatica Celtica, 1853 ; Zimmer, Glossæ Hibernicæ.

Service Books : The Antiphonary of Bangor and Stowe Missal (Warren) ; The Irish Liber Hymnorum (Bernard and Atkinson), pub. by the H. Bradshaw Soc.

Martyrologies : Calendar of Angus the Culdee (Wh. Stokes), R.I.A., Ir. MSS. Series, 1880, and *H. Bradshaw Soc.* ; Mart. of Gorman (Wh. Stokes), *H. Bradshaw Soc.*, 1895 ; Mart. of Donegal, O'Clery (Todd and Reeves), *Ir. Arch. Soc.*, 1864.

Saints' Lives (1) Collections : Colgan's Trias Thaumaturga, and Acta Sanctorum ; Migne, *Pat. Lat.* 53, 80, 87, 88, etc.

Fleming, Collectanea Sacra, 1667.

Lives of the Saints from the Book of Lismore (Wh. Stokes) ; Latin Lives (E. Hogan), R.I.A., *Todd Lectures*, V., 1894.

(2) St. Patrick : Tripartite Life (Wh. Stokes), Rolls Series ; Eng. Trans. of Mairchu's Life (A. Barry) ; Confessio (N. White), Pro. R.I.A., 1905.

(3) S. Columcille: Adamnan's Life (W. Reeves), *Ir. Arch. Soc.*, 1857, and Historians of Scotland, Vol. VI., 1874, and (J. T. Fowler), 1894, Clar. Press; Eng. Tr., D. Mac Carthy; O'Donnell's Life (Henebry), *Zeit. für Celt. Phil.* III., IV., V.; Amra Columcille (Wh. Stokes), R.C. xx.

(4) Other Saints: St. Molling (Wh. Stokes), 1906; St. Finan (Macalister), *Zeit. für Celt. Phil.*, II.; SS. Ciaran of Saighir, Molaise, Cellach, Magnenn (S. H. O'Grady), Sil. Gad.

Homilies, etc. Passions and Homilies from the L. Breac (Atkinson), R.I.A., *Todd Lectures*, 1885; Homilies and Legends from ditto (E. Hogan), *ibid.* 1895; Keating's Three Shafts of Death (Atkinson), *ibid.* 1890; Keating's Defence of the Mass (P. O'Brien), 1898; Fragments of Monastic Rules, hymns, etc., will be found in Eriu (in progress).

MISCELLANEOUS PROSE AND VERSE.

Senchus Mór or Ancient Laws of Ireland (Brehon Law Commissioners), 1865-1901; Book of Rights (O'Donovan), *Celtic Soc.*, 1847; Saltair na Rann (Wh. Stokes), Anec. Oxon., 1883; Triads of Ireland and Cáin Adamnan (K. Meyer); Metrical Dindsenchus (E. Gwynn), R.I.A., Todd Lectures, 1900, etc.; The Rennes Dindsenchus, R.C. xv., xvi.; The Edinburgh Dind., 1893; The Bodleian Dind., 1892; Coir Anmann, Ir. T., Vol. III., Pt. I.; Cormac's Glossary, *Ir. Arch. Soc.*, 1868; Dialogue of the Two Sages, R.C. xxvi. (all ed. by Wh. Stokes).

CLASSICAL AND MEDIÆVAL TRANSLATIONS.

Vol. II., Chapter VIII.

(1) *Classical*—Tale of Troy (Wh. Stokes), Calcutta, 1882, and Ir. T., II., Pt. 1, 1884; Alexander Saga (K. Meyer), Ir. T., Vol. II., Pt. 2; The Irish Odyssey (K. Meyer), 1886; Virgil's Æneid (G. Calder), *Ir. Texts Soc.*, Vol. VI., and cf. Episode of Dido (T. Hudson Williams), *Zeit. für Celt. Phil.* II.

(2) *Mediæval*—The Gaelic Maundeville, and the Gaelic Marco Polo (Wh. Stokes), *Zeit. für Celt. Phil.* II. ; The Gaelic Bevis of Hampton (Robinson), *ibid ;* Irish version of Nennius (J. H. Todd), Ir. Arch. Soc., 1848, and (E. Hogan), R.I.A., Todd Lecture Ser., 1895.

HISTORIES AND ANNALS.

Vol. II., Chapters X.—XII

Annals of the Four Masters (O'Donovan), 6 vols. ; Annals of Ulster (W. Hennessy and B. MacCarthy), 4 vols.

In the Rolls Series, Annals of Lough Cé and Chronicum Scotorum (W. Hennessy) ; Wars of the Gaedhil with the Gaill (J. H. Todd).

Ann. of Clonmacnois, Eng. trans. by MacGeoghegan (ed. by D. Murphy) ; Ann. of Tighernach (Wh. Stokes), R.C. xvi.-xviii.

Mac Firbis' Annals of Ireland (O'Donovan), Ir. Arch. Soc., 1860 ; Leabhar Oiris, Eriu, Vol. I., Pt. I. ; Career of Cellachan of Cashel, and The Fomorians and Norsemen, A. Bugge, Christiana, 1905 ; O'Clery's Life of Red Hugh O'Donnell (D. Murphy), 1893 ; P. O'Sullivan-Beare's Historiæ Catholicæ Iverniæ Compendium, Latin (M. Kelly) ; Extracts of ditto in English in " Ireland under Elizabeth " (M. Byrne); R. O'Flaherty's Ogygia, 1685 ; John Lynch, Cambrensis Eversus (M. Kelly), Celtic Soc., 1848.

G. Keating's History of Ireland, Part 1 (D. Comyn), *Ir. Texts Soc.*, 1901, Parts ii., iii. (P. S. Dinneen), in press ; Introduction only (D. Comyn), Gaelic League ; Part 1 (Joyce), 1900 ; Eng. Trans. only (O'Mahony), 1857.

BARDIC AND OLDER IRISH POETRY.

Vol. I., Chapters XIII.—XV. Vol. II., Chaps. XIII., XIV.

Examples of the older poetry of the bards and of the official poets will be found in the following works :—O'Curry, " Mans. Cust.", and " MS. Mat. " ; Petrie's " Tara " ; *Atlantis*, Vol. IV. ;

Miss Brooke's " Reliques of Irish Poetry " ; Hardiman's " Irish Minstrelsy," 1831 ; Miscellany of the *Celtic Soc.*, 1846 ; *Kilkenny Arch. Jl.*, Vol. I., etc. ; Skene, Celtic Scotland, Appen. ; Gaelic Soc. Pub., 1808 ; Book of the Dean of Lismore ; Reliquæ Celticæ ; Topographical Poems (O'Donovan), *Irish Arch. and Celtic Soc.*, 1862, and 1841 ; Bardic Poems from Copenhagen MS. (L. C. Stern), *Zeit. für Celt. Phil.*, II. ; Catalogue of MSS. in the British Museum (S. H. O'Grady) ; Otia Merseiana (K. Meyer) ; Eriu, etc.

Separate poems ; King and Hermit, 1901 ; Liadan and Curither, 1902 ; Songs of Summer and Winter, 1903 (K. Meyer) ; Vision of Mac Conglinne (K. Meyer), 1892 ; cf. Thurneysen's Mittelirische Verslehen, Ir. Texte III., Pt. 1, and pieces in Eriu, Gaelic Journal, etc.

MODERN POETRY.

Vol. II., Chapters XV.-XVI.

The following have been published by the Gaelic League :— Keating's Poems (J. Mac Erlean), Geoffrey O'Donoghue of the Glen, Pierce Ferriter, Seaghan Claragh Mac Donnell, Owen Roe O'Sullivan, Tadhg Gaedealach O'Sullivan, Poets of the Maigue, *i.e.*, John O'Tuomy and Andrew M'Grath (all ed. by P. S. Dinneen), Pierce Mac Gerald (R. Foley), John O'Neachtan (A. O'Farrelly), John O'Murchada na Raithineach (T. O'Donoghue), Colm de Wallace (J. Lloyd).

Egan O'Rahilly's Poems (P. S. Dinneen), Ir. Texts Society, 1900 ; Brian Merriman's " Midnight Court " (C. L. Stern), *Zeit. für Celt. Phil.* V., 1905, and (F. W. O'Connell) ; Raftery's Songs (D. Hyde), 1903 ; Poems of Donagh Roe Macnamara (T. Flannery), 1897.

A good number of T. O'Carolan's Poems will be found in Hardiman's Irish Minstrelsy, II. (1831).

Collections.—Besides Hardiman's two volumes, the following, among others, contain a good number of the Jacobite or popular songs and lyrics : Reliques of Irish Jacobite Poetry, 1844 ; The Pious Miscellany of T. G. O'Sullivan (1868), and the Irish

Language Miscellany (J. O'Daly), 1876; Poems written by Clare Bards (B. O'Looney), 1863; Reliques of Irish Poetry (Brooke); Poets and Poetry of Munster (Mangan), 1849; Love Songs of Connacht and Religious Songs of Connacht (D. Hyde); Amhráin Chlainne Gaedheal (M. and T. O'Malley), Irish Popular Songs (E. Walsh), 1847; Ceól-Sídhe (N. Borthwick); cf. Bunting's and Joyce's collections of Ancient Irish Music, and Dr. A. Carmichael's " Carmina Gadelica."

Translations.—Bards of the Gael and Gall (Sigerson); Spirit of the Nation (Duffy); Lays of the Western Gael (Ferguson); Irish Song-book (Graves); cf. Lyra Celtica (Sharp); Treasury of Irish Poetry (Brooke and Rolleston).

WORKS OF REFERENCE.

D'Arbois de Jubainville, Cours de Litterature Celtique, Vols. I., II.,* V., VI., VII., VIII.; and Essai d'un Catalogue de la litt. épique de l'Irlande, 1883.

E. O'Curry, Manuscript Materials of Irish History, and Manners and Customs of the Ancient Irish.

D. Hyde, Literary History of Ireland, Three Centuries of Gaelic Literature, and Mac Ternan Prize Essay on Irish Poetry.

P. W. Joyce, Social Life in Ireland, and Old Celtic Romances.

A. Nutt, Voyage of Bran, and Popular Studies in Mythology, Nos. 3, 8.

E. O'Reilly, Irish Writers (Iberno-Celtic Soc., 1820).

Sir James Ware, The Writers of Ireland, 1746.

J. C. Walker's Memoirs of the Irish Bards.

Irish Articles in Dictionary of National Biography.

S. H. O'Grady's Catalogue of Manuscripts in the British Museum.

* Vol. II. " Le cycle mythologique-irlandais," has been translated into English by R. I. Best.

WALES.

Lady Guest's Mabinogion ; New Ed., A. Nutt.

W. F. Skene, The Four Ancient Books of Wales.

T. Stephen's Literature of the Cymri, and the Gododin of Aneurin.

Anwyl's Celtic Religion.

Sir J. Rhys, Celtic Heathendom (Hibbert Lectures, 1888) ; Celtic Folk-lore, Welsh and Manx.

Ivor B. John, The Mabinogion (Popular Studies).

INDEX.

" Finic o'an rgníobar aniam go fóil

    Agur Finic oaníníb o'án bfiábnur bnóín

   . . Agur Cníorca o'án n-óíoeán an an cníab Sióín.''